Critical Issues in Police Civil Liability

Third Edition

Victor E. Kappeler

Eastern Kentucky University

WAVELAND

PRESS, INC.

Prospect Heights, Illinois

For information about this book, write or call:
Waveland Press, Inc.
P.O. Box 400
Prospect Heights, Illinois 60070
(847) 634-0081
www.waveland.com

Contents

Preface   vii
Acknowledgments   ix

1   The Scope and Impact of Police Civil Liability   1
The Incidence of Civil Suit   3
Police Fear of Litigation   5
The Cost of Civil Liability   8
The Benefit of Civil Liability   11
The Process of Civil Litigation   12
Summary   14

2   The Fundamentals of State Tort Law   17
Police Liability and State Tort Law   17
Historical Barriers and Defenses to Police Liability   28
Summary   33

3   The Fundamentals of Federal Liability Law   35
The Civil Rights Act of 1871   35
Municipal Liability under Section 1983   45
Administrative Negligence
    and Deliberate Indifference   52
Municipal Liability for Failure to Train   54
Defenses to Section 1983 Lawsuits   60
Summary   64

4   Civil Liability for Police Use of Excessive Force   65

Excessive, Deadly, and Nondeadly Force   66
State and Federal Claims   67
Federal Standards Governing
    the Use of Deadly Force   71
Standards Governing the Use of Nondeadly Force   76
Liability for Indirect Excessive Force   78
Summary 80

**5   Police Civil Liability for High-Risk
     Drug Enforcement Operatons   81**

Search and Seizure Law in Drug Operations   82
Drug Detection and Probable Cause   98
Summary   105

**6   Police Liability for Abandoning Citizens
     in Dangerous Places and Situations   107**

Governmental Liability for
    Third-Party Criminal Victimization   108
Abandoning Vehicle Occupants
    and Qualified Immunity   110
Abandoning Children and Severity of Injury   113
Abandoning Assault Victims and
    Knowledge of Impending Victimization   115
Case Analysis   117
Summary   119

**7   Legal Issues in Police Negligent Operation
     of Vehicles in Emergency Situations   121**

Statutory Immunities   122
Negligence Principles and Police Pursuit   125
Defenses to Negligent Operation   134
Summary   135

**8   Police Civil Liability for Failure
     to Arrest Intoxicated Drivers   137**

Traditional Barriers to Liability   138
The Public Duty Doctrine   144
Special Relationship   148
Summary   153

Contents   v

9 The Liability of Traffic Officers: Negligence at Accident Scenes — 155

The Duty to Warn and Protect   155
The Duty to Render Assistance   160
The Duty to Investigate Accidents   163
The Duty to Secure Accident Scenes   166
Summary   168

10 Police Liability for Failure to Prevent Detainee Suicide — 171

The Framework of Negligence Litigation   172
The Special Duty of Care   173
Police Conduct and Breach of Duty   178
Defenses to Detainee Suicide   186
Summary   187

11 Shifting Conceptions of Police Civil Liability and Law Enforcement — 189

Legal Assumptions and Police Civil Liability   190
Implications for the Future Police Executive   199

References   203
Cases   207
Index   215

Preface

If asked, most students of criminal justice can provide an adequate legal definition of crime. If pressed, students can usually recite and even question the process by which behavior is made criminal. Students can recall the level of proof necessary to convict a person of a crime as well as defenses to criminal charges. Criminal justice students are well-versed in the administration of criminal justice agencies and can easily distinguish between a policy and procedure as well as the other essentials of administration. Far fewer students can provide a definition of *tort* or the elements necessary for a finding of civil liability. Seldom can they provide an adequate answer to "what level of proof is required for a civil judgment, or what defenses are available to police officers facing claims of false arrest?" Students are often at a loss when asked to discuss the relationships between developing agency policy, operationalizing that policy, and judicial findings of civil liability.

These observations do not necessarily represent student deficiency but rather reflect their educational experience and our orientation to the study of crime and justice. While criminal justice is still a new and perhaps evolving discipline, it has for the past twenty-five years or so concentrated more on criminal rather than civil law. While the discipline has matured by the introduction of the scientific method, it has yet to mature fully in the realm of legal studies. Largely we have ignored an entire body of law in our pursuit to understand *justice.* We have spent countless hours studying, debating and measuring the effects of the exclusionary rule on police misconduct but have left relatively untouched the effects of civil damage awards. This, however, may be changing—not so much from design but from experience. As

more and more criminal justice personnel are being exposed to civil litigation, the need and pressure to educate students of justice in areas
beyond the criminal law becomes evident.

Critical Issues in Police Civil Liability is an attempt to aid in the
integration of civil law, social science, and police studies. The book was
written to be used in either legal courses that focus on the police or in
management and administration courses. Law, administrative practice,
and police operations have become so entangled that a modern police
administrator can no longer be effective without a basic understanding
of the principles of civil liability. Although the text is predominantly
legal in nature, I have attempted to address some of the many issues
confronting modern law enforcement officers. Toward this end, the
work includes many items that demonstrate the "real world" impact of
judicial decisions. Whenever possible, I have attempted to place the law
in a context meaningful to the future police officer or executive.

Victor E. Kappeler
Eastern Kentucky University

Acknowledgments

This book made its way into print through the vision of many people who either directly contributed to the work or contributed to the author's early career. Rolando V. del Carmen of Sam Houston State University played critical roles as both mentor and friend. His patient guidance, a free flowing red pen, and an occasionally well-timed grunt of approval as I stumbled through the educational process are debts that will forever go unpaid, and his influence is clearly evidenced throughout the pages of this book. Rolando was one of the first legal scholars to give police civil liability a serious consideration and he remains arguably one of the best.

Substantial contributions to this work and many other projects were made by Carol and Neil Rowe of Waveland Press. Thanks to Carol for nearly a decade of encouragement, friendship, and very fine editing. Carol always seems more of a colleague in these projects than an editor. If it were not for Carol making it a delight to produce books, I would have stopped writing long ago. I would also like to extend my gratitude to Neil having the foresight to produce this book when we were in front of the "market curve." He has nurtured this and other projects into mainstays of the field and has silently affected the course of criminal justice education.

A debt of gratitude is owed to several of my colleagues, particularly Donald Wallace, Larry Gaines, Michael S. Vaughn, Richard Holden, Bankole Thompson, and Stephen Ryals for their support, input, or careful readings of early drafts of this manuscript. The book is much improved for their contributions and balanced critiques. I would also like to thank several of my former research assistants and graduate students who, over the years, collected much of the information that made its way into this book. Most recently, William Oakley provided me with an outstanding level of support during the last revision of this book.

Some of the material appearing in this work was originally written with coauthors—Rolando V. del Carmen, Mike Vaughn, and Mike Kaune. I would like to thank these coauthors for their permission to use portions of our earlier works.

Last—but foremost in my mind—are my wife Jana and son Aaron to whom I dedicate this book. When the first edition of this book was published Aaron was just a toddler; with the publication of the third edition he embarks on his academic career, and his future looks very bright. Aaron has always been a source of great pride for me, not only as a father but also as an academic. While writing this edition, Jana and I celebrated our twentieth anniversary. Over the years, Jana has been a continual source of light in my life. I look forward to the years to come. Jana and Aaron, more than anyone else, give meaning to my work.

The Scope and Impact of Police Civil Liability   1

Policing is a difficult and challenging occupation. Police officers perform duties that include apprehending suspected criminals, providing citizens with protection, aiding people in distress, and maintaining the safety of our streets and communities. Police officers in the United States are called upon to make some very tough decisions. Routinely, police officers must handle traffic accidents, decide whether to arrest citizens, and search suspected drug traffickers. In a less routine fashion, police officers must make decisions about whether to engage in high-speed vehicular pursuits and about when to use force—even deadly force. These are difficult tasks and decisions in themselves. Matters become even more complicated since police officers are increasingly the target of varied lawsuits. Civil suits against the police arise out of many situations and for a variety of reasons; some of these reasons are inherent in the nature of the police role; others arise from the services officers provide the public; still others result from the status of officers as governmental employees.

When police officers fail to perform their assigned duties, perform them in a negligent fashion, abuse their authority, or just make poor decisions, the possibility of civil liability exists. Police liability, however, is not always the product of performing a complicated task or making an honest error in judgment. An alarming number of police civil liability cases are filed that allege misconduct, abuses of authority, false arrest, and brutality. Trautman (1997) reports that during a five-year period at least 3,000 of approximately 600,000 U.S. police officers were officially sanctioned for misconduct ranging from theft to sexual assaults. Certainly a large number of these cases resulted in lawsuits. Many lawsuits often allege intentional violations of constitutional, civil, or statutory rights.

There are, unfortunately, police officers who engage in acts of misconduct and step beyond the scope of their official authority. The videotaped beating of motorist Rodney King by Los Angeles police officers

1

following a police pursuit captured the nation's attention. As a result of this beating, attorneys for Mr. King filed a federal civil rights lawsuit against the police—asking for a multimillion-dollar damage award. King was eventually awarded $3.8 million in a civil judgment against the City of Los Angeles. During the same year, the public was exposed to at least three other videotaped police beatings. Police officers in Kansas City, Missouri, were taped using excessive force to arrest a traffic violator; an officer in Texas was filmed beating a handcuffed prisoner; and a police officer in Trenton, New Jersey, was captured on film repeatedly slapping a man in the face after he inquired about his son's arrest.

In 1995, the conduct of federal law enforcement officers at Ruby Ridge, where police snipers used deadly force to seize two citizens, resulted in the federal government's agreement to pay survivors almost $4 million because of unconstitutional police use of deadly force. More recently, after 11 years of litigation against the City of Philadelphia, a federal jury awarded Ramona Africa $1.5 million. Ms. Africa was the sole adult survivor of a 1985 bombing of her residence by Philadelphia police. This judgment followed on the heels of the city's $1.7 million settlement with a child who survived the bombing. In this case, city police officers dropped C-4 explosives from a helicopter in an attempt to make members of the MOVE group leave their home. The bombing resulted in the destruction of 61 homes and the deaths of 11 people (Terry, 1996).

At the close of the century, police misconduct was once again in the public spotlight. The sexual assault of a Abner Louima by New York City Police officers, the investigation into the corruption of the Los Angeles Police Department's Rampart CRASH unit, and the national concern with the issue of Driving While Black have all contributed to a renewed interest in controlling police misconduct. In 1999, a jury acquitted four white New York police officers of criminal changes in the shooting of Amadou Diallo, a West African immigrant. The undercover police officers confronted Diallo standing in the vestibule of his Bronx apartment. Allegedly mistaking Diallo's wallet for a gun, the officers opened fire on the unarmed man discharging 41 rounds and striking him 19 times. Diallo, a 22-year-old street vendor with no criminal record, died at the scene. Following the officer trial, Diallo's parents filed an $81 million civil liability suit against the officers and city, accusing them of deprivation of constitutional rights, racial profiling, and inadequate police training. In 2000, after years of litigation as a result of the FBI's siege of the Branch Davidians' compound in Waco, Texas, a federal court found that governmental officials were not liable for the deaths of over 60 people. These incidents keep the issue of police misconduct and civil liability in the forefront of public attention. There is growing public concern about the misconduct of police officers in U.S. society and a well-evidenced trend toward suing law enforcement officials for acts of misconduct and abuse of authority.

Civil suits against the police are not solely the product of an inability or failure to perform assigned duties in a responsible manner. The mere filing of a lawsuit against a police officer does not always mean the officer has engaged in some obvious and intentional wrongdoing. Some people perceive governmental bodies as having "deep pockets" and the ability to pay out-of-court settlements or large punitive damage awards. Therefore, some lawyers and citizens are quick to bring litigation against local governments and their most visible agents—the police. This, coupled with a rise in court findings of police liability, has led some to conclude that no other group of governmental employees is more exposed to civil lawsuits and liability than are police officers. Indeed, civil liability can be an occupational hazard even for well-meaning officers and professional police departments, leading some to maintain that "suing public officials has become the second most popular indoor sport in the country" (del Carmen, 1994, p. 409).

This chapter explores the scope and impact of police civil liability. In the sections to follow, consideration will be given to the frequency of civil litigation against the police, the costs of liability litigation to society, and the fear some law enforcement officers have over the possibility of being sued. The social benefits and some of the rationales for allowing the police to be sued will be raised. The chapter then turns to a brief review of the litigation process and the roles of the various actors in that process.

The Incidence of Civil Suit

The potential for occupational misconduct and a judicial trend toward allowing governmental liability has led to an explosion in the number of lawsuits filed against the nation's police. Accurate information regarding the actual number and types of lawsuits filed is difficult to obtain. Even so, several trends can be found in the available literature on police civil liability. First, since the 1960s there has been a sharp increase in the number of civil suits filed against the police. Second, there has been an increase in civil cases successfully litigated against police officers, police departments, and municipalities (Kappeler, 1989; Kappeler and Kappeler, 1992; Littlejohn, 1976). Finally, while police officers and their departments have had a good record in defending themselves from civil lawsuits, there are still a significant number of judgments handed down against the police, and there is reason to believe that the number may be growing.

According to one survey of police departments, the number of civil suits filed against the police from 1967 to 1971 increased by 124 percent (AELE, 1974) and averaged more than 6,000 cases each year. In

1976 there were over 13,400 civil suits filed against law enforcement officers in the United States. Between 1967 and 1976, the yearly number of civil suits brought against law enforcement officers increased by over 500 percent (AELE, 1982). Studies conducted by the IACP (1976) and other organizations indicate that within this time frame one in 34 police officers was sued. Studies like these predicted that by the 1980s there would be over 26,000 civil lawsuits filed against the nation's police annually (AELE, 1980). According to one legal scholar, the police are currently faced with more than 30,000 civil actions annually (Silver, 2000).

While these trends are expected to continue in the years to come, police administrators have taken a guarded view of potential liabilities. A survey conducted by the Police Foundation found that while police chiefs thought liability was an important issue for law enforcement, they did not feel that it had reached the point of crisis (McCoy, 1987). Similarly, David Carter's (1994) informal survey of police executives found that civil liability ranked 20th on their top-twenty list of concerns.

These views may be the result of a perception that the police have a good record in defending themselves from civil suits. Early estimates were that only about 4 percent of the cases alleging police wrongdoing result in a verdict against the police (AELE, 1980; del Carmen, 1981; Schmidt, 1974). More current research shows that police lose about 8 percent of the cases reported (Kappeler, Kappeler and del Carmen, 1993). While the percentage of cases the police lose seems small, these cases represent a great strain on the resources of police departments and municipal governments—especially since the number of lawsuits and the percentage of cases the police lose are increasing. A recent study of police lawsuits in Texas found that of 630 lawsuits filed by the public, police lost 22 percent of these cases (Vaughn, Cooper, del Carmen, 2001, p. 7). Hiring attorneys to defend a case is an expensive proposition—both in terms of money expended and time directed away from other activities. A study of all the officially reported and published police liability cases decided by the federal district courts between 1980 and 2000 found that plaintiffs prevailed in a much higher percentage of the cases than previous reports indicate. Figure 1.1 presents the number of published Section 1983 cases decided by the federal district courts and the percentage in which plaintiffs prevailed on at least one issue.

While published district court decisions represent only a small fraction of all the claims filed against the nation's police, there is some evidence of a growth in their numbers and a trend toward plaintiffs prevailing in a greater number of these cases. This does not mean all these cases resulted in police liability; there was, however, enough evidence to warrant a jury's consideration of the alleged police misconduct. Given the statistics on litigation, the lack of concern about the issue of civil liability expressed by some police chiefs seems shortsighted.

Figure 1.1

Published Section 1983 Cases Decided by the Federal District Courts, Selected Years*

Year	Total Cases Published	Percent of Cases Plaintiffs Prevail[a]	Frequency Plaintiffs Prevail
1980	46	45.7	21
1984	106	52.8	56
1988	129	46.5	60
1992	117	49.6	58
1996	135	48.1	65
2000	129	53.4	69
Totals/Mean	662	49.6	329

*Data excludes employment based actions and prisoner/detainee conditions of confinement cases.

[a]The term *prevail* does not mean the decision always resulted in a finding of liability against the police, only that there was sufficient evidence to warrant a jury trial or that plaintiffs prevailed on a substantive issue or motion before the court.

Police Fear of Litigation

One irony of current thinking on civil liability is that while police chiefs have taken a guarded view of the liability situation and generally feel that civil liability has yet to reach a point of crisis (McCoy, 1987), their officers are less confident. This may be due, in part, to the fact that municipal police chiefs are afforded some insulation from personal liability for the actions of their officers. Research shows that some police officers fear civil litigation. A study of 101 police cadets, conducted by Scogin and Brodsky (1991), found that 9 percent of the officers interviewed felt that their fear of civil litigation had reached a point of being irrational and excessive. Several of the officers interviewed expressed a very simplistic understanding of prevention measures, as well as a fatalistic sentiment regarding potential litigation. This research noted that, "Typical [officer] responses were, for example, '. . . what seems to be the only word in the English language is sue' and 'we can be sued for anything.'" Other officers expressed their risk management precautions in terms of "treating people fairly" and "going by the book." These researchers concluded "the percentage of litigaphobic candidates is considerably higher than the 9 percent self-identified figure" (p. 44).

A survey of 50 police officers from three different law enforcement agencies in Pennsylvania conducted by Garrison (1995) found that 28 percent of the officers agreed with the statement that "the idea that a police officer can be sued bothers me" (p. 26). A replication of these studies in Kentucky found that 50 percent of 220 police cadets in a state-wide training academy were worried about civil liability, and 31 percent thought they worried to excess (Kappeler, 1996). Female police officers showed less anxiety over the potential to be sued even when controlling for age, education, years of experience, and job assignment. In all, lower-ranking police officers seem more concerned with the potential of civil liability than do their chiefs. More recently, a survey of 658 sworn police officers from 21 agencies across the United States found that 15 percent of the officers ranked civil liability third among the top ten serious challenges they face on the job (Stevens, 2000). Likewise a study of over 800 Texas police chiefs found that 53 percent thought that "lawsuits or the fear of lawsuits made it more difficult for them or their officers to do their job" (Vaughn, Cooper, and del Carmen, 2001, p. 6).

Such fears are promoted by a lack of understanding of the nature and consequences of police civil liabilities, a general feeling by police officers that they can be "sued and found liable for anything," and that frivolous lawsuits are commonplace. Such misplaced notions are promoted by police officers who feel unjustly threatened by civil litigation. Consider a few of the remarks made by police commanders in very popular police magazines: "Every time a police officer engages in a confrontation with a citizen or performs other official duties, he runs the risk of possible civil litigation . . . only a small percentage of such suits have any reasonable justification. The remainder are brought by overzealous citizens who perceive some personal harm, however so slight. . . ." (Reynolds, 1988, p. 7). Another police commander remarks: "Any perfectly law-abiding police officer can be sued, perhaps maliciously, by just about anybody at just about any time. That's an unfortunate and unjust side effect of pinning on a badge" (Garner, 1991, p. 34). This view of civil liability appears to be much more extensive than the occasional comment in a policing magazine. Vaughn, Cooper and del Carmen's (2001) study of Texas police chiefs found that 76 percent of the chiefs they surveyed believed that most of the lawsuits filed against the police were frivolous (p. 7).

These views, based on inaccurate information and false perceptions, express unrealistic fears of litigation and can have negative effects. Some have argued that unrealistic fears of civil liability

> can seriously erode the necessary confidence and willingness to act. Even worse, law enforcement officers who have an unrealistic or exaggerated fear of personal liability may become overly timid or indecisive and fail to arrest or search to the detriment of the public's interest in effective and aggressive law enforcement. (Schofield, 1990, p. 26-27)

Besides the chilling effect fear of liability may have on "aggressive" law enforcement, these views may foster protectionism, police cover-ups, and a division between the police and community.

Although some have claimed that the fear of being sued may negatively affect law enforcement practice, research seems to suggest otherwise. Garrison's (1995) survey of police officers found that most police officers did not believe that "civil suit against police officers is an impediment to effective law enforcement" (p. 25). In fact, while a slight majority of officers indicated that they thought civil liability had a deterrent effect on police misconduct, the vast majority said that the possibility of being sued "did not affect their thinking in the field" (p. 26). Stevens's (2000) survey of police officers in 21 agencies found that only 11 percent of the officers reported that concern about civil liabilities promoted alternatives to arrest. Likewise, Vaughn et al.'s study (2001, p. 6) of Texas chiefs of police found that 61 percent thought lawsuits had little or no effect on their departmental functions. Some might argue that the social objective for holding police officers liable for their misconduct is to make them think about the consequences of their actions. It would seem that the prospect of civil liability has a deterrent effect in the abstract survey environment, but that it does not have a major impact on field practices. This may be due in part because many police officers believe that most lawsuits filed against the police are frivolous.

An examination of published cases decided by the federal district courts indicates that less than one-half of one percent of those cases resulted in a judicial sanction, because plaintiffs brought cases that clearly lacked merit (Kappeler and Kappeler, 1992). In 2000, for example, the issue of sanctions was only brought up once in police liability cases reported by the federal district courts. In 1995, two cases mentioned sanctions. In one case the court refused to impose sanctions on a plaintiff and in the other case the court refused to impose sanctions against the defendant-sheriff (*Singer v. Fulton County Sheriff*, 1995). One must remember that just as a few clearly frivolous claims are brought against the police, police officers and their legal counsel can also engage in sanctionable misconduct during the litigation of a police liability case (see, *Jocks v. Tavernier*, 2000).

One must also consider the millions of interactions that take place between citizens and the police each day and the number of incidents that result in litigation. With approximately 17,000 state and local law enforcement agencies in the United States employing over 800,000 people (Gaines, Kappeler, and Vaughn, 1999), the rate of litigation would seem relatively small compared to the potential. A study conducted by the International Association of Chiefs of Police (1976) concluded that about 40 percent of the liability cases were brought against the police for officer misconduct—not just technical error or minor rights violations.

There are good reasons for a healthy concern over potential civil liability, but not when the concern is premised on the notion that citizens file an inordinate number of unjustified claims against the police. As noted later in this chapter, the civil litigation process has safeguards to prevent and, if necessary, punish frivolous and unjust claims brought against the police (see, Kritzer, Marshall, and Zemans, 1992). Comments such as those cited above divide the police from citizens and close minds to an understanding of the complex issues of police civil liability and the need for accountability.

The Cost of Civil Liability

The cost of a civil suit goes beyond expenses incurred by individual police officers. State and municipal governments are also at risk. Such factors as the cost of liability insurance, litigation expenses, out-of-court settlements, and punitive damage awards make civil liability an extremely expensive proposition for police officers, law enforcement agencies, governments, and—ultimately—taxpayers. A survey conducted by the National Institute of Municipal Officers found that the 215 municipalities surveyed had over $4.3 billion in pending liability lawsuits. One criminal justice scholar reasoned that if these figures were applied to the existing 39,000 local governments, there could be as much as $780 billion in pending liability litigation against local government (Bates, Culter, and Clink, 1981 as cited in Barrineau, 1994). A 1996 survey of city managers and clerks (MacManus, 1997) found that police liability was the biggest contributor to the rising cost of municipal liability.

Facing potential judgments amounting to millions of dollars, municipalities are forced to secure liability insurance to protect themselves from civil litigation. Insurance policies of this type are extremely expensive. After several lawsuits are filed against a police department, premium prices can skyrocket, or companies may refuse to insure the high-risk police department. In some states municipalities have banded together to create self-insurance pools to avoid the expense of insurance and to spread the financial risk of liability across cities.

Figure 1.2

Section 1983 Awards against the Police as Reported by the Federal District Courts*

Civil Rights Violations	Average Award**
False Arrest/Imprisonment/Unlawful Detention	90,312
Excessive Force	178,878
Assault/Battery	117,013
Unlawful Searches/Seizure	98,954
Inadequate Supervision	119,114
Strip Search	24,329
Malicious Prosecution	53,306
Inadequate Training	105,450
Vehicle Pursuit	1,250,000

*1978–1996; includes awards and attorney fees when they were reported. Amounts were recorded as presented by the courts and include any reduction or enhancement of award or fee by the court.
**Mean of all cases containing this particular civil rights claim.

The cost of an average jury award of liability against a municipality is reported to be about $2 million. While early studies of police liability indicated that individual judgments against the police averaged only about $3,000, it is not uncommon for police liability cases to result in six- or seven-figure awards against cities. In 1982 there were over 250 cases where juries awarded at least $1 million (National League of Cities, 1985). A more contemporary study of published police liability cases handed down by the federal district courts from 1978 through 1995 indicated that the average reported award and attorney fees against police departments was $118,698. During this time, awards ranged from a single dollar to judgments of over $1.6 million (Kappeler, Kappeler and del Carmen, 1993, updated 1996). A more recent study of 1,525 federal liability cases for police failure to train officers adequately found the average award against a police-defendant was about $492,000 and attorney fees for the prevailing party averaged just over $60,000 (Ross, 2000). A 2001 study of Texas police chiefs reported that the average jury or court award in a police liability case was $98,100 (Vaughn, Cooper, and del Carmen, 2001, p. 10).

These figures, of course, do not represent the growing trend toward settling cases outside the courtroom and are based only on cases officially reported by the courts. A study of police liability in Texas found that of 630 lawsuits filed against the police 159 or 25 percent resulted in an out-of-court settlement with the average payment to a police-plaintiff being $55,411 (Vaughn, Cooper, and del Carmen,

2001, p. 10). A study of the New York City Police Department found
that between 1987 and 1991 the city paid out $44 million in claims to
settle police misconduct cases. Over the five-year period the "average
settlement or judgment on police misconduct cases more than dou-
bled, from $23,000 to $52,000." Also during the same period, "the
comptroller's office saw a jump from 977 to 1,498 in the number of
claims alleging misuse of force" (Staff, 1992). New York City is not
alone. The Christopher Commission's investigation into the Los Angeles Police Department found that in 1991 the city paid out $13 million
in damage awards for police misconduct (Christopher, 1991), but by
1997 they had reduced that figure to $9.8 million (Katz, 1998). In 1990,
the City of Detroit paid $20 million in damage awards.

Figure 1.3
The Cost of Police Liability in Selected Cities and Years

City	Year(s)	Payments	Type of Cases
Chicago	1991–94	29 million	excessive force, false arrest
Detroit	1986–97	100 million	all law suits
Los Angeles	1991–95	179.2 million	excludes traffic
	1996–97	9.8 million	
Minneapolis	1994	1.4 million	excessive force, false arrest
New York	1994–95	44 million	excludes traffic
Philadelphia	1994–95	20 million	unknown
San Francisco	1993–95	1.9 million	settlements
Washington, DC	1993–95	4.1 million	false arrest only

Sources: Gaines, L. K., Kappeler, V. E., and Vaughn, J. B. (1999); Katz, D. M. (1998).
Human Rights Watch (1998); various newspaper reports.

In an attempt to prevent such large judgments, many cities and
their sureties have made it a routine practice to settle many claims of
police misconduct out of court for a minor portion of what a jury might
award if the case went to trial. Such practices can lead cities to pay relatively large sums of money even in cases where the police might not
be found liable in a civil proceeding. Given the cost of litigation and the
potential of multimillion-dollar awards, many municipalities are not
willing to gamble on whether juries will find in favor of their police
officers or award judgments against them. A Justice Department study
of Los Angeles County found that county officials settled 61 police misconduct cases, paying plaintiffs between $20,000 and $1.75 million a
case. Such settlements can encourage the filing of frivolous civil suits,
create morale problems in police organizations, and lead to an unfavor-
able public perception of police conduct. In addition, automatically set-

tling cases brought against a police department can send the wrong message to line officers. They may sense that they can engage in street justice and that if a citizen complains or files a lawsuit, the city will make it "go away." In all, police liability is an expensive proposition for officers, police departments, governmental agencies, and taxpayers.

The Benefit of Civil Liability

There is, however, another side to the police liability issue. Although litigation against the police can be costly and great resources are often expended by the justice system to resolve these cases, there are benefits in allowing citizens to sue the police. Proponents of police civil liabilities argue that when the government takes on a responsibility to provide service or to protect the public, people injured by the government's negligent performance of those responsibilities deserve compensation for their injuries. It would be unjust to allow governmental officials to escape their responsibilities while holding citizens accountable for their conduct. Similarly, when the government develops policy in the realm of social control and law enforcement (aggressive drug enforcement practices, for example), innocents who are injured or have their rights violated in pursuit of such policies should have an avenue of redress.

Proponents of this position often make several compelling arguments. First, if citizens' rights are to have real meaning, there must be some form of enforcement mechanism or avenue for redress for citizens who are injured. If there are no consequences for police misconduct, there is no deterrence to lawless police behavior. Second, allowing citizens to sue the police for misconduct has fostered better police training and more responsible law enforcement practices. Many argue that municipalities would not have increased training and raised required education levels for the police if they were not faced with the potential of huge liability judgments. The courts have made it a less expensive proposition to provide police with proper training than to pay the damages of a civil judgment. As one text instructs, "suits against the police that prove inadequate administrative controls, deficient policies, or customs and practices that are improper or illegal, can force the department to correct its specific deficiencies and review all policies, practices and customs" (Alpert and Dunham, 1996, p. 244). Advocates also argue that society is spreading the cost of accidents and injuries from individuals to the entire community. Taxpayers, it is reasoned, can collectively shoulder a financial burden that would destroy an individual or single family. Finally, when the police are held liable for their misconduct the courts set standards for acceptable and unacceptable behavior and by doing so they establish the bounds of professional police practice.

The Process of Civil Litigation

Unlike a criminal proceeding, police liability cases are tried in civil court. Jurors selected from the community in which the alleged wrong-doing occurred generally decide the outcome of their cases; they determine the facts of a case and ultimately decide whether the police will be held liable. A judge acts as the referee or moderator for the proceeding, instructing the jury on the law of civil liability and ruling on the motions of attorneys representing the parties involved in the litigation. The citizen who is injured and brings a lawsuit against the police is the plaintiff. Plaintiffs may include any citizen who has had his/her rights violated. In some cases, police officers themselves bring lawsuits against other police officers, their departments, or the local government. The person, agency, or government entity that has allegedly violated the plaintiff's rights is the defendant. In police liability cases, defendants may include individual officers, supervisors, law enforcement administrators, agencies, and governmental entities.

It is common practice for plaintiffs filing a police liability lawsuit to name as many defendants as possible. Anyone associated with the injury or damage, such as the police officer, department, supervisor, chief of police or mayor, may be named in the lawsuit. This practice allows plaintiffs to include the person or agency with the "deepest pockets." While an individual officer may have limited financial resources, high-level police administrators and governments have the ability to pay larger damage awards either personally, through insurance, or by raising taxes.

While variations exist, the typical process by which civil liability is determined follows a logical, step-by-step sequence. When a person is injured or has his/her rights violated, the first step in the litigation process is to secure the advice of legal counsel. This involves a meeting between the would-be plaintiff and an attorney to discuss the facts of the case and the potential for a successful lawsuit. After this initial meeting and a presuit investigation of the matter by the counsel (Ryals, 1995), the attorney may file a complaint with the court on behalf of the plaintiff. The attorney files a formal written document outlining the facts given by the client and lists the specific rights that have been violated by the police. Following the filing of the complaint, the police officers named in the complaint become the defendants. Each defendant is served with a copy of the complaint, which provides formal notice of the allegations. Each police officer then retains counsel or is provided representation by the department or the employing municipality. After service of the complaint to the defendant, the defendant's counsel then prepares a written response to the complaint for the court. This written response usually consists of a denial of the allegations made by the plaintiff or a claim of immunity from liability.

Following the defendant's response to the complaint, the officer may ask the court to consider a motion to dismiss. At this point in the process, the defendant argues to the court that the complaint has not sufficiently stated a legal claim. Unless the complaint is poorly drafted or obviously frivolous, the motion is usually denied. Alternatively, the court may allow the plaintiff to amend the complaint to include additional facts or allegations. At this point, the court accepts all the information in the complaint to be factual and basically views the complaint from the plaintiff's standpoint.

Once a complaint has survived a motion for dismissal based either on its own merit or by amendment, the defendant may request the court to grant a motion for summary judgment. In a motion for summary judgment, the defendant argues that the facts of the plaintiff's case as stated in the complaint cannot possibly support a jury's consideration of the issues. Unlike a motion to dismiss, the motion for summary judgment allows the parties to provide additional facts so that a judge can determine whether the case warrants a jury's consideration of the issue. Summary judgment is appropriate only if the evidence taken in the light most favorable to the plaintiff "fails to yield a trialworthy issue as to some material fact" (*Martinez v. Colon*, 1995, pp. 983–84) or if "it is so one-sided that one party must prevail as a matter of law" (*Anderson v. Liberty Lobby, Inc.*, 1986, pp. 251–52; *Zambranan-Marrero v. Suarez-Cruz*, 1998).

If, in the estimation of the presiding judge, the plaintiff's complaint has not stated sufficient factual evidence of a claim or there are not factual issues to be resolved at trial, judgment will be entered in favor of the defendant. On the other hand, if the plaintiff's claim survives a motion for summary judgment the case will proceed to trial.

The ability of a police or municipal defendant to appeal a denial of summary judgment has been restricted by the United States Supreme Court (*Johnson v. Jones*, 1995; *Swint v. Chambers County Comm'n*, 1995). This restriction may have at least two effects on police liability litigation. First, cases may now move faster through the system because police-defendants will no longer be able to file an automatic appeal of a denial of summary judgment. Second, more cases will be settled if the only alternative is to proceed with a trial.

If a case moves sufficiently into the process to warrant a trial, jury selection begins. Prospective jurors are interviewed by the judge and sometimes by counsel to determine whether they are fit to serve as jurors in the particular case. On some occasions, members of the potential jury pool may be dismissed if it is found that they cannot deliberate the case in a fair and unbiased fashion.The remaining jurors are impaneled, and the trial starts.

The trial begins with opening statements by the plaintiff's lawyer, which are followed by statements by the defendant's counsel. In these opening remarks, counsel provides the jury with an overview of the case. Following opening comments, the plaintiff presents the facts of the case; the defendant later presents the opposing viewpoint. After all witnesses have been called and testimony has been given, both sides are allowed to make closing arguments to the jury. These arguments are designed to persuade the jury one last time why they should find for the plaintiff or for the defendant. Following counsels' closing remarks, the judge instructs the jury on the law pertinent to the case and advises what the law requires.

The jury then deliberates the facts of the case and reaches a conclusion about the plaintiff's allegation. Although a jury may find against a police officer, a judge can enter a directed verdict or a judgement of law in favor of the officer. A judgement of law is only granted where there is a complete lack of evidence supporting the jury's verdict or when the overwhelming evidence would not lead a reasonable minded person to the verdict rendered (*Jocks v. Tavernier*, 2000). There is still the possibility that the decision will be appealed to a higher court. Either side can, given certain circumstances, appeal an adverse court or jury ruling. Upon appeal, a higher court may determine that the jury's verdict was correct and let that verdict stand, or it may require a new trial.

Our brief walk though the civil litigation process seems orderly and straightforward. In reality, it was an oversimplification of a complex process. The nature of the process is highly technical, and cases can be tied up for years. It is not unusual for a police liability case to take anywhere from three to ten years from the time of the alleged police misconduct to its final disposition. Filing numerous motions and prolonging the time to trial can have several advantages. Each motion upon which a judge rules can later form the basis for an appeal to a higher court. Stringing out the process can result in witnesses who die, documents that are destroyed, or employees who leave their jobs and are no longer available to serve as witnesses. Such tactics can serve the interests of the litigants but will increase the cost of processing the case.

Summary

The difficulty of performing law enforcement duties in an often hostile environment places officers in vulnerable positions and exposes them to charges of misconduct. Civil litigation against the police arises for a number of reasons, some of which are inherent in the police role. Trends in police liability litigation include the following: (1) a sharp increase in the number of civil suits filed against the nation's police since the 1960s; (2) an increase in civil cases successfully litigated against police officers, police departments and municipalities; and (3) a significant number of judgments handed down against the police despite a good record by police officers and their departments in defending themselves from civil lawsuits. In the final section of the chapter, the roles of various actors in civil litigation were outlined, and the civil process was described.

Unrealistic fears of civil liability have a number of negative effects: morale problems; erosion of confidence; alienation from the public; and barriers to reflective understanding of complex issues. Despite some frivolous suits, civil litigation does provide an avenue of redress for misconduct. Without consequences for unsanctioned behavior, there is no deterrence. The possibility of litigation has also created better training and more responsible practices.

The Fundamentals of State Tort Law 2

There is no better way for officers, a department, or police executives to insulate themselves from the threat of civil liability than to have a good understanding of the framework of liability law. There are generally two avenues for litigating municipal police misconduct. First, plaintiffs may file lawsuits in state court claiming that the police negligently or intentionally failed to perform their duties in violation of state law. These types of lawsuits are brought under state tort law. Second, a civil suit can be brought in federal court where the plaintiff claims police violated either a constitutional or federally protected statutory right.

This chapter presents the framework of state tort law. After a discussion of the different types of tort we will explore some of the most common claims of police negligence and a brief historical overview of the legal barriers to suing governmental officials. The chapter concludes with a discussion of defenses available to police officers facing claims of state torts.

Police Liability and State Tort Law

The term tort is derived from the Latin word *tortus*, which means twisted or bent. The term was first used in the English language following the Norman Conquest of 1066. The direct antecedent was the French term *tort*, which means "wrong." Originally, crimes and torts were identical, and people handled both types of wrongdoing by taking private action against the injuring party. "Gradually the custom of private vengeance was replaced with the concept of criminal law, that is the community as a whole is injured when one of its members is injured" (Barrineau, 1994, p. 1). As the law evolved, torts and crime

17

became distinguishable. Torts are now civil legal actions between private parties not arising from written contract.

The concept of torts is best understood when compared to crimes. Crimes are harms punished by the state and codified in written form. They are viewed as offenses against the state and not against a particular crime victim. The underlying assumption is that when a person is victimized by a criminal act, not only are the victim's rights violated, but so are the rights of the community and society as a whole. Therefore, the state may step in and take charge of the prosecution of criminal offenses. Crimes are punishable by sanctions such as community service, fines, probation, incarceration, or death. In order for a person to be convicted of a crime, a court must find the defendant guilty beyond a reasonable doubt. This requires the state to present a high level of proof that the accused party committed the crime.

A tort, on the other hand, is conduct that interferes with the private interests of people or their property. Persons suffering private interest harms can bring legal action against the party inflicting damage in a civil rather than a criminal proceeding. Torts are redressed by money awards and are not subject to criminal punishments. People bringing tort actions must show by a mere preponderance of evidence that the defendant caused the harm by acting in an unreasonable manner contrary to law. This level of proof is much lower than that needed to convict a person of a criminal offense.

While torts are distinguishable from crimes, some torts can also be crimes. Consider the situation where a police officer intentionally discharges a firearm and kills an innocent bystander. If the officer is tried in criminal court, a finding of manslaughter or murder is possible depending on the circumstances surrounding the incident. If the officer is convicted of the crime, this would mean the imposition of a criminal sanction by the state—a fine, probation, or incarceration. The family of the shooting victim may also file a civil lawsuit claiming the officer's conduct violated the victim's personal rights. In this civil process, the officer might be found liable for the death of the victim, and the family might be awarded money to help compensate for their loss. The officer's conduct would be a violation of criminal law (an offense against the state) and at the same time a tort where injury was inflicted on another person.

There are generally three types of torts under state law: (1) strict liability tort, (2) intentional tort, and (3) negligence tort. Each of these torts requires plaintiffs to establish different elements and to meet different levels of proof to sue a police officer successfully. Figure 2.1 presents the basic differences between the three levels of state torts.

Figure 2.1
Differences Between Levels of State Torts

Type of Tort	Behaviors	Elements
Strict liability	Extremely dangerous	Conduct and damage or injury
Intentional	Purposive behaviors likely to result in damage	Knowledge, foreseeability, and damage or injury
Negligence	Inadvertent and unreasonable behaviors	Legal duty, breach, proximate cause, and damage or injury

Strict Liability Tort

Strict liability torts are normally associated with behaviors that are so dangerous or hazardous that a person who engages in such behavior can be substantially certain the conduct will result in injury or damage (Silver, 2000). Since behavior of this type is socially and legally unacceptable, persons engaging in these behaviors are held liable for any harm. Under strict liability tort the defendant's mental state—whether he or she intended to engage in the conduct—is not a judicial consideration. Under strict liability, fault on the part of the defendant need not be established. When courts decide strict liability cases, they concern themselves with whether the officer or the agency should bear the burden of the financial costs of the damage or injury.

Strict liability torts do not usually apply to police officers, even though many of the services they provide and duties they perform obviously involve great danger. There have, however, been law enforcement policies that could render the police liable under strict liability torts. One such scenario is the use of military or military-style tactics to control drug trafficking. At the height of the war on drugs, some people advocated the use of military warplanes to seek out and destroy planes used to import illegal drugs. Another possible scenario is the use of chemical agents to control illegal drug crops. Although there never has been a case litigated, if a person became seriously ill after using an illegal drug that had been purposely treated with a chemical by the police, such conduct could approximate a strict liability tort.

Intentional Tort

A contrast to strict liability tort is intentional tort. Intentional tort requires the plaintiff to prove that an officer's behavior was intentional. The police officer must have intended to engage in the conduct that led to damage or injury. It is important to note that this requirement does not mean the officer "intended" to inflict the injury or damage, only that the officer intended to engage in the conduct that led to the injury. The distinction between strict liability tort and intentional tort is drawn by the foreseeability of danger associated with engaging in a particular behavior and the extent to which the officer's behavior was intentional. Intentional torts are usually those behaviors that are substantially certain to cause injury or damage where the officer knowingly engaged in the behavior. For example, the police officer who shoots an unarmed fleeing burglar may have intended to discharge the firearm but may not have intended to kill the suspect. For purposes of proving an intentional tort, it must only be shown that the officer intended to discharge the firearm. For liability purposes, it makes little difference whether the officer intended to kill, wound, or merely scare the suspect. Since the officer intended to discharge the firearm and could be substantially certain damage or injury would follow, liability would be found, absent an adequate defense.

There are various forms of intentional torts that can be brought against police officers. The type of intentional tort action filed depends on the officer's conduct and the existing law. Some intentional torts are based on state statutes that require officers to perform their duties in a certain fashion while others prohibit officers from engaging in certain behaviors. Other litigation is based on previously decided judicial decisions that, as a matter of legal policy, make certain types of conduct unacceptable (*Narney v. Daniels*, 1992). Some of the most common forms of intentional torts filed against police officers include wrongful death, false arrest, false imprisonment, and assault and battery.

Wrongful Death. Wrongful death lawsuits are based on state statutes. The family of the deceased often brings this type of civil lawsuit. Police officers who either take the life of a citizen or fail to prevent the death of a citizen can be held liable for wrongful death under certain circumstances (*Donaldson v. City of Seattle*, 1992).

Wrongful death claims often arise as a result of police use of deadly force or because of high-speed police pursuits (*Medina v. City of Chicago*, 1992; *Stewart v. City of Omaha*, 1995). In most states, the law permits persons to bring civil action against an officer who intentionally and unlawfully kills someone. These laws are intended to compensate the family of victims who are wrongfully killed by improper police action. Depending on the officer's behavior and state law, punitive damages can also be awarded against the officer and the police department.

Many states used to allow police officers to use deadly force to apprehend suspected felons attempting to flee the scene of a crime. However, in *Tennessee v. Garner* (1985) the Supreme Court curtailed the use of deadly force by police officers. The Court held that certain state fleeing felon laws were unconstitutional. In the *Garner* decision, the Court said that police officers were allowed to use deadly force only to prevent the escape of a dangerous felon or to protect themselves or others from serious physical harm. Since the *Garner* decision, it has become easier for the families of shooting victims to succeed in civil actions against police officers who improperly use deadly force.

Assault and Battery.   Assault is behavior that causes a person to fear the infliction of immediate injury. It is sufficient for a finding of liability to show that the officer's actions caused an individual to fear for his or her safety; damage need not be shown in a civil action, other than the distress associated with fear or apprehension of injury. If they are not acting within the scope of their lawful authority, police officers can be found liable for assault when they engage in conduct that either inflicts injury or causes fear of injury. Consider the situation where a police officer is interrogating a criminal suspect. During the investigation the officer moves toward the defendant, grabs him, and threatens to throw the suspect from a second floor window. This type of behavior could result in liability under an intentional tort claim of assault.

Battery, on the other hand, is offensive or harmful contact between two persons. This form of intentional tort does not require that the officer intended to inflict harm or that the officer realized the conduct to be offensive to a person. It need only establish that the officer acted without the consent of the party and made some form of offensive contact. Consider the situation where a male police officer performs an illegal search of a female without her consent and over her protests. If the officer was not legally entitled to conduct the search and was not acting within the scope of police authority, such a search may constitute a battery as well as other violations of civil law. An intentional tort claim could therefore be filed against the officer, and liability could be imposed by a court.

False Arrest and Imprisonment.   False arrest is the unlawful seizure and detention of a person. It is any unlawful restraint of a person's liberty without his or her consent. To demonstrate false arrest, it is not necessary for the officer to physically restrain the person. It need only be established that a reasonable person under similar circumstances would conclude that he or she was no longer free to go about normal activities, even though no physical contact between the officer and the suspect may have occurred. A police officer who places a person inside a patrol car with a screened cage, several police officers surrounding an individual, or an officer ordering someone to remain at the police station are all examples of behavior where a person would not feel free to leave. The courts could interpret these behaviors, for purposes of liability, as making an arrest.

Plaintiffs claiming false arrest, however, must establish several factors to succeed in a civil action against the police: (1) the police willfully detained them, (2) their detention was against their will, (3) the detention was made without authority of law, and (4) the person being detained was aware of the confinement (*Bordeau v. Village of Deposit*, 2000). If these four elements are established, then a plaintiff is likely to succeed in a false arrest lawsuit. One should be mindful, however, that there is no checklist for determining when an investigative detention turns into an arrest situation that requires probable cause. The courts will consider the features of the detention, such as the use of force to restrain and the length of time detained, when deciding whether a detention became an arrest (*Nelson v. City of Cambridge*, 2000).

Most false arrest claims allege the arresting officer did not have probable cause to make the arrest and detain the person (*Abrahante v. City of New York*, 1994). To make a warrantless arrest, police officers must have probable cause to believe the suspect has committed or is in the process of committing a crime. If the officer makes an arrest without a warrant, probable cause is always a legal issue. Whether probable cause to arrest existed at the time of arrest is a determination made by the courts. If it is found the officer did not have probable cause to make the arrest, liability may follow.

One way to limit the likelihood of a liability for false arrest is to secure a warrant before making an arrest. Here, a magistrate determines whether probable cause exists for the arrest. Normally, an arrest made pursuant to a valid warrant provides the officer with a total defense to a claim of false arrest. This is because a judge has made the determination that probable cause existed and issued a warrant for the arrest. There are, however, situations where a warrant does not totally shield an officer from liability. If a police officer provides a magistrate with false information to secure an arrest warrant, the officer may be found liable for false arrest. Another potential form of liability is the situation where a police officer knowingly serves a warrant on someone other than the person named on the warrant. If the officer cannot show reasonable diligence in securing the identity of the person or the validity of the warrant, liability may be imposed (*Plaza v. City of Reno*, 1995). Usually if an officer is acting in good faith and believes the warrant is valid and is intended for the person arrested, civil liability is barred.

False imprisonment is similar to false arrest in that it requires an unlawful detention by a police officer. Claims of false imprisonment are distinguished from false arrest in that an officer may have had probable cause to arrest but may still be found liable for false imprisonment. A successful claim of false imprisonment generally requires: (1) an intent to confine, (2) acts resulting in confinement, and (3) knowledge of the confinement or harm (*Brown v. Bryan County, Okl.*, 1995). An officer who makes a valid arrest may later violate certain rights during a person's detention. Failure to release an arrested person at an appointed time, preventing an arrested person access to a judge, or preventing a person from posting bail or a bond may result in a lawsuit for false imprisonment. False imprisonment lawsuits have been supported by the courts where police officers: (1) fail to follow proper booking procedures, (2) prevent defendants from being properly arraigned, (3) restrict a defendant's access to court, or (4) improperly file criminal charges against a suspect. False imprisonment claims are usually based on the conduct of an officer following an arrest, where the officer either unlawfully prolongs detention or violates the rights of a detained person.

Negligence Tort

Negligence is inadvertent behavior that results in damage or injury. The distinction between strict liability and intentional torts leaves negligence torts as a residual category. Negligence requires a lesser degree of foreseeability of danger than does intentional tort. In negligence tort the mental state of the police officer is not an issue— even inadvertent behavior resulting in damage or injury can lead to liability. The standard applied in negligence tort is whether the officer's act or failure to act created an unreasonable risk to another member of society. Consider the situation where a police officer is driving a vehicle. If the officer inadvertently exceeds the posted speed limit and becomes involved in an accident, the officer could be found liable for negligence in the operation of a motor vehicle. Even though the officer was unaware of the vehicle's speed, liability could be found based on negligence.

Negligence is, however, more complicated than demonstrating inadvertent behavior and injury or damage. There are four elements needed to establish a case of negligence. Each of these elements must be shown before a police officer can be found liable for a claim of negligence: (1) a legal duty, (2) a breach of duty, (3) proximate cause, and (4) actual damage or injury (*Estate v. Willis*, 1995).

Legal Duty.   When one speaks of a police officer's duty, the term is often used loosely. One may speak of a duty to serve our community and to protect lives and property. Legal duty, however, is very specific. Legal duties are those behaviors recognized by the courts that require police officers either to take action or to refrain from taking action in particular situations. Police legal duties arise from a number of sources. Laws, customs, judicial decisions, and departmental policy can create duties for police officers.

Criminal law can be a source of police duty. Consider the case where a state law prohibits drunk driving. A typical state law might read, "police officers shall arrest and take into custody any persons operating a motor vehicle under the influence of intoxicants." A court examining this law may conclude it creates a duty on the part of police officers to arrest intoxicated drivers. Similarly, a police department policy may require officers who stop suspected drunk drivers to perform field sobriety tests at the scene of traffic stops. If an officer stops a drunk driver, fails to perform a field sobriety test, and fails to make an arrest, the officer could be held liable for any subsequent injury, if that driver is later involved in an accident. The court might conclude that the officer had a duty to perform the field test under departmental policy and a duty to arrest the drunk driver because of state law. Had the officer performed the duties, the injury and damage may not have occurred.

In the past, most plaintiffs were unsuccessful in establishing that the police owed them a legal duty of protection. Courts had ruled that while police officers owe a duty to protect the general public, this duty was not owed to specific individuals. This, however, has changed, and many courts now recognize that under certain circumstances police may owe a special duty to individual citizens where the actions of the police set that individual apart from other members of society. For example, if a police officer becomes involved in an investigation and an informant provides the officer with information that leads to the arrest of a fugitive, the police officer may owe a duty to protect the informant from future harm. Likewise, if a police officer stops an intoxicated driver but fails to arrest that driver, the courts may find that as a result of stopping the driver a special relationship had been created between the officer and the motoring public. In such a case, the officer could be held liable for any damage the drunk driver caused. Recently, some courts have held that the duties of law enforcement officers are not limited to the protection of identifiable victims of a crime or injury. In fact, some courts have held that duty may be established even in the absence of a specific and identifiable danger that affects a unique segment of the public (*Torres v. State*, 1995).

Breach of Duty.   The existence of a duty alone is not sufficient to lead to a police officer's liability. A plaintiff in a negligence lawsuit must establish that the officer breached a duty to the citizen. Breaches of duty are determined from factual situations. In the case of police failure to arrest a drunk driver, the injured party must show that the officer either acted or failed to act according to an existing duty. Police officers may have a duty to arrest drunk drivers, but that does not mean that if the police do not arrest every drunk driver, liability is incurred for every injury. For example, if a drunk driver with whom the police had no contact injures an individual, the police cannot be held liable for the injury. The same reasoning holds true for crime victims. A rash of burglaries in a community does not mean the police are liable to people whose homes have been invaded. There must exist some special knowledge or circumstance that sets the individual citizen apart from the general public and shows a relationship between that citizen and the police. For example, if a home owner called the police and advised that a person threatened burglary that evening and the police failed to take any action to prevent the crime, a court might find that police inaction created a breach of duty.

Proximate Cause. Once a plaintiff has demonstrated the existence of a police duty and has shown the officer breached that duty to a specific citizen, he or she must still prove that the officer's conduct was the proximate cause of the injury or damage. The proximate cause of an injury or damage is determined by asking "but for the officer's conduct, would the plaintiff have sustained the injury or damage?" If the answer to this question is no, then proximate cause is established. If proximate cause is established, then the officer can be held liable for the damage or injury.

This requirement of negligence is designed to limit liabilities in situations where damage would have occurred regardless of the officer's behavior. Consider the case where a police officer is involved in a motor vehicle chase. If the officer chases the suspect and the suspect's vehicle strikes an innocent third party, is the officer liable? Generally, if the officer was not acting in a negligent fashion and if the officer's conduct cannot be shown to have been the cause of the injury, there would be no liability on the officer's part (*Fielder v. Jenkins,* 1993). The accident may have occurred regardless of the officer's behavior. There are, however, exceptions that will be discussed in greater detail in later chapters.

Damage or Injury. Providing a plaintiff has shown the existence of a duty, the breach of that duty, and the proximate cause of injury, the civil suit will still not succeed unless the plaintiff can show actual damage or harm, which substantially interfered with an interest of an individual or his/her property. General or technical rights' violations that do not significantly interfere with the interests of a specific individual do not satisfy the damage element under negligence tort. Similarly, potential but uncertain future damage or harm is not sufficient to satisfy the damage element of a negligence action. For example, if the police refuse to provide a victim of a crime with police protection, the victim could not succeed in a negligence action until some actual damage or injury occurred. The potential for future damage alone is not sufficient to satisfy the damage element in a negligence action. There must be actual damage or injury.

Common Claims of Police Negligence

There are various types of police behaviors that can form the basis of a negligence claim. The following are a few of the most frequent claims of negligence brought against the police. When reviewing this list, one must remember that the law of police negligence is highly unique to legal jurisdictions, and every form of negligence listed is not always actionable in all jurisdictions. We will revisit many of these forms of negligence in greater detail in later chapters in the context of police pursuits, failure to arrest drunk drivers, police duties at traffic accident scenes, and failure to prevent detainee suicides.

Negligent Operation of Emergency Vehicles. Under this claim of negligence, a plaintiff argues that a police officer failed to operate an emergency vehicle with due care for the safety of the public. As a result of the negligent operation and because the officer's actions were unreasonable, the plaintiff sustained injuries. Claims of police negligent operation of emergency vehicles can be brought against the police by innocent third parties who are injured when police officers engage in high-speed pursuit driving. Under such circumstances, if a police officer becomes involved in an accident with an innocent motorist or causes the fleeing suspect to injure an innocent motorist, there is a potential for civil liability. In rare cases, even the fleeing suspect can sue if injured while attempting to elude officers.

Negligent Failure to Protect. This form of negligence may occur if a police officer fails to take adequate actions to protect a person from a known and foreseeable danger. These claims most often arise when police officers fail to protect battered women. There are, however, other circumstances that can create a duty on the part of police officers to protect people from crime. Informants, witnesses, and other people dependent upon the police can be a source of police liability if an officer knows of a potential threat and fails to take reasonable action to prevent victimization. Additionally, police officers may owe a duty of protection to the people they have taken into custody. In some cases, police officers may have a legal duty to prevent self-inflicted injury or death.

Negligent Failure to Arrest. A claim of negligent failure to arrest or apprehend is similar to a claim of negligent failure to protect. Under this form of negligence, a plaintiff argues that he or she was injured as a result of a police officer's failure to enforce the law. These claims are usually brought as a result of police failure to arrest suspected criminals. Plaintiffs argue that while there existed probable cause to arrest the suspect and the officer could reasonably foresee that inaction would lead to injury or damage, the officer still failed to take action. One of the most frequent claims of police failure to arrest occurs in situations where a police officer fails to arrest a drunk driver and that driver later injures an innocent motorist or pedestrian.

Negligent Failure to Render Assistance. In certain circumstances, the police may have a duty to render assistance to sick or injured people. If officers undertake a duty to provide assistance or medical attention and if they do not provide that assistance in a reasonable manner they can be subject to civil liability. This type of claim most often arises as a result of traffic accidents, injuries, or when illnesses strike people in custody.

Negligent Selection, Hiring, and Retention. Police administrators may have a duty to use appropriate and reasonable methods of selecting and hiring police officers. This duty may include the use of proper selection standards and tests as well as conducting adequate background investigations of police applicants. If a police officer is hired in a negligent fashion and that negligence is directly related to a later incident of police misconduct or illegal behavior, administrators may be held civilly liable for unreasonable selection and hiring practices. Likewise, police administrators who knowingly retain or promote employees who have committed illegal acts or patterns of illegal acts can be held liable for negligent retention. This is especially the case if the illegal act committed is clearly related to past acts of misconduct by the same employee.

Negligent Police Supervision and Direction. Negligent supervision and direction involves breaching a duty to provide effective systems for the evaluation, control, and monitoring of police employees' performance. Evidence of a breach of this duty may come in the form of failure to provide written and verbal directives, failure to develop adequate departmental policies and guidelines, or failure to articulate clearly to employees how duties are to be performed. It may also involve a supervisor's direction to an employee to engage in an illegal activity or the supervisor's approval of an illegal activity.

Negligent Entrustment and Assignment. Police administrators may have a duty to ensure that officers are properly trained and capable of using equipment or carrying out a given responsibility before they entrust or assign them to that responsibility. A police administrator, for example, who entrusts an officer with a motor vehicle knowing that the officer is incapable of using the vehicle with an ordinary amount of care could be held liable for negligent entrustment. Likewise, assigning an officer to a duty that the officer is incapable of performing can result in liability if the officer or a citizen is injured while the officer is performing that assignment. An example of negligent assignment would be assigning an officer to conduct a bomb sweep of a building knowing that the officer had no training in the proper execution of that assignment.

Negligent Failure to Discipline and Investigate. Negligent failure to discipline and investigate relates to a police department's failure to provide an effective system of police accountability. This breach of duty could arise by a department's failure to have adequate citizen complaint processes, adequate internal affairs investigative practices, or failing to take effective and progressive steps to sanction police misconduct.

Historical Barriers
and Defenses to Police Liability

Governmental entities and their police officers are afforded some protection from state claims of intentional or negligence tort. Legal barriers to police liabilities are established doctrine that either bar liability claims from being considered by a jury or mitigate a damage award. The most common legal doctrines barring police liability are the doctrines of sovereign immunity and public duty. Defenses to claims of police misconduct are offered during the trial. Defenses act either to excuse the behavior based upon a legal justification or to mitigate a finding of liability even where the officer's actions are shown to be unreasonable. The most common defenses to claims of police negligence include: (1) contributory negligence, (2) comparative negligence, (3) assumption of risk, and (4) sudden peril. Figure 2.2 shows the possible effect of successfully applying established doctrine or raising one of the defenses.

Figure 2.2
Traditional Barriers and Defenses to State Tort Claims

Type of Doctrine or Defense	Behavioral Focus	Possible Legal Effect
Sovereign immunity	All conduct absent waiver	Bars claims
Sudden peril	Defendant's conduct	Bars recovery
Assumption of risk	Plaintiff's conduct	Bars recovery
Contributory negligence	Plaintiff's conduct	Bars recovery
Public duty doctrine	Relationship between defendant and plaintiff	Bars recovery absent special relationship
Comparative negligence	Plaintiff's and defendant's conduct	Mitigates damages

Sovereign Immunity

The origin of the doctrine of sovereign immunity is open to debate. Some scholars believe the doctrine is traceable to Roman law, while others contend the doctrine originated with English common law. It is generally thought, however, that the doctrine was based upon the belief that "the king can do no wrong" and prevented private parties from suing the English crown. This maxim was in keeping with the prevailing belief in the divine rights of kings. Another explanation for the doctrine's creation is that it was thought unacceptable practice for a king to be sued in a court that he himself created and governed. While exceptions to absolute sovereign immunity were maintained under the English system of justice, the early American experience was markedly different.

The transmission of the doctrine of sovereign immunity from English to American common law occurred relatively early in the nation's development. The United States Supreme Court decided one of the first cases involving the doctrine of sovereign immunity. In *Chisholm v. Georgia* (1793) the Court held that Article III of the Constitution of the United States gave the federal courts jurisdiction over any lawsuit brought against a state by citizens of another state, regardless of whether a state had given its consent to be sued. The decision caused negative reaction from state legislators who viewed the decision as limiting the rights of states, and accordingly it set the states in opposition to the Court. While conflicting theories exist, it is generally believed that this decision and concerns about potential lawsuits against the government arising from debts acquired from financing the Revolutionary War prompted Congress to enact the Eleventh Amendment to the Constitution. With the enactment of the Eleventh Amendment, the power of the judiciary was limited and an economic shield of sovereign immunity was raised between the states and its citizens. The Eleventh Amendment to the United States Constitution states that:

> The judicial power of the United States shall not be construed to extend to any suit in law or equity, commenced or prosecuted against one of the United States by citizens of another State, by citizens or subjects of any foreign state.

Later in *Cohens v. Virginia* (1921), Chief Justice Marshall held that no lawsuit could be brought against the United States government but that citizens could bring civil suit against a state if the action reached a constitutional level. The doctrine was later refined to prohibit lawsuits against the states absent their expressed consent. Eventually, even suits that reached a constitutional level were barred by the Supreme Court's construction of the doctrine of sovereign immunity. In *United States v. Clark* (1834) the Court stated that the shield of sovereign immunity was applicable to the federal as well as the state governments, and in *Siren* (1869), Justice Field stated that: "It is obvious that the public service would be hindered, and public safety endangered, if the [state] could be subjected to suit at the insistence of every citizen. . . . The exemption from direct suit is, therefore, without exception" (p. 154).

By the close of the nineteenth century, the doctrine of sovereign immunity was firmly entrenched in American case law. The states were quick to adopt this doctrine and shroud themselves with similar immunities. Eventually, even municipal governments were protected by the doctrine, and citizens injured by governmental officials had no legal avenue of redress for their injuries. Historically the doctrine has provided police officers with a protection from lawsuits. However, during the past fifty years, sovereign immunity has been in decline, and recently this immunity protection has been eroded by federal and state voluntary legislative waivers of the immunity or by forced waivers due to judicial decisions. Today, while states are protected by the doctrine, municipalities are not, and police officers have become susceptible to civil suits by citizens.

The Public Duty Doctrine

The public duty doctrine has its origin in both English and American case law. Some of the first decisions to resemble a doctrine of public duty are found in English case law decided in the early nineteenth century. In *Daniels v. Wilson* (1810), an English court held that the conduct of an excise officer in assaulting an innocent person whom he mistakenly believed to be a smuggler was not actionable. The court reasoned "perhaps [the officer was] too hasty, yet it manifestly appears that he acted in the supported execution of his office." Therefore, legal liability could not attach. Early American case law in New York indicates that the position of no liability in the performance of public duties was questionable. In the case of *People v. Schuyler* (1850), a New York court held that a lawsuit against a sheriff's surety for negligent performance of an official duty could succeed; four years later, a New York court applied the precedent set out in *Schuyler* and ruled that if a lawsuit had been brought against the sheriff and his surety, the surety would have been found liable (*Dennision v. Plumb*, 1854).

The liability of a public official in the performance of an official public function was first addressed by the United States Supreme Court in 1856 in the case of *South v. Maryland* (1856). In that case, a lawsuit was brought against a sheriff for failure to prevent a breach of the peace. The plaintiff had been kidnapped and held for ransom by a violent mob. The plaintiff had requested that the sheriff provide him with protection from the mob before the incident. The sheriff declined the request; as a result, the plaintiff was severely injured and a $2,500 ransom had to be paid for his release. Justice Grier delivered the opinion of the Court, and he discussed the origin of the common-law position of nonliability for the execution of public duties by stating, "It is an undisputed principle, that for a breach of a public duty, an officer is punishable by indictment; but where he acts ministerially, and is bound to render certain services to individuals for a compensation or fee in salary, he is not liable for acts of misfeasance or nonfeasance to the party who is injured by them" (*South v. Maryland*, 1856, p. 400). The Court ruled that the "sheriff as conservator of the public peace is not liable to the plaintiff . . . even if it should appear that [the sheriff] unreasonably omitted or neglected to exert his authority to suppress it" (p. 400).

The Supreme Court's decision in *South* established several principles that have become the cornerstones of decision making for police negligence in the performance of public duties. The Court's decision in *South* is not surprising considering that the decision was rendered during an era of expanding use of sovereign immunity. The already formidable blanket of immunity that had been established by the federal and state courts initially muted the significance of the *South* decision. It remained relatively dormant until the decline of sovereign immunity in the 1940s and the rise of government-related liability litigation. Over the last 120 years, thirteen states and six circuits have directly adopted the public duty doctrine as enunciated by the Supreme Court in 1856.

The contemporary interpretation of the public duty doctrine holds that governmental functions, such as police protection, are owed to the general public and not to specific individuals. Where a duty is owed to the general public and not to any particular person, there can exist no cause of action or subsequent liability for failure to protect individuals from injury. Under the public duty doctrine there is no liability for a police officer's negligent conduct unless it can be shown that there was a duty owed to the injured person as an individual, as opposed to a duty owed to the public in general (*Torres v. City of Anacortes*, 1999). There are exceptions to the public duty doctrine that remove the protection granted to police officers in the performance of their duties. While state law varies on the requirements for exceptions to the public duty doctrine, most states recognize a special relationship as removing the protection of the public duty doctrine. Several states recognize that a special relationship is created by:

1. an explicit assurance by the municipality, through promises or actions, that it would act on behalf of the injured party;
2. knowledge on the part of the municipality that inaction could lead to harm; and,
3. justifiable and detrimental reliance by the injured party on the municipality's affirmative undertaking (*Cuffy v. City of New York*, 1987).

A word of caution is warranted at this point. First, some states require (in addition to the above three requirements) "direct contact" between a police officer and a citizen as well as "express assurances" of assistance by the police to give rise to a special relationship (*Torres v. City of Anacortes*, 1999). Some states recognize a "volunteer rescue exception" to the public duty doctrine when a government agency gratuitously assumes the duty to warn an individual of a danger or to come to the aid of the individual and then breaches the duty (*Babcock v. Mason County Fire Dist.*, 2000). Finally, other states are split on whether or not reckless or malicious police conduct should be litigated within the four corners of the doctrine or outside its protections. The public duty doctrine and its exceptions will be discussed in greater detail in subsequent chapters.

Although the doctrine has suffered some erosion in recent times, it still represents a formidable hurdle that plaintiffs must clear before they successfully can sue the police for negligent behavior that results in injury or damage.

Contributory Negligence

The defense of contributory negligence holds that if an officer can show that the plaintiff was also negligent in causing the damage or injury, the officer will not be held liable for the damage or injury. This defense is based on the idea that all persons owe a duty to carry out their day-to-day activities in a reasonable manner. It is thought that if the plaintiff was engaged in unreasonable behavior that increased the likelihood of damage or injury, the officer should not be held liable. Consider the situation where a police officer is in pursuit of a speeding suspect. Although the officer might be negligent in the operation of the vehicle, other motorists owe a duty to operate their vehicles in a reasonable manner. If the pursuing officer became involved in an accident with another motorist who did not pull over to the side of the road, a court might find that the citizen's behavior contributed to the damage. In such a situation, liability would be prevented due to the citizen's own contributory negligence.

Comparative Negligence

Comparative negligence does not totally bar an officer's liability; rather, it mitigates the size of the damage award. Consider the situation where the officer is in pursuit of a suspect. When the issue comes to court in a jurisdiction using the comparative negligence defense, the court would attempt to determine the degree of negligence of both the officer and the injured party. If the officer was 30 percent negligent and the citizen was 70 percent negligent, the court would proportion the damage award accordingly. If the award were $1,000, the officer would be liable for $300. The comparative negligence defense allows the court to assess fault to both parties and to determine the extent to which each party contributed to the accident.

Assumption of Risk

The assumption of risk doctrine is another method by which liability is limited. The general principle behind the doctrine is that one who knowingly participates in a dangerous behavior cannot expect to recover damages sustained in conjunction with engaging in that behavior. For example, a suspect injured while fleeing from the police following an armed robbery cannot expect to sue police to recover damages resulting from the chase. In such a situation, a court applying the assumption of risk doctrine could hold that the suspect had assumed the risk of injury by choosing to commit the robbery and attempting to flee from the police. Since the suspect assumed the risk of injury, the police would not be liable to the suspect for any damages received (see generally, Kappeler and Vaughn, 1989).

Sudden Peril

In a very limited number of police liability cases, especially cases involving the use of force, officers may be able to bar liability by using the sudden peril or emergency defense doctrine. Courts and juries have recognized that certain behaviors of law enforcement officers entail split-second decisions. It would be unfair to allow liability in cases where officers have to make quick decisions on how to react to a situation (*Scott v. City of Opa Locka*, 1975). This form of defense is, however, tentative. Many courts and juries will fail to recognize the sudden peril doctrine. While the sudden peril defense is a possibility in cases where officers react instinctively to a sudden emergency, police officers should never rely on its adequacy. Additionally, the defense is not available to officers who create the sudden emergency or peril by their own misconduct.

Summary

Under state law, there are three types of torts: strict liability, intentional, and negligence. The four basic elements of a negligence action are legal duty, breach of duty, proximate cause, and actual damage. After a brief consideration of the common forms of police negligence, the chapter outlined the traditional barriers to governmental liability: the doctrine of sovereign immunity and the public duty doctrine. Defenses to claims of negligence include contributory negligence, comparative negligence, assumption of risk, and sudden peril. These elements, defenses, and liability-limiting doctrines constitute the traditional common-law theory of negligence and reflect the conceptual framework for litigating claims of police negligence.

The Fundamentals of Federal Liability Law 3

One of the most common avenues of suing the police for misconduct is federal law. While there are several federal statutes that allow citizens to bring claims against law enforcement officers and their employers, one of the most commonly used is the Civil Rights Act of 1871, which has since been codified as Title 42 of the United States Code. Even though criminal charges can be brought against the police for violating a citizen's constitutional rights, litigation under civil sections is far more frequent and represents a greater threat. While juries are sympathetic to the violation of a citizen's constitutional rights, they are less willing to impose criminal sanctions on police officers absent a very heinous violation of rights.

In this chapter, we take a quick look at the history of the Civil Rights Act of 1871 and the general framework of litigation under the provisions of that legislation. A brief presentation of the elements necessary for a federal civil rights action is followed by a discussion of the judicial requirements for successfully litigating a federal lawsuit against a municipality. Attention is given to the requirements for suing a municipal government for inadequate training of police officers as well as for other common forms of administrative misconduct that may result in federal liability. The chapter concludes with a discussion of the various defenses available to police officers who are alleged to have violated the constitutional rights of citizens.

The Civil Rights Act of 1871

Following ratification of the Thirteenth and Fourteenth Amendments of the United States Constitution, which abolished slavery and provided due process safeguards, Congress enacted the Civil Rights Act of

1871 primarily to assist in controlling the conduct of people affiliated with the Ku Klux Klan. The legislation allowed a remedy for deprivation of civil rights and was later codified as Section 1983.

Although the legislation was largely unused before the 1960s, it is now the cornerstone of police federal liability litigation. The increasing use of the Civil Rights Act may be attributable to an expanded interpretation of the legislation by the Supreme Court, enhanced further by the passage of the Attorney's Fees Act of 1976. The courts have interpreted the Civil Rights Act to allow persons who have had their constitutional rights violated by government officials acting under color of state law to bring civil suit in federal court against law enforcement officers, police agencies, and municipalities. Additionally, the Attorneys Fee Act allows counsel representing these parties to collect their fees from judgments against defendants found liable for constitutional rights violations. These two factors have led to an explosion in the number of federal cases filed against the police claiming violations of constitutional or federally protected rights.

Title 42 of the United States Code, Section 1983 reads:

> Every person, who under color of any statute, ordinance, regulation, custom, or usage, of any State or territory, subjects, or causes to be subjected, any citizen of the United States or other persons within the jurisdiction thereof to the deprivation of any right, privileges, or immunities secured by the Constitution and laws, shall be liable to the party injured in an action at law, suit in equity, or other proper proceeding for redress.

This seemingly simple passage has a number of important elements. First, the plaintiff must be a protected person within the meaning of the legislation. This requirement has virtually no limitation because anyone under the jurisdiction of the United States is considered a person with the right to bring a civil rights lawsuit. Second, the defendant must also be a person within the meaning of the legislation. This second element has more profound implications. As we will discuss in later portions of the chapter, the courts have gone back and forth on whether governments are considered "persons" within the meaning of the statute. Three critically important elements of the statute remain. Citizens seeking redress for civil rights violations can sue police officers successfully if they can show that: (1) the officer was acting under color of state law, (2) that the alleged violation was of a constitutional or federally protected right, and (3) the alleged violation reached a constitutional level. If each of these elements is not established, then liability is barred under the provisions of the legislation. If these elements cannot be established, civil suit may still be brought at the state level under a tort action (as discussed in chapter 2) provided that the elements of a tort can be established.

Acting Under Color of Law

Defendants in a Section 1983 action must be acting under "color of state law" to be held liable for constitutional violations. The Supreme Court defined the concept of color of law as it pertains to Section 1983 actions in the case of *West v. Atkins* (1988). The Court states that,

> The traditional definition of acting under color of state law requires that the defendant in a 1983 action have exercised power "possessed by virtue of state law and made possible only because the wrongdoer is clothed with the authority of state law . . ." To constitute state action, "the deprivation must be caused by the exercise of some right or privilege created by the State . . . or by a person for whom the State is responsible," and "the party charged with the deprivation must be a person who may fairly be said to be a state actor." "[S]tate employment is generally sufficient to render the defendant a state actor." It is firmly established that a defendant in a 1983 suit acts under color of state law when he abuses the position given to him by the State. Thus, generally, a public employee acts under color of state law while acting in his official capacity or while exercising his responsibilities pursuant to state law. (*West v. Atkins*, 1988, pp. 49–50, citations omitted)

Acts of private individuals, unless they conspire with state actors, or the acts of law enforcement officers not related to employment, usually are not actionable under the provisions of the legislation. In order to establish the liability of a private citizen under the provision of Section 1983 it must be shown that the individuals conduct is "fairly attributable to the state" (*Lugar v. Edmondson Oil Co.*, 1993, p. 937), that the private citizen and state acted together, or that the private citizen obtained significant aid from the state (see generally, *Pino v. Higgs*, 1996). This, however, does not mean that an off-duty police officer performing a police function cannot be held liable for a constitutional violation (*Jocks v. Tavernier*, 2000). Off-duty police officers employed on second jobs can be found to be acting under color of law if they perform police functions. Consider the situation where an off-duty police officer has accepted employment as a bank security guard. If the bank is robbed and the officer attempts to apprehend the suspect, the officer may be found to be acting under color of law.

Many police actions that lead to the filing of a Section 1983 suit are based on conduct outside the scope of an officer's official authority. For example, a police officer who brutalizes a citizen is not acting within the scope of lawful police authority. Nonetheless, courts interpret this type of conduct as being under color of state law even though it is illegal. A color of law determination does not depend on "whether an officer stays strictly within the line of duty, or oversteps it" (*Martinez v. Colon*, 1995, p. 986). Often the distinction between official state action and private action is difficult to make. Generally, if officers are carrying out a police function, such as making an arrest or conducting a search, it can be said that they are acting under color of state law for purposes of liability.

Historically, the courts determined whether officers were acting under color of law by considering their duty status. Today they consider many factors when making this determination. Courts have repeatedly instructed:

> no single, easily determinable factor will control whether a police officer was acting under color of state law. While certain factors will clearly be relevant—for example, a police officer's garb, an officer's duty status, the officer's use of a service revolver, and the location of the incident—these factors must not be assessed mechanically. (*Bouye v. Marshall*, 2000; *Jocks v. Tavernier*, 2000; *Parrilla-Burgos v. Hernandez-Rivera*, 1997, p. 45; *Rivera v. Vargas*, 1999)

Rather, when making a color of law determination the courts consider a number of factors as well as the context of the situation that gave rise to the lawsuit. In *Martinez*, the First Circuit Court of Appeals stated "whether a police officer is acting under color of state law turns on the nature and circumstances of the officer's conduct and the relationship of that conduct to the performance of his official duties" (*Martinez v. Colon*, 1995, p. 986). Such an evaluation requires an assessment of the totality of the surrounding circumstances, "'[t]he key determinant is whether the actor, at the time in question, purposes to act in an official capacity or to exercise official responsibilities pursuant to state law" (*Rivera v. Vargas*, 1999, citing *Martinez v. Colon*, 1995, p. 986).

The following are among the most important factors considered by the courts:

1. Did the police identify themselves as law enforcement officers?
2. Did the police file official documents in the case?
3. Did police attempt an arrest, conduct a search, or engage in an investigation?
4. Were the police on patrol?
5. Was police power or authority used and was it in their jurisdiction?
6. Did the police display weapons or other police equipment?
7. Did department policy indicate duty status?
8. Did the department remove the officer's authority to act in an official capacity?
9. Did the department authorize the act?
10. Were the police in uniform or wear clothing that identified them as officers?
11. Were the police operating a marked police vehicle? (see, Vaughn and Coomers, 1995; *Jocks v. Tavernier*, 2000; *Martinez v. Colon*, 1995; *Parrilla-Burgos v. Hernandez-Rivera*, 1997; *Rivera v. Vargas*, 1999).

Although the courts consider these factors when making a determination of whether an officer was acting under color of law, the factors are not applied in formulaic fashion. The courts are free to consider the plaintiff's subjective reactions to the defendant-officer's conduct as well as the extent to which any or all of these factors spanned the police-citizen encounter (*Zambranan-Marrero v. Suarez-Cruz*, 1998). Although the subjective reactions of the victim and the frequency with which the factors detailed above occurred during an encounter have relevance, "the primary focus of the color of law analysis must be on the conduct of the police officer" (*Parrilla-Burgos v. Hernandez-Rivera*, 1997, p. 47) and whether it "related in some meaningful way either to the officer's governmental status or to the performance of his duties" (*Martinez v. Colon*, 1995, p. 987).

Violation of a Constitutional Right

Conduct that can be redressed under Section 1983 is limited to violations of constitutional or federally protected rights. This means violations of state laws or city ordinances by a police officer are not actionable under the Civil Rights Act. For example, a police officer arrests an intoxicated driver and lawfully impounds the motor vehicle. If under state law it is unlawful for the officers to conduct an inventory search of the contents of the vehicle and the officer does so anyway, a state law has been violated. However, since inventory searches of motor vehicles are permissible within the provision of the Fourth Amendment of the United States Constitution, the officers conduct would not be a violation of a constitutional or federally protected right. While the drunk driver may have grounds for a civil action under state tort law, a Section 1983 lawsuit could not succeed since the conduct did not violate a constitutional right.

Figure 3.1 presents select amendments of the United States Constitution most commonly violated by police officers. A violation of any of the provisions of these amendments can form the basis for civil litigation under the provision of Section 1983. It is important to note that the courts interpret these amendments to prohibit various types of police conduct. Often these judicial interpretations are not obvious from a cursory reading of the amendments. For example, a quick reading of the Fourth Amendment might lead one to conclude that its provisions relate only to the search and seizure of evidence. Courts have, however, interpreted the Fourth Amendment to prohibit police officers from using unreasonable and excessive force in effecting arrests, a topic discussed in some detail in chapter 4.

Figure 3.1

Selected Amendments to the United States Constitution

Amendment I: Congress shall make no law respecting an establishment of religion, or prohibiting the free exercise thereof; or abridging the freedom of speech, or of the press; or the right of the people peaceably to assemble, and to petition the Government for a redress of grievances.

Amendment IV: The right of the people to be secure in their persons, houses, papers, and effects, against unreasonable searches and seizures, shall not be violated, and no warrants shall issue, but upon probable cause, supported by oath or affirmation, and particularly describing the place to be searched, and the persons or things to be seized.

Amendment V: No person shall be held to answer for a capital, or otherwise infamous crime, unless on a presentment or indictment of a Grand Jury, except in cases arising in the land or naval forces, or in the militia, when in actual service in time of war or public danger; nor shall any person be subject for the same offense to be twice put in jeopardy of life or limb; nor shall be compelled in any criminal case to be a witness against himself, nor be deprived of life, liberty, or property, without due process of law; nor shall private property be taken for public use, without just compensation.

Amendment VI: In all criminal prosecutions; the accused shall enjoy the right to a speedy and public trial, by an impartial jury of the State and district wherein the crime shall have been committed, which district shall have been previously ascertained by law, and to be informed of the nature and cause of the accusation; to be confronted with the witnesses against him; to have compulsory process for obtaining witnesses in his favor, and to have the assistance of Counsel for his defense.

Amendment VIII: Excessive bail shall not be required, nor fines imposed, nor cruel and unusual punishments inflicted.

Amendment XIV: Section 1. All persons born or naturalized in the United States, and subject to the jurisdiction thereof, are citizens of the United States and of the State wherein they reside. No State shall make or enforce any law which shall abridge the privileges or immunities of citizens of the United States; nor shall any State deprive any person of life, liberty, or property, without due process of law; nor deny any person within its jurisdiction the equal protection of laws.

Determining the exact constitutional provision allegedly violated by a police officer is another important aspect of evaluating a constitutional violation. Law enforcement officers perform a variety of tasks that can seem to fall under several provisions of the Constitution. For example, the provisions of the Fourth Amendment govern intentional seizures by means of deadly force. While many police actions may seem to be seizures on their face, closer inspection of the conduct of the officer, the status of victim, and the circumstance surrounding the constitutional violation may indicate otherwise. A classic example of this situation is the case where a police officer is pursuing a suspect in a motor vehicle chase. If the officer unintentionally strikes the suspect's vehicle killing the driver or even killing a passenger, the courts are not likely to find that the officer's actions constituted a seizure (*County of Sacramento v. Lewis*, 1998). In this case the litigation would proceed under the substantive due process clause of the Fourteenth Amendment rather than under Fourth Amendment provisions. Likewise, the conduct of an officer who physically abuses a prisoner would fall under either the Fourteenth Amendment's due process clause or the Eighth Amendment's prohibition against cruel and unusual punishment. Because the standards for establishing liability differ depending on the constitutional provision violated, it is important to determine the exact constitutional provision under which a law enforcement officer's actions fall.

In *Graham v. Connor* (1989) the Supreme Court established the "more-specific provision rule." The Court held that "[w]here a particular amendment provides an explicit textual source of constitutional protection against a particular sort of government behavior, that Amendment . . . must be the guide for analyzing" liability claims (p. 395). The Court later explained:

> [*Graham*] does not hold that all constitutional claims relating to physically abusive government conduct must arise under either the Fourth or Eighth Amendments; rather, *Graham* simply requires that if a constitutional claim is covered by a specific constitutional provision, such as the Fourth or Eighth Amendment, the claim must be analyzed under the standard appropriate to that specific provision, not under the rubric of substantive due process. (*United States v. Lanier*, 1997, slip op. p. 13)

Nor does this rule make all police pursuits that end in injury impossible to litigate under the provisions of the Fourth Amendment. Rather it means that "all claims that law enforcement officers have used excessive force—deadly or not—in the course of an arrest, investigatory stop, or other 'seizure' of a free citizen should be analyzed under the Fourth Amendment and its 'reasonableness' standard, rather than under a 'substantive due process' approach" (*Albright v. Oliver*, 1994, p. 276).

Figure 3.2 shows many of the specific federal claims brought against the police and the outcome of these cases in Federal District Court.

Figure 3.2

Section 1983 Claims Against the Police: Decisions of the Federal District Courts*

Allegation Against the Police	Frequency of Claim	Percent of Cases With Claim[a]	Percent of Cases Plaintiffs Prevail[b]	Frequency of Plaintiffs Prevail
False Arrest/Imprisonment	740	39	46	341
Excessive Force	540	29	56	304
Unlawful Search and Seizure	383	20	48	183
Assault/Battery	285	15	55	157
Malicious Prosecution	217	12	47	102
Inadequate Training	203	11	55	112
Conspiracy To Violate Civil Rights	201	11	50	100
Inadequate Supervision	183	10	59	108
General Negligence	141	8	48	67
Infliction of Emotional Distress	135	7	56	75
Unlawful Detention/Delay	133	7	49	65
Inadequate Investigation	111	6	48	53
Inadequate Policy	86	5	57	49
Inadequate Medical Attention	67	4	49	30
Perjury/False Reporting	67	4	48	32
Strip Searches	64	3	72	46
Invasion of Privacy	63	3	49	31
Failure to Protect	58	3	52	30
Failure to Prevent Detainee Suicide	46	2	46	21
Vehicular Pursuits	42	2	31	13
Civil Processes	42	2	43	18
Libel/Slander	33	2	46	15
Coercion	14	1	64	9
All Others	193	10	46	88

*Cases from 1978–1994; percentages are rounded.

[a]Percentage of cases in which this issue was raised. Total equals more than 100 because cases often include multiple issues.

[b]Percentages total more than 100 because they are based on win/lose ratio by type of claim against the police.

Source: Kappeler, V. E., Kappeler, S. F., and del Carmen, R. V. (1993).

Constitutional Level

To sue a police officer successfully under the provisions of Section 1983, a plaintiff must be able to counter the claim that the conduct of the police did not reach a level of significance to violate the constitution (*Dunn v. Denk*, 1995; *Simpson v. City of Pickens, Mississippi*, 1995). This means that negligent acts by the police or acts that result in very minor injury, in and of themselves, normally cannot form the sole basis of a Section 1983 lawsuit (*Cathey v. Guenther*, 1995). Additionally, as the Supreme Court has pointed out, "not every push or shove" is a constitutional violation (*Graham v. Connor*, 1989). Some courts have, however, carried the principle to its extreme to protect police officers from liability.

In the case of *Hinton v. City of Elwood, Kansas* (1993) Kenneth Hinton was arrested by several police officers for disorderly conduct. Hinton was informed that his dog had been tranquilized and impounded by an Elwood animal control officer. Hinton approached the officer on three separate occasions to inquire about the incident and to retrieve his dog. Each time he was told to wait for his day in court and to talk to the judge. On the final encounter and in the company of his three children and two neighbors, Hinton became angry. Hinton told the animal control officer that the daughter of a prior landlord had become ill after she called the animal control officer about his dog. The control officer interpreted this as a threat and called the police.

Elwood police responded to the call and located Hinton walking home with his children. One officer informed Hinton that he wanted to discuss a complaint that had been filed against him for disturbing the peace. Allegedly, the officer poked Hinton in the chest several times and instructed him that if he did not stop walking, he was going to jail. The officer testified that Hinton jerked off his shirt as if he was ready to fight. About this time the mayor arrived and told Hinton to calm down, go home, and that if he engaged in one more outburst he would be arrested for disorderly conduct. At the end of this exchange, Hinton shoved the officer out of his way, picked up his daughter, and started to walk away. The officer seized Hinton and a struggle ensued. The officer shoved Hinton's face into the asphalt and twisted his arm behind his back. The officer eventually used a stun-gun to subdue Hinton. Hinton asserted that the officer used the stun-gun on him numerous times.

Hinton filed an excessive force claim against the mayor, the city, and the arresting officer under Section 1983. The district court granted the officer's motion for summary judgment, but Hinton appealed. On appeal, the Tenth Circuit Court held that the alleged deprivation suffered by Hinton at the hands of the police did not reach a constitutional level. Accordingly, the court affirmed the lower court's summary judgment decision.

Hinton stands in opposition to a more recent case where a police officer arrested a female motorist. During the course of the arrest, the officer threw her facedown into a ditch, put his knee in her back, handcuffed her, and called her a bitch (*Dunn v. Denk*, 1995). The motorist brought a Section 1983 action against the officer asking for money damages because of the post-traumatic stress and injuries she suffered as a result of the arrest. Considering the case on appeal, the United States Court of Appeals for the Fifth Circuit stated that although in another case it found the fear caused by a police officer when he pointed a gun at a citizen "did not rise to the level of a constitutional level . . . the case at bar, however, is exceptional; the evidence of record was sufficient for the jury to find significant injury . . ." (p. 25). The case was remanded to the federal district court. On rehearing the case, the Fifth Circuit further muddied the waters of determining significant injury by ruling that because the plaintiff suffered merely the aggravation of a preexisting injury that could only be attributable to the officer's reasonable use of force and not his excessive use of force, liability could not attach (*Dunn v. Denk*, 1996; see also, *Johnson v. Morel*, 1989; *Wells v. Bonner*, 1995). The dissent in *Dunn* was sharp, declaring the decision "open season on the infirm" (p. 408).

In contrast to the Fifth Circuit's position, the United States Court of Appeals for the Ninth Circuit has a history of taking the position that an alleged constitutional deprivation that results in minor damage or no actual harm or injury is actionable and should result in the plaintiff's compensation (*Floyd v. Laws*, 1991; *George v. City of Long Beach*, 1992). "In this Circuit, nominal damages must be awarded if a plaintiff proves a violation of his [or her] constitutional rights" (*George v. City of Long Beach*, 1992, p. 708). The trier of fact must award nominal damages to the plaintiff "as a symbolic vindication of her constitutional rights" (*Floyd v. Laws*, 1991, p. 1403). In *Macias v. Ihde* (1999) the court held that plaintiffs can prove a Section 1983 violation without showing that the deprivation of constitutional rights caused actual harm.

The cases of the Fifth, Ninth, and Tenth Circuit Courts illustrate the divide among many lower courts when they attempt to interpret the requirement that any alleged police misconduct must reach a significant level of constitutional violation before an officer can be held liable under the provisions of Section 1983. One of the factors contributing to the confusion among the lower courts is their failure to distinguish adequately between what acts reach a level of constitutional deprivation and an injury requirement for a successful excessive force lawsuit brought under the Fourth Amendment.

Historically, both state governments and municipalities could not be sued under the statute because they enjoyed immunity. Today, states still enjoy immunity. While this immunity protects the states from civil suit based on the conduct of state officers, it does not protect individual state officers from civil liability. Like local police officers, state officials can be sued in their personal capacities; the state itself, however, cannot be held liable under Section 1983. Two Supreme Court decisions have held that states cannot be sued under the provisions of Section 1983, but lawsuits can be brought against state officers in their personal capacities as private individuals (*Hafer v. Melo*, 1991; *Will v. Michigan Department of State Police*, 1989).

Municipal Liability under Section 1983

Municipal liability is a relatively new form of civil liability under Section 1983. In 1961 the United States Supreme Court held that municipalities are not "persons" under the meaning of Section 1983 legislation. Therefore municipalities were not subject to civil suit under the statute (*Monroe v. Pape*, 1961). Today, however, this is not the case. In 1978, the United States Supreme Court held that municipalities could be held liable for constitutional violations by their employees, thus depriving local governments of the protection of sovereign immunity and making municipalities "persons" within the meaning of the legislation (*Monell v. Department of Social Services*, 1978). In *Monell v. Department of Social Services* (1978) the Supreme Court stated that,

> Our analysis of the legislative history of the Civil Rights Act of 1871 compels the conclusion that Congress did intend municipalities and other local government units to be included among those persons to whom 1983 applies. Local governing bodies, therefore, can be sued directly under 1983 for monetary, declaratory, or injunctive relief. (p. 657)

Municipal governments can be held liable under the provisions of Section 1983 if police conduct results in the violation of a citizen's constitutional rights due to the "deliberate indifference" of a municipality. To establish municipal liability for the behavior of a police officer, plaintiffs must establish that there existed a policy or custom promoted by the city's designated policymaker that caused the constitutional deprivation. More specifically, to hold a municipality liable for a constitutional deprivation plaintiffs must show that:

1. they possessed a constitutional or federally protected right;
2. they were deprived of their constitutional or federally protected right;
3. the municipality had an unconstitutional policy or custom;
4. the policy or custom amounted to deliberate indifference to plaintiff's constitutional or federally protected right; and
5. the policy or custom caused the deprivation of a constitutional or federally protected right (see, *Estate of Macias v. Lopez*, 1999; *Macias v. Ihde*, 1999).

Municipal Policy and Policymakers

In *Monell* (1978), the Supreme Court held that civil liability under Section 1983 may be imposed on a municipality for the actions of its employees, if:

... the action that is alleged to be unconstitutional implements or executes a policy statement, ordinance, regulation, or decision officially adopted and promulgated by that body's officers. Moreover, although the touchstone of the 1983 action against a government body is an allegation that official policy is responsible for a deprivation of rights protected by the Constitution, local governments, like every other 1983 "person," by the very terms of the statute, may be sued for constitutional deprivations visited pursuant to governmental "custom" even though such a custom has not received formal approval through the body's official decision-making channels. (citations and footnotes omitted; p. 657)

The Supreme Court's decision means that municipalities can be held liable for the acts of their police officers if the acts are the product of either official policy or organizational custom and practice. This requires that the policy or custom be the "moving force" behind the officer's violation of the constitutional rights. One court has interpreted the Supreme Court's decision to require either of the following elements to establish municipal liability:

(1) A policy statement, ordinance, regulation, or decision that is officially adopted and promulgated by the municipality's lawmaking officers or by an official to whom the lawmakers have delegated policymaking authority; or

(2) A persistent, widespread practice of city officials or employees which, although not authorized by officially adopted and promulgated policy, is so common and well settled as to constitute a custom that fairly represents municipal policy. Actual or constructive knowledge of such custom must be attributable to the governing body of the municipality or to an official to whom that body had delegated policymaking authority. (*Bennett v. City of Slidell*, 1984, p. 862)

Such an interpretation of the statute requires that an officer's violation of a citizen's constitutional right be attributed to a municipal policy or custom that was either created or condoned by a high-level municipal policymaker.

On several occasions the Supreme Court has specifically ruled on the issue of who is a policymaker for purposes of municipal liability. In *Pembaur v. City of Cincinnati* (1986), the Court held that only those public officials who have final policymaking authority could render a municipality liable under the provisions of Section 1983. In *City of St. Louis v. Praprotnik* (1988), the Court held that a municipality may be held liable where authorized policymakers "approve a subordinate's decision and the basis for it" (p. 127). The Court further instructed that federal judicial decisions of who is a policymaker for purposes of liability are to be made by examining state law (*Bennett v. Pippin*, 1996; *City of St. Louis v. Praprotnik*, 1988). When making a decision of who is a policymaker the court must "identify those officials or governmental bodies who speak with final policymaking authority for the local governmental actor concerning the action alleged to have caused the particular constitutional or statutory violation at issue" (*Jett v. Dallas independent School Dist.*, 1989). Deliberation of whether a law enforcement official is a policymaker for the local unit of government, either municipal or county, requires the courts to address the following issues:

1. Does the law enforcement official have the power to set policy?
2. Does the law enforcement official have final policymaking authority?
3. Is the law enforcement official's power and authority to establish policy within the particular area or issue under litigation?; and
4. Does state law describe the policymaking power and authority of the law enforcement official?

Because laws vary across states and are specific to different employment positions, not every police supervisor or law enforcement official can be considered a policymaker for purposes of Section 1983 liability. Several courts have, however, ruled that a police chief is "one whose acts or edicts may fairly be said to represent official policy" (*Bordanaro v. McLeod*, 1989, p. 1157). Thus, police chiefs are usually considered municipal policymakers (*Eversole v. Steele*, 1995) when they have final decision-making authority (*Comfort v. Town of Pittsfield*, 1996). There is much more confusion among the court on whether sheriffs are policymakers of county governments. Some courts have held that sheriffs are policymakers, thus county government can be held liable for the policy and custom promoted by a sheriff (*Bennett v. Pippin*, 1996; *Brown v. Bryan County, Okl.*, 1995; *Marchese v. Lucas*, 1985; *Navarro v. Block*, 1996). Other courts have held that sheriffs are not policymakers of county government and accordingly a county cannot be held liable for the constitutional violations of sheriffs or their appointees (*Strickler v. Waters*, 1993; *Thompson v. Duke*, 1989). Likewise, constables or city marshals may or may not be considered policymakers since they often have very limited control over recruitment, selection, and training of law enforcement personnel. Therefore, what a constable or marshal promulgates is not normally construed as official policy (*Rhode v. Denson*, 1985).

There are, however, exceptions to the general proposition that police chiefs and sheriffs are municipal policymakers. In *Hill v. Clifton* (1996), a Gainesville police officer sued her city employer for alleged discrimination, equal protection violations, and retaliation for exercising her First Amendment rights. The police chief allegedly retaliated against Hill for her investigation and grand jury testimony concerning misconduct in the police department. Addressing the issue of who is a policymaker, the United States Court of Appeals for the Eleventh Circuit stated, "Because the Police Chief was not the final policymaking authority, and because there is no evidence the City Manager approved of any illegal or improper motive the Police Chief may have had" it affirmed the district court's grant of summary judgment to the city (p. 1151). The court's analysis was based on a narrow reading of *City of St. Louis v. Praprotnik* (1988), interpreting that case as requiring a demonstration that the city manager approved or ratified not only the police chief's actions but the basis or underlying "improper motive" of that action (*Hill v. Clifton*, 1996, p. 1152). Other courts have attempted to exclude sheriffs from the category of policymakers. Despite the Supreme Court's questioning of position, some courts continue to use novel legal language to exclude sheriffs from liability (see, *McMillian v. Johnson*, 1996).

One of the major conflicts among the lower courts on whether a particular law enforcement official is a policymaker of the local unit of government comes from an attempt to delineate between general and final policymaking authority in a specific area of practice. Some courts, for example, have held that while a police chief or sheriff may have the power and authority to hire, fire, and demote employees, that power may be distinct from the power and authority to make policy for the municipality or the county (*Morro v. City of Birmingham*, 1997; *Venter v. City of Delphi*, 1997). In this form of analysis it is possible for a police executive to have authority over some administrative aspects of the agency or law enforcement practice but still lack the power to make policy for the municipality. In these cases, it is possible that a law enforcement official can be the final policymaking authority for enforcement practices (*J. B. v. Washington County*, 1997) but not have final policymaking authority over employment practices. It is equally possible that a law enforcement official can be the final policymaking authority for a local government in employment policy (*Brady v. Ft. Bend Cty.*, 1998) but not in all aspects of law enforcement practice. The Supreme Court has attempted to clarify the conflict among the lower courts on the policymaker issue.

In 1997, the Supreme Court attempted to bring some uniformity to the policymaker issue when it is applied to law enforcement officials. In *McMillian v. Monroe County, Alabama* (1997), the Court took up the issue of whether Alabama sheriffs are policymakers of county government. Ronda Morrison was murdered in Monroe County, Alabama, and the plaintiff was indicted, convicted, and sentenced to death for the crime. After two remands, the Alabama Court of Criminal Appeals reversed the conviction, holding that the state suppressed statements and other exculpatory evidence. After six years in prison, the plaintiff was released.

The plaintiff brought a Section 1983 lawsuit in the District Court for the Middle District of Alabama against Monroe County and numerous officials, including the three men who investigated the murder.

Tom Tate, the sheriff of Monroe County, was among these men and was sued in his official capacity. The district court dismissed the claims against Monroe County and Tate in their official capacities holding that "any unlawful acts of Defendants Tate and Ikner cannot be said to represent [Monroe] County's policy," because "an Alabama county has [no] authority to make policy in the area of law enforcement" (App to Pet. for Cert. 55a). Tate appealed the decision to the Court of Appeals for the Eleventh Circuit, which affirmed the District Court's decision that Sheriff Tate was not the "final policymaker for Monroe County in the area of law enforcement, because Monroe County has no law enforcement authority" (McMillian v. Johnson, 1996, p. 1583).

The Supreme Court granted certiorari. The Court noted that two principles guided its decision.

> First, the question is not whether Sheriff Tate acts for Alabama or Monroe County in some categorical, "all or nothing" [manner]. Our cases on the liability of local governments under §1983 instruct us to ask whether governmental officials are final policymakers for the local government in a particular area, or on a particular issue. . . . Thus, we are not seeking to make a characterization of Alabama sheriffs that will hold true for every type of official action they engage in. We simply ask whether Sheriff Tate represents the State or the county when he acts in a law enforcement capacity . . . Second, our inquiry is dependent on an analysis of state law . . . This is not to say that state law can answer the question for us by, for example, simply labeling as a state official an official who clearly makes county policy. But our understanding of the actual function of a governmental official, in a particular area, will necessarily be dependent on the definition of the official's functions under relevant state law. (*McMillian v. Monroe Cty., Ala.,* 1997, pp. 7–8)

The Court went on to examine three sources of state law—the Alabama Constitution, the Alabama Code, and Alabama Supreme Court decisions. Considering these sources of state law, the Court concluded:

> In sum, although there is some evidence in Alabama law that supports petitioner's argument, we think the weight of the evidence is strongly on the side of the conclusion reached by the Court of Appeals: Alabama sheriffs, when executing their law enforcement duties, represent the State of Alabama, not their counties. (p. 12)

The petitioner argued that this conclusion will create a lack of uniformity in Alabama and throughout the country, but the Court reasoned that "since it is entirely natural that both the role of sheriffs and the importance of counties vary from State to State, there is no inconsistency created by court decisions that declare sheriffs to be county officers in one State, and not in another" (p. 14).

Knowledge of Policy and Custom

Obviously when a policymaker designs and implements a formal written policy or directive, it can be assumed that the policymaker had actual knowledge of that policy. In cases alleging custom or unwritten practices, there are two avenues that plaintiffs can pursue to demonstrate the requisite knowledge for establishing municipal liability. First, some courts recognize that a combination of repeated violations of constitutional rights by police employees and failures of policymakers to take corrective actions can by itself establish custom, irrespective of the official policymaker's knowledge of the police practices (*Gillette v. Delmore*, 1992; *Navarro v. Block*, 1996; *Thompson v. City of Los Angeles*, 1989). Second, some courts cling to the principle that it is necessary for plaintiffs to demonstrate that the policymaker had actual or constructive knowledge of a practice or custom within the organization (*Hill v. Clifton*, 1996). Factors indicating such knowledge may include:

1. the presence of supervisory personnel at the violation;
2. the extent to which the policymaker oversees operational aspects of the organization;
3. the incident review process used by the policymaker; and
4. the method used to gain control and compliance of employees (del Carmen and Kappeler, 1991).

Even if plaintiffs can establish repeated acts or constructive knowledge of the custom by policymakers, it must be shown that the custom was the moving force behind the individual officer's constitutional violation. For plaintiffs to succeed in Section 1983 actions they must demonstrate a nexus between the officer's constitutional violation and the municipal custom or practice. Factors indicating that the action of a lower-ranking employee was based on a custom attributable to the municipality or its policymakers include:

1. the frequency of the violations;
2. the extent to which the practice was routinized by employees;
3. the extent to which the practice was accepted by supervisors;
4. the extent to which the action represented shared beliefs of employees;
5. the number and unanimity of employees involved in the violation;
6. retention of, failure to discipline, or failure to investigate the violating employee; and
7. failure to prevent future violations (del Carmen and Kappeler, 1991).

While these factors indicate the existence of an official policy or custom as well as actual or constructive knowledge on the part of the policymaker, courts view custom in the totality of the circumstances surrounding the constitutional violation. The presence or absence of a single factor usually does not determine liability (*Hegarty v. Somerset County*, 1995; *Santiago v. Fenton*, 1989). Although it was shown in one case that a police department had six incidents of police brutality within a single precinct, the court concluded that the time encompassed by the incidents (ten years) and the number of officers employed by the department (over 10,000) precluded a finding that these violations showed a pattern or custom indicating tolerance for police brutality (*Ramos v. City of Chicago*, 1989). Here, the court could not say that the six incidents in and of themselves were evidence of a widespread custom or a generally accepted practice by police employees. Likewise, in *Sova v. City of Mt. Pleasant* (1998) the court awarded a municipality summary judgment on a "failure to supervise and train" case involving the use of deadly force. The city was able to show that this was only the second time a city officer had used deadly force.

Under these judicial decisions, liability for municipal policy generally does not attach unless it can be demonstrated that an individual officer's constitutional violation was a product of official policy or custom promoted by a high-level policymaker within the police department. This necessarily requires that plaintiffs establish a pattern of constitutional violations and an awareness of the violations by high-ranking police officials. Demonstrating a municipal policy or custom can be a very formidable task. "For example, a plaintiff trying to prove a city custom must show that an unconstitutional practice has become 'permanent' throughout and 'well-settled' within local government activities. Accordingly, the plaintiff needs to obtain empirical or testimonial evidence proving the city's custom. . . . Such evidence may be difficult to gather" (Comment, 1990, pp. 767–68 [citations omitted]).

An alternative to establishing municipal liability through the pattern of practices requirement is the "single act" exception. Single acts of constitutional violation are usually (although there are exceptions) insufficient to establish municipal liability (*Bordeau v. Village of Deposit*, 2000; *Cornfiled by Lewis v. Consolidated High School District No. 230*, 1993; *Jackson v. Marion County*, 1995; *Jordan v. Jackson*, 1994; *McNabola v. Chicago Transit Authority*, 1993; *Nelson v. Strawn*, 1995; *Ramos v. City of Chicago*, 1989; *Snyder v. Trepagnier*, 1998). In some cases municipalities can be held liable based on a single unconstitutional act by a police employee. Such a situation arose in the case of *Oklahoma City v. Tuttle* (1985). In that case, civil action was brought because of the fatal shooting of a citizen by a police officer. During the course of the litigation, it was learned that the citizen was unarmed and did not threaten the officer in any way. During the trial, evidence supported a finding of official policy or custom of gross negligence, but such finding was based on the single incident in question. The Supreme Court said that "proof of a single incident of unconstitutional activity is not sufficient to impose liability. . . unless it was caused by an existing unconstitutional municipal policy, which policy can be attributed to a municipal policymaker" (p. 814).

The United States Court of Appeals for the Second Circuit addressed the same issue of single incident customs in a police training case and stated that, "While some causal link must be made between the county's failure to train and the violation of constitutional rights, a single brutal incident . . . may be sufficient to suggest that link" (*Owens v. Haas*, 1983, p. 1246). More recently, the United States Court of Appeals for the District of Columbia considered a case where a police officer ordered a suspect to "freeze" and then immediately shot him (*Atchinson v. District of Columbia*, 1996). Deciding whether a single constitutional violation could state a case of municipal custom, the court remarked:

> Atchinson's allegation that Officer Collins shot him in broad daylight so quickly after ordering him to "freeze" states facts that may reasonably suggest misconduct sufficiently serious and obvious to justify an allegation of improper training in the use of force. . . . Moreover, Atchinson's complaint is adequate even though it alleges only one instance of unconstitutional conduct. (pp. 422–23)

While there is conflict among the lower courts on whether or not a single incident of police misconduct can result in a municipality's liability, the United State Supreme Court has held that under the single incident exception one violation of a constitutional or federally protected right may be sufficient to prove deliberate indifference and hence municipal liability (*Board of County Comm'rs. of Bryan County v. Brown*, 1997). "The single incident exception requires proof of the possibility of recurring situations that present an obvious potential for violation of constitutional rights and the need for additional or different police" practices (*Gabriel v. City of Plano, Texas*, 2000). Additionally, to establish municipal liability for a single constitutional violation, plaintiffs must establish that the decision, practice, or policy of the municipality was the "moving force" behind the constitutional violation (*Board of County Comm'rs. of Bryan County v. Brown*, 1997). Given the fact that the Supreme Court has had several opportunities to rule out the single incident basis for municipal liability but has not done so, there is ample reason for caution even in single act situations.

Administrative Negligence and Deliberate Indifference

While there is some confusion among the federal courts on what level of culpability (if any) is required for a finding of liability under the provisions of Section 1983, the recognized standard—although poorly defined—is deliberate indifference. While the courts have never adequately defined this legal concept, they have identified behaviors that, in their totality, may result in a finding of deliberate indifference, which can lead to civil liability. The federal courts have recognized that mere negligence on the part of a police officer or a municipality cannot form the basis of a finding of liability under Section 1983. Having made this statement, there are exceptions. The courts have recognized that gross negligence or an accumulation of related incidents of mere negligence may rise to a level of deliberate indifference. This means that generally a single act of administrative negligence cannot result in a finding of liability under the provisions of Section 1983. However, if in the totality of the circumstances there are numerous and related incidents of negligence, such accumulation may evidence deliberate indifference to the constitutional rights of citizens. If this is the case, a municipality may be held liable in federal court.

There are many forms of administrative negligence that may in their totality evidence deliberate indifference to citizens rights. Virtually any administrative function of the police executive can be carried out in such a fashion as to contribute to a constitutional violation. The key to determining liability under Section 1983 as opposed to mere negligence is whether the administrative policy or practice was the moving force behind the violation and whether the practice rises to the level of deliberate indifference. In single decision cases of administrative misconduct it must be "plainly obvious" that the act or decision of the policymaker will lead to the specific constitutional deprivation alleged by the plaintiff.

In *Board of the County Commissioners of Bryan County, Oklahoma v. Brown* (1997) the Supreme Court addressed the issue of administrative inadequacy in the hiring of law enforcement officers. In that case, Jill Brown and her husband were returning home to Bryan County, Oklahoma, from a trip to Texas. Mr. Brown was driving and after seeing a police check point he decided to turn the vehicle around and return to Texas. Bryan County Deputy Sheriff Robert Morrison and Reserve Deputy Stacy Burns saw the turn around and began to pursue the vehicle. The deputies claimed that the pursuit reached speeds of over 100 miles per hour, but Brown was unaware that the police were behind him. The chase ended about four miles from the checkpoint when Brown stopped the vehicle. After the vehicle stopped, Deputy Morrison pointed his gun at the Browns' vehicle and ordered the Browns to raise their hands. Deputy Burns was on the passenger's side of the vehicle and ordered Jill Brown to exit. When she did not exit, he used an "arm bar" technique and pulled her from the vehicle to the ground. The arrest resulted in severe injury causing Mrs. Brown to have knee replacement surgery.

Jill Brown sued Bryan County under 42 U.S.C. Section 1983 claiming that the county was liable for Burns's use of excessive force based on Sheriff Moore's decision to hire Burns who was the son of his nephew. Specifically, she claimed that Sheriff Moore failed to consider Burns's background. Burns had a record of driving violations and various misdemeanors, including assault and battery, resisting arrest, and public drunkenness. Sheriff Moore testified that while he had Burns's criminal record he did not review it very closely. The county argued that a single hiring decision by a municipal policymaker could not give rise to municipal liability under 1983.

The district court denied the county's motions, and the jury found that Burns effected the arrest of Mrs. Brown without probable cause and used excessive force. It also found that the hiring policy of Bryan County was so inadequate as to amount to deliberate indifference to Mrs. Brown's constitutional rights. The Court of Appeals for the Fifth Circuit affirmed the judgment against the county on the basis of the hiring claim. The Supreme Court granted certiorari to decide whether the county was liable for the injuries based on Sheriff Moore's single decision to hire Burns.

Considering the evidence presented at trial, the Supreme Court reasoned that while a jury could find that Sheriff Moore's assessment of Burns's background was inadequate, an instance of inadequate screening is not enough to establish deliberate indifference.

> A plaintiff must demonstrate that a municipal decision reflects deliberate indifference to the risk that a violation of a particular constitutional or statutory right will follow the decision. Only where adequate scrutiny of an applicant's background would lead a reasonable policymaker to conclude that the plainly obvious consequence of the decision to hire the applicant would be the deprivation of a third party's federally protected right can the official's failure to adequately scrutinize the applicant's background constitute "deliberate indifference." (p. 644)

The Supreme Court held that Bryan County was not liable for the sheriff's isolated decision to hire Burns without adequate screening, because it was not demonstrated that "his decision reflected a conscious disregard for a high risk that Burns would use excessive force in violation of respondent's federally protected right" (p. 646). The Court vacated the judgment of the court of appeals and remanded the case.

Municipal Liability for
Failure to Train

One of the most common forms of municipal liability is not for actions taken by policymakers but for their failure to act. The allegation of inadequate or improper training of police officers is frequently the basis of a failure to act claim brought under Section 1983. This issue was addressed by the United States Supreme Court in *City of Canton v. Harris* (1989). In the *Canton* case, the plaintiff was arrested and brought to the police station in a police wagon. Upon arrival at the station, she was found sitting on the floor of the wagon. When asked if she needed medical attention she responded with an incoherent remark. During the booking process, the plaintiff slumped to the floor. She was later released and taken by an ambulance to a hospital. The plaintiff was diagnosed as suffering from several emotional ailments. The plaintiff brought a Section 1983 suit against the city and its officials, claiming that they violated her constitutional right to due process. Evidence was presented during the trial showing that shift commanders in the police department were authorized to determine, solely at their discretion, whether a detainee required medical care. Testimony was also presented stating that the commanders were not provided with any special training to make such determinations. The district court decided in favor of the plaintiff on the medical claim, and the Sixth Circuit Court of Appeals affirmed that decision.

The case was appealed to the United States Supreme Court, which held that failure to train can be the basis of liability under Section 1983 if that failure is based on "deliberate indifference" to the rights of those with whom the police come into contact. The Court stated that

> it may happen that in light of the duties assigned to specific officers or employees the need for more or different training is so obvious, and the inadequacy so likely to result in violation of constitutional rights, that the policymakers of the city can reasonably be said to have been deliberately indifferent to the need. (*City of Canton v. Harris*, 1989, p. 1205)

The Court then set forth what may be considered requisites for liability based on "deliberate indifference." These include:

1. the focus must be on the adequacy of the training program in relation to the tasks the particular officer must perform;
2. the fact that a particular officer may be unsatisfactorily trained will not alone result in city liability because the officer's shortcoming may have resulted from factors other than a faulty training program;
3. it is not sufficient to impose liability if it can be proved that an injury or accident could have been avoided if an officer had better or more training; and
4. the identified deficiency in a city's training program must be closely related to the ultimate injury (del Carmen and Kappeler, 1991).

Using the *Canton* case as precedent, the United States First Circuit Court of Appeals decided *Bordanaro v. McLeod* (1989). In the summer of 1982 an off-duty police officer and a female were at a motel bar. Shortly after their arrival, an altercation began between the officer and two other patrons. The officer was badly beaten in the fight and ejected from the bar. He then called the police department to report the incident; the entire night-watch of the department was dispatched to the scene. Upon arrival at the bar, the officers found the glass front door locked; they demanded admittance. When the manager hesitated, they shattered the door and threatened to kill the occupants of the lounge. Those involved in the earlier altercation had fled to a room within the motel and the officers pursued them, brandishing "nightsticks, clubs, bats, tire-irons and an ax in addition to their service revolvers" (p. 1153). Instead of accepting the manager's offer to open the door with a pass key, officers drilled a hole and sprayed mace into the room while firing shots into the door. After the officers forcibly entered the room, the plaintiffs were beaten unconscious, and one died from the injuries.

A civil rights action was brought under Section 1983 against the municipality, the mayor, the police chief, and several individual officers, claiming that the police action constituted numerous constitutional violations. On appeal, the First Circuit Court discussed in detail the issue of municipal liability for police misconduct. The court reviewed the trial evidence and affirmed the jury's finding of municipal liability for failure to train, as well as the imposition of punitive damages against the chief of police and the mayor. Liability was based on the following findings:

1. the department was operating under rules and regulations developed and distributed to the officers in the 1960s;
2. the department's rules and regulations failed to address modern issues in law enforcement;
3. the department failed to provide officers with training beyond that received in the police academy;
4. the city actively discouraged officers from seeking training;
5. there was no supervisory training;
6. the chief of police haphazardly meted out discipline and failed to discipline the officers in the current incident until after they were indicted; and
7. there was no internal investigation of the incident until one year after its occurrence (del Carmen and Kappeler, 1991).

The court found liability for failure to train based on the "deliberate indifference standard" as well as liability for the promotion of an "official" policy based on a custom of unconstitutional use of force and unlawful search and seizure. The *Bordanaro* case applied the standards set forth by the United States Supreme Court in *Canton* to a specific set of facts and concluded that there was deliberate indifference.

In 1992, the Supreme Court revisited the issue of a municipality's failure to train its employees adequately in the context of workplace safety. The case of *Collins v. City of Harker Heights, Texas* (1992) arose because of the death of Larry Collins, an employee in the city's sanitation department. Collins died of asphyxia while working in a manhole trying to unstop a city sewer line.

Collins's widow sued under 42 U.S.C. 1983, alleging that the city violated her husband's rights under the due process clause of the Fourteenth Amendment. The complaint alleged that Collins had the right to be free from unreasonable risks of harm in the workplace that were the product of the city's deliberate indifference toward employee safety. Specifically, the complaint alleged that the city had a custom and policy of not training its employees about the dangers of working in sewers; that it failed to provide employees with safety equipment; and that it failed to warn employees about the dangers of their work.

The district court dismissed the complaint, ruling that it did not allege a constitutional violation. The court of appeals affirmed, finding that a Section 1983 action required an "abuse of governmental power." In making this decision, the appeals court never reached the issue of whether the city violated Collins's constitutional rights.

On appeal, the Supreme Court held that because a city's failure to train or warn its employees about workplace hazards does not violate the due process clause of the Fourteenth Amendment, no remedy was available under Section 1983 when a municipal employee is killed in the course of employment. The Court rejected the appeals court's reasoning that 1983 required an abuse of governmental power separate from an alleged constitutional violation. Citing *City of Canton v. Harris*, (1989), as precedent, the Court reasoned that the characterization of the city's failure to train as "deliberate indifference" was sufficient to hold the city liable if the city also violated the Constitution. Failing to find a constitutional violation, the Court reasoned that nothing in the due process clause supported the claim that municipalities have a substantive duty to provide minimal levels of safety in the workplace. The Court, however, distinguished voluntary acceptance of employment from situations where a citizen has been deprived of his/her liberty, noting that the due process clause guarantees a right to a minimal level of safety in custodial situations. Finally, the Court rejected the argument that the city's failure to train or warn employees about risks in the workplace constituted "conscience-shocking" behavior that rose to a violation of the Fourteenth Amendment.

This Supreme Court decision answered a single question about the obligation of an employer to maintain a safe workplace. The Court held that there was no constitutional obligation to do so and that a failure to train on the part of a municipality that results in the death of an employee while performing work duties does not violate the due process clause of the Fourteenth Amendment. It should be noted, however, that this case does not bar claims of inadequate training that result in constitutional violations. Just because the facts of *Collins* did not demonstrate a Fourteenth Amendment violation does not mean failure to train cannot result in the violation of another constitutional right. In essence, by answering one question the Court generated many other unanswered questions.

The limited applicability of the *Collins* decision and the difficulty of applying this decision in the context of law enforcement were recently addressed by the United States Court of Appeals for the Ninth Circuit. In *Jensen v. City of Oxnard*, (1998), the Oxnard police department's SWAT team conducted a raid of an unoccupied, two-story townhouse. As the officers stormed the residence, Officer Jensen, who was standing in a staircase, threw a "flash-bang" grenade onto a second floor landing. The grenade exploded, emitted a blast of light, and engulfed the area and surrounding rooms in smoke. The officers charged the staircase and moved up to the second floor. In the turmoil and confusion Sergeant Christian, a member of the SWAT team, mistook Jensen for a gun-wielding suspect and fired three rounds from his shotgun killing Officer Jensen.

Officer Jensen's widow filed a Section 1983 lawsuit against the city of Oxnard, the chief of police, and the individual officers. She alleged the police actions constituted an intentional and reckless act that was the product of the city of Oxnard's indifference in training and controlling the officers who conducted the raid. The city moved to dismiss the claim, arguing that Jensen failed to state a cause of action because she failed to allege specific constitutional violations. In the alternative, the city argued that the officers were entitled to qualified immunity. The district court ruled in favor of the plaintiff, and the city appealed to the United States Court of Appeals for the Ninth Circuit.

The circuit court held that the complaint adequately stated a cause of action under the Fourth and Fourteenth Amendments by alleging that Sergeant Christian used excessive and unreasonable deadly force and that the city acted with deliberate indifference in regard to its SWAT teams. The court noted that the complaint alleged that the city

> (1) failed adequately to train or equip the members of the SWAT team; (2) failed to control those members of the SWAT team who have a known propensity for violence; and (3) failed to investigate SWAT team members for potential substance abuse and/or mental problems. Moreover, the complaint specifically alleges that the police chief, assistant police chief, and police commander assigned Sergeant Christian to the SWAT team knowing that he was using mind-altering drugs, including phenobarbital and other substances. (*Jensen v. City of Oxnard*, 1998)

Relying on *Collins*, the city of Oxnard maintained that the allegations did not state a constitutional violation because the Supreme

Court has held that there is no constitutional right to a safe work-place. The city argued that public employees cannot bring Section 1983 claims against employers for on-the-job injuries because munic-ipalities have no obligation to provide employees with certain minimal levels of safety and security. Therefore, the city argued, Jensen could not have had his rights violated because he was injured performing police duties.

The appeals court acknowledged that the Constitution does not guarantee a right to a safe workplace but rejected the city's attempt to turn the case into a safe workplace issue, noting that this case involved the allegedly intentional or reckless acts of a government employee directed against another government employee. The appeals court noted that while this case is distinguishable from a case in which the state owes a duty to care because it has deprived someone of his/her liberty,

> Officer Jensen did not forfeit all constitutional rights when he be-came a member of the police force. Rather, like all individual police officers, Officer Jensen maintained some constitutional rights (in-cluding Fourth Amendment rights) which, if violated by a state ac-tor, can result in liability under Section 1983. In particular, he retained the right at issue here—"the Fourth Amendment right to be free from unreasonable seizure by fellow officers while performing police work. (*Jensen v. City of Oxnard*, 1998)

The court affirmed the decision holding that Jensen properly stated a claim.

For a Section 1983 action, regardless of who the plaintiff is, a police officer or a civilian, he or she must show five basic elements to establish municipality liability for failure to train. A plaintiff must prove that:

1. the training was in fact inadequate;
2. the officer's actions exceeded constitutional limits;
3. the officer's actions arose in a typical situation with which offic-ers must deal;
4. the training demonstrates a deliberate indifference toward per-sons with whom the police come into contact; and
5. there is a direct causal link between the constitutional depriva-tion and the inadequate training (*Allen v. Muskogee*, 1997, pp. 841–42; *Brown v. Gray, Denver Manager of Public Safety*, 2000; *City of Canton v. Harris*, 1989, pp. 389–91).

When considering these elements of a failure to train case it should be noted that showing a pattern of constitutional violations is not necessary to put a municipality on notice that its training program is inadequate. In failure to train cases where the departmental policy is itself not unconstitutional, single incidents of constitutional violations can establish the existence of an inadequate training program when the violation is coupled with other evidence of the program's inadequacy (*Allen v. Muskogee*, 1997, pp. 844-45).

Plaintiffs are required to establish that the constitutional violation constitutes a usual situation with which officers must deal. This merely means that the situation is "common," "likely," "foreseeable," or "predictable." The situation need not be frequent or constant; it must merely be of the type that officers can reasonably expect to confront while performing police work. The courts have recognized individuals requiring medical care while in custody, arrests of fleeing felons, and encounters with armed mentally ill people as constituting usual and recurring situations for police officers (citations omitted, *Brown v. Gray, Denver Manager of Public Safety*, 2000).

Plaintiffs must show that the municipality was deliberately indifferent to the training of its officers (*Hockenberry v. Village of Corrollton*, 2000). This means that plaintiffs are required to show that "the need for more or different training is so obvious, and the inadequacy so likely to result in the violation of constitutional rights, that the policymakers of the City can reasonably be said to have been deliberately indifferent to the need" (*City of Canton v. Harris*, 1989, p. 390). This showing, however, does not require the plaintiff to prove the existence of a pervasive problem. Nor is the plaintiff required to present explicit evidence that the chief of police was personally aware of and chose to ignore the problem. Rather, the plaintiff must show that a policymaker was deliberately indifferent.

Finally, a plaintiff must prove that there was a causal connection between the constitutional violation and the inadequate training. Municipalities are subject to liability only for their official policies or customs "when [the] execution of a government's policy or custom . . . inflicts the injury" (*Monell v. Department of Social Services*, 1978, p. 694). For liability to attach in a failure to train case, "the identified deficiency in a city's training program must be closely related to the ultimate injury" so that it "actually caused" the constitutional deprivation (*City of Canton v. Harris*, 1989, p. 391).

Defenses to Section 1983 Lawsuits

There are a number of defenses police officers can use when they are confronted with a claim of liability under Section 1983. Each of these defenses bars recovery of damages by plaintiffs. There are four primary defenses to Section 1983 actions: (1) absolute immunity, (2) qualified immunity, (3) probable cause, and (4) good faith. Each of these defenses is available to individual police officers but are not afforded to the municipalities that develop policy or customs within a police organization.

Absolute Immunity

The concept of absolute immunity means that if a civil action is brought against a person protected by this form of immunity, the court will dismiss the lawsuit. This form of immunity is usually reserved for persons involved in the judicial process. Since the role of law enforcement officers in the judicial process is limited, there is only one circumstance under which the court will recognize absolute immunity of police officers. If a police officer is testifying in a criminal trial and commits perjury or provides the court with incorrect information, the officer cannot be held liable. In *Brisco v. LaHue* (1983), the Supreme Court granted absolute witness immunity from liability under Section 1983 to police officers alleged to have deprived citizens of due process rights by committing perjury at trial. The Court noted that other circuit courts had already accorded police such immunity (see, *Burke v. Miller*, 1979) and that this immunity was necessary in order not to deter witness testimony, lest censorship destroy the truth-finding function of the courts (*Imbler v. Pachtman*, 1976). The courts reason that it is difficult enough to get people to testify at a criminal trial without imposing the threat of civil liability. Also, the courts reason that there exist alternative criminal actions that can be taken against a person who commits perjury. Officers who intentionally provide perjured testimony are immune from civil liability but may be charged and convicted of a criminal offense.

Qualified Immunity

A lesser form of immunity than absolute is qualified immunity. Qualified immunity extends to police officers who are performing duties of a discretionary nature. Discretionary duties are those tasks performed by police officers that require deliberation or judgment. Qualified immunity for public officials serves important societal purposes and is intended to protect "all but the plainly incompetent or those who knowingly violate the law" (*Malley v. Briggs*, 1986, p. 341). The qualified immunity of an individual police officer is determined by a two-part analysis (*Harlow v. Fitzgerald*, 1982; *Johnson v. Jones*, 1995).

The first step in the decision-making process is to determine whether the alleged constitutional violation was a breach of a clearly established constitutional right at the time of the deprivation.

> This does not mean that a right is clearly established only if there is precedent of considerable factual similarity. . . . It does mean, however, that the law must have defined the right in a quite specific manner, and that the announcement of the rule establishing the right must have been unambiguous and widespread, such that the unlawfulness of particular conduct will be apparent ex ante to [based on expected results from] reasonable

public officials. (*Brady v. Dill*, 1999; *Nereida-Gonzalez v. Tirado-Delgado*, 1993; *Ringuette v. City of Fall River*, 1998; see also, *Wilson v. Layne*, 1999)

The determination of whether a right is clearly established can by made by considering the following questions:

1. Is the right defined with reasonable clarity?
2. Has the Supreme Court or a court of appeals affirmed its existence?
3. Would a reasonable police officer understand from existing law that the conduct was illegal (*Dickerson v. Monroe County Sheriffs Dept.*, 2000)?

It must be established that law enforcement officers had ample opportunity to know what behaviors were proper before holding them accountable (*Anderson v. Creighton*, 1987).

If the law was clearly established at the time of the alleged misconduct, the court moves to the second step in the decision-making process: determining whether the officer's conduct was objectively reasonable. It asks the question, would a reasonable law enforcement officer know that his or her conduct was a violation of a constitutional right? If a court determined that the law was not clearly established or that the officer's conduct was reasonable, the officer is to be afforded immunity from liability (see, *Bonner v. Anderson*, 1996; *Vera v. Tue*, 1996).

Probable Cause

Police officers who face claims of false arrest or unlawful search are afforded qualified immunity if they can show probable cause. If an officer can show that probable cause existed either to make an arrest or to search a residence, liability will be barred by the courts. Probable cause, in the context of a Section 1983 action, means the officer has a "reasonable good faith belief in the legality of the action taken" (*Rodriguez v. Jones*, 1973, p. 599). In *Hunter v. Bryant* (1991), the United States Supreme Court addressed the issue of police immunity for making arrest decisions. The facts of *Hunter* revealed that in 1985, Secret Service agents received a copy of a handwritten letter that threatened the assassination of Ronald Reagan, then president of the United States. The Secret Service agents assigned to the case began an investigation that included interviewing university officials who had originally received the letter. Based on these interviews, agents determined the letter had been delivered by a James Bryant and that he had made several incriminating statements concerning President Reagan. Armed with this information, Secret Service agents interviewed Mr. Bryant at his residence, the address of which appeared on the letter, but he failed to incriminate himself or admit to composing the letter. Mr. Bryant further refused to tell the agents whether or not he intended to harm the president. Based on the investigation and the discovery of the original letter at the address, Mr. Bryant was arrested for making threats against the president of the United States.

Bryant brought a civil lawsuit against the agents in federal district court claiming that his Fourth Amendment rights were violated when the agents arrested him without probable cause or a warrant. The agents moved for summary judgment on the grounds of immunity but that motion was denied. The decision was appealed to the court of appeals, which affirmed the lower court's decision. The United States Supreme Court granted certiorari and reversed the court of appeals decision finding that the Secret Service agents were entitled to qualified immunity from the claim of false arrest. The Court held that "Secret Service agents Hunter and Jordan are entitled to immunity if a reasonable officer could have believed that probable cause existed to arrest Bryant" (p. 537). The Court reasoned that even if there lacked probable cause for the arrest, "the agents nevertheless would be entitled to qualified immunity because their decision was reasonable, even if mistaken" (p. 537).

The best way to demonstrate probable cause is to secure a warrant either for an arrest or search. By securing a warrant, a judge makes the determination of whether probable cause exists for the proposed police action. Police searches and arrests based on warrants also provide an officer with the defense of good faith.

Good Faith

When the defense of good faith is used by police officers, the officer in effect argues that at the time the act was committed he could not have reasonably known that the act was unconstitutional or against the law (*Harlow v. Fitzgerald*, 1982). A good faith defense can be used where an officer executes an arrest warrant believing the warrant is valid. Later, if it is determined that the warrant is defective and invalid, the officer can raise the defense of good faith. There are a number of factors the courts will consider as evidence of an officer's good faith actions. These factors include:

1. the officer's actions were based on departmental policy and regulations;
2. the officer was acting pursuant to a valid law which is later invalidated by a court;
3. the officer was acting on the orders of a supervisor and believed the orders to be legal; or
4. the officer was acting on advice of legal counsel and felt the advice was valid. (del Carmen, 2001, p. 418)

Agency defendants have argued that even though their policies may have been unconstitutional, they should be afforded the defense of "good faith." In *Owen v. City of Independence* (1980), however, the Supreme Court said that a municipality sued under Section 1983 cannot invoke the good faith defense, which is available to its officers and employees. In that case, a police chief was dismissed by the city manager and city council for certain misdeeds while in office. The police chief was not given any type of hearing or due process rights because the city charter under which the city manager and city council acted did not give him any rights before dismissal. The Court held that the city manager and members of the city council acted in good faith because they were authorized by the provisions of the city charter, but that the city itself could not invoke the good faith defense, hence the city could be liable.

Summary

This chapter considered the framework of federal lawsuits brought against the police under Section 1983. After a brief presentation of the elements necessary for a federal civil rights action, the chapter turned to a discussion of the judicial requirements for successfully litigating a federal lawsuit against municipalities. The Supreme Court's major decision in the area of police training was discussed, as was the relationship between police administrative negligence and findings of municipal liability. The chapter concluded with a discussion of the various defenses available to police officers who are alleged to have violated a citizen's civil rights under Section 1983.

Civil Liability for Police Use of Excessive Force 4

Policing is one of the few occupations granted the legal right to use force to accomplish its objectives. In the course of their work, police officers must sometimes resort to the use of force to subdue violent arrestees, to prevent escape, or to protect themselves and innocent victims from injury. Egon Bittner (1970: 40) has remarked:

> Whatever the substance of the task at hand, whether it involves protection against an undesired imposition, caring for those who cannot care for themselves, attempting to solve a crime, helping to save a life, abating a nuisance, or settling an explosive dispute, police intervention means above all making use of the capacity and authority to overpower resistance to an attempted solution in the native habitat of the problem. There can be no doubt that this feature of police work is uppermost in the minds of people who solicit police aid or direct the attention of the police to problems, that persons against whom the police proceed have this feature in mind and conduct themselves accordingly, and that every conceivable police intervention projects the message that force may be, and may have to be, used to achieve a desired objective.

Since the use of force is a fixture of the police occupation, most officers have had to use some level of physical force to effect an arrest—far fewer have had to use deadly force. Although police officers may use various levels of force to accomplish legal objectives, sometimes police officers exceed their legal authority and abuse their prerogative to use force.

When police officers use force, they are expected to use only the amount of force necessary and reasonable to accomplish a lawful objective. Police officers, however, often stray from this requirement. Unfortunately, there are no reliable national statistics that describe how often police officers use justifiable force against citizens—and even less data on how often police misuse force. As a consequence, it is difficult to determine how many people are killed or wounded by the police each year. Researchers have had to rely on data collected for other purposes as well as on information that has voluntarily been supplied by police departments in order to estimate the annual number of police killings.

We do know, however, that police shootings are relatively rare events. Although shootings of citizens by the police are rare, the use of firearms is only one type of force available to officers. Regardless of the type of force used, these events have obvious and serious consequences. One of these consequences—and an important consideration in the decision to use force—is the possibility of civil liability. Whenever a police officer kills or injures a citizen, there is a high probability that a civil lawsuit will be filed against the officer and the police department. These lawsuits can end in enormous damage awards against the police.

Historically, court decisions regarding the civil liability of police officers who use excessive force lacked cohesiveness. There were differing legal standards of proof and interpretations of liability for excessive force. Plaintiffs would file cases under a number of different amendments. These often included the Fourth, Eighth, and Fourteenth Amendments. Three Supreme Court decisions, *Tennessee v. Garner* (1985), *Graham v. Connor* (1989) and *Brower v. Inyo County* (1989) have produced guidelines that clarify some of the issues surrounding police liability for the use of excessive force. In this chapter, we will first distinguish deadly from nondeadly force. Next we will explore the major avenues of suing the police for use of force—federal actions. Finally, we highlight the major Supreme Court decisions governing police use of force.

Excessive, Deadly, and Nondeadly Force

For an act to constitute excessive force, it need not result in death or even serious injury. Excessive force is any force that is unreasonable or unnecessary to accomplish a legal objective. Excessive force is a matter of judicial interpretation. If the force is determined to be excessive, the officer is liable for the consequences of its use. If the force is reasonable and required to achieve a legally justifiable goal, the officer is justified in using it. While police uses of force can range from merely moving a citizen without his/her consent to shooting a suspect with fatal consequence, any level of force used to carry out an illegal act is considered excessive force. A police officer who uses a reasonable and necessary amount of force to effect an illegal arrest has still used excessive force (*Atkins v. New York*, 1998). As this example illustrates, there are some incidents of police misconduct that clearly cannot be excused as justifiable under any interpretation.

The courts have distinguished between police use of deadly force and nondeadly force. *Deadly force* is defined as "force likely or intended to cause death or great bodily harm" (Black, 1990, p. 398). Such force can range from the use of a firearm to striking a suspect with a police baton. *Nondeadly force* is that force which is neither likely nor intended to result in death or great bodily injury. Behaviors that constitute nondeadly force can range from merely touching or moving a suspect to the use of equipment like stun-guns and tazers. Obviously, the use of deadly force does not always result in death or great bodily harm. Conversely, nondeadly force can be lethal. In this chapter, deadly force generally denotes the use of firearms with fatal consequences. Nondeadly force will refer to the use of other police equipment and control techniques that do not end in a fatality or serious injury.

State and Federal Claims

Lawsuits alleging the use of excessive force, brutality, assault, and battery can be filed in state or federal courts either as state tort actions or as Section 1983 claims. Each jurisdiction requires different elements of proof, uses different cases for precedent, and relies on different legal standards for determining police civil liability. The major distinction between state and federal actions is the element of constitutional deprivation. To be successful in a federal action, the plaintiff must prove that the officer's actions caused the deprivation of a constitutionally guaranteed right. State actions require that plaintiffs demonstrate the elements of a tort action, that is, a civil wrong. Depending on the circumstances surrounding police use of force, a plaintiff may file a lawsuit in either federal or state court.

The required proof of constitutional deprivation is a product of legal history. As we discussed in chapter 3, the Supreme Court in the 1960s began to employ a seldom-used section of the United States Code for deciding lawsuits brought against the government. Title 42 of the United States Code, Section 1983—Civil Action for Deprivation of Civil Rights, requires the plaintiff to prove: that the conduct complained of was committed by a person acting under color of state law; that this conduct deprived a person of rights, privileges, or immunities secured by the Constitution or laws of the United States; and that the violation reached a constitutional level. Because of the reliance on this section of the United States Code, many of the lawsuits brought against police officers are called Section 1983 suits.

Until recently, there was some confusion over which constitutional right was being deprived when officers used excessive force. Many courts relied on the "due process" guarantee of the Fourteenth Amendment when determining legal liability (*Gumz v. Morrissette*, 1985; *Johnson v.*

Glick, 1973; *Schillingford v. Holmes,* 1981); other courts followed the Fourth Amendment's prohibition against unreasonable searches and seizures. A few courts would allow claims to be brought under the Eighth Amendment's prohibition against cruel and unusual punishment. Still other courts eschewed the use of a specific guarantee and proposed that Section 1983 alone was a source of substantive rights (*Graham v. Connor,* 1989). This confusion led to a large body of law that was inconsistent and left police officers with little direction in the proper application of force. The conflict among court decisions and the confusion in standards for the use of force called for Supreme Court intervention.

James Fyfe's (1983) observation prior to the Supreme Court's decision in *Tennessee v. Garner* is insightful. He stated:

> Perhaps because of the seeming analogy between deaths caused by police shootings of fleeing felons and deaths effected by the system by executions after trial, plaintiffs' attorneys and scholars have frequently argued that fleeing felon police shootings are punishment and should be subject to Eighth Amendment protections. There are faults in this analogy, however, because execution is a court-ordered final disposition of an offender who has been given all the benefits of due process, and who has been found guilty beyond a reasonable doubt of a capital offense. Shootings to apprehend felony suspects, by contrast, occur earlier in the process, and are a last resort means of seizing suspected offenders. Thus, they are clearly subject to Fourth Amendment restrictions. (p. 528)

The exact constitutional guarantee used is important because how the court interprets the guaranteed right dictates its determination of police liability. For example, a claim of excessive force brought under the Fourth Amendment would require the plaintiff to show that the force used was unreasonable, and a claim under the Eighth Amendment would require showing that the force used inflicted cruel and unusual punishment. The same case brought under the provisions of the Fourteenth Amendment would require a demonstration that the force used violated due process to the extent that it shocked the judicial conscience.

Not only were the courts divided over which amendment was violated when a police officer used excessive force, but there was also substantial confusion among them about the extent to which use of force had to result in serious injury to be a constitutional violation. Some courts held that many claims of police use of excessive force do not reach the level of a constitutional deprivation (*Dunn v. Denk,* 1995; *Hinton v. City of Elwood, Kansas,* 1993), either because they were not the product of deliberate indifference to the violation or because they did not result in a (judicially determined) meaningful injury (*Cathey v. Guenther,* 1995). Several courts required that plaintiffs must have suffered meaningful injuries before police liability could be imposed (*Hinton v. City of Elwood, Kansas,* 1993; *Palmer v. Williamson,* 1989).

For example, merely shoving, pushing, restraining, or using a stun-gun on a suspect was not always actionable under federal law (*Brown v. Noe*, 1989; *Eberle v. City of Anaheim*, 1990; *Evans v. Hawley*, 1990; *Hinton v. City of Elwood, Kansas*, 1993; *Trout v. Frega*, 1996). In fact, courts are fond of remarking "not every push or shove, even if it later seems unnecessary in the peace of a judge's chambers, subjects defendants to Section 1983 liability for excessive force" (*Trout v. Frega*, 1996, p. 121). On the other hand, some courts held that a claim of improper use of handcuffs, slamming someone onto the ground, or twisting a suspect's arm causing stress or the need for medical attention could serve as viable claims of excessive force (*Brown v. Glossip*, 1989; *Browning v. Snead*, 1995; *Harsen v. Black*, 1989; *Thornton v. City of Macom*, 1998).

Further confounding the issue of what type of injury is required to claim excessive force in federal court is the ruling in *Martin v. Board of County Commissioners* (1990). In Martin, the court ruled that although police officers never touched the plaintiff-patient, serving a warrant on her and subsequently forcing her to be removed from a hospital despite medical professionals' advice against it could constitute unreasonable and therefore excessive force on the part of the police officers. At the other extreme, one court has held that the actions of a police officer who placed a gun in the plaintiff's mouth and threatened to blow his head off did not meet the "significant injury" requirement (*Wisniewski v. Kennard*, 1990).

The United States Supreme Court addressed the issue of just how severe an injury must be to form the basis of a Section 1983 lawsuit. In *Hudson v. McMillian* (1992) the Court granted certiorari to decide "whether the use of physical force against a prisoner may constitute cruel and unusual punishment when the inmate does not suffer serious injury" (p. 1). In *Hudson*, an inmate who had been handcuffed and shackled was kicked and punched repeatedly by correctional officers. During the beating, the correctional officers' supervisor "merely told the officers 'not to have too much fun'" (p. 1). As a result of the beating the inmate sustained "minor bruises and swelling of his face, mouth and lips. The blows also loosened Hudson's teeth and cracked his partial dental plate."

After concluding that the correctional officers' use of force was unnecessary and constituted the wanton infliction of pain, the Court reasoned that, "When prison officials maliciously and sadistically use force to cause harm, contemporary standards of decency are always violated. This is true whether or not significant injury is evident" (p. 6). Unfortunately, the Supreme Court's decision was grounded in the Eighth Amendment's cruel and unusual punishment clause rather than under the protections of the Fourth Amendment. Therefore it is not certain that such a ruling would apply to police officers when they use force to seize free citizens. One can only infer that the Court would grant an equal and consistent standard to free citizens who suffer from excessive force at the hands of police officers. At least that is the position taken by some Circuits following the Supreme Court's opinion in *Hudson* (see, *Harper v. Harris County, Texas*, 1994). For example, after the Supreme Court's decision, other courts have ruled that pushing, handcuffing, and dragging an arrestee constitute excessive force *(Sheth v. Webster*, 1998). Police restraint techniques intentionally designed to inflict injury, like "hog-tying," have also been deemed to constitute excessive force (*Gutierrez v. City of San Antonio*, 1998).

Perhaps the remarks of the United States Court of Appeals for the Fourth Circuit best capture current judicial thought on the extent of injury and level of force necessary to constitute a constitutional violation.

> The suggestion that . . . constitutional rights are transgressed only if he suffers [serious] physical injury demonstrates a fundamental misconception. . . . Police can violate a suspect's constitutional rights . . . without leaving [a visible sign of any beating]. (*Riley v. Dorton*, 1996, p. 117)

Lawsuits claiming improper use of force are often filed in state courts as torts of assault and battery or wrongful death. When actions are brought against the police in a state court, existing state statutes or tort law governs them. Normally, the degree of injury sustained by the plaintiff does not bar a state tort action for assault and battery. Again, a tort is a civil wrong in which the action of one person causes injury to the person or property of another, in violation of a legal duty.

The standard of proof in a state case is often less restrictive than that needed in a federal lawsuit. Having to prove the deprivation of a constitutional right is a high legal hurdle. Despite the difficulty of a federal action, most excessive force lawsuits are filed in federal court. There are a number of reasons for this—the major one being that attorney's fees may be included in the judgment and are not deducted from the settlement, as is true of many alternative actions. In other words, a million-dollar award in a federal suit actually goes to the plaintiff. The attorney's fees, often significant, are "tacked on" in addition to the award. In a similar state tort, the attorney's fees are first subtracted from the award, and the plaintiff retains the balance. Therefore, while the requirements for successfully litigating a Section 1983 lawsuit are restrictive, the potential rewards are high. In addition, many states have enacted immunity statutes that either restrict the lawsuits that can be brought against the police or limit the amount of damage awards that can be levied against them.

Federal Standards Governing the Use of Deadly Force

Tennessee v. Garner (1985) is the definitive Supreme Court decision on police use of deadly force. Briefly, the facts of the case are that a Memphis police officer shot and killed an unarmed fifteen-year-old who was fleeing the scene of a burglary. While investigating a call from a neighbor, the officer had walked behind the unoccupied house and spotted the child climbing a chain link fence. The officer called out to the child to stop. When he did not, the officer shot him in the back of the head. Although it was dark outside, the officer admitted that he had no reason to believe the decedent was armed or dangerous and explained that his reason for firing was that the decedent would have escaped and very likely never would have been apprehended. The officer's actions were thought justifiable under an existing state fleeing felon statute that authorized the police to use deadly force to prevent the escape of felony suspects.

Garner's father filed a lawsuit in federal court following the incident. The original *Garner* suit alleged violations of the Fourth, Fifth, Sixth, Eighth, and Fourteenth Amendments to cover a number of rights violated by the police shooting. The Sixth Circuit Court of Appeals concluded that the officer's actions amounted to a seizure, and the officer's actions were governed by the provisions of the Fourth Amendment that requires all seizures be reasonable. The Fourth Amendment states:

> The right of the people to be secure in their persons, houses, papers, and effects, against unreasonable searches and seizures, shall not be violated, and no Warrants shall issue, but upon probable cause, supported by Oath or affirmation, and particularly describing the place to be searched, and the persons or things to be seized.

The United States Supreme Court also adopted this interpretation. The Supreme Court ruled that the police officer used excessive force when he seized Garner by gunshot and was thus liable for his actions. For the first time police and plaintiffs alike had a single legal standard from which to judge police use of force.

In *Garner*, the Court introduced a new standard—the balancing test—for determining liability. The balancing test requires a court to "balance the nature . . . of the intrusion on the individual's Fourth Amendment interests against . . . the governmental interests alleged to justify the intrusion" (p. 8). The principle of the balancing test is fairly straightforward. Imagine the scales of justice with the individual's interests on one end and the government's interests on the other. If the citizen's rights and interests outweigh the government's interests, liability for use of force probably exists. Conversely, if the government has a substantial reason for using force, the citizen has no grounds for alleging liability.

The interests of a citizen are simple but substantial; he or she does not wish to die from a police bullet. To overcome this significant interest, the Court held that the officer may seize the suspect by using deadly force only when the officer "believe[s] that the suspect poses a threat of serious physical harm, either to the officer or to others" (*Tennessee v. Garner*, 1985, p. 11). A threat of serious harm is evident in two situations: first, when there is immediate and serious danger to the officer or bystanders; and second, when the suspect demonstrates dangerousness by the previous use or threatened use of force. These two elements or justifications for the use of deadly force are cornerstones of the *Garner* decision and warrant some detailed consideration.

Immediate and Serious Danger

There are two points to consider in determining immediate danger: the nature of the danger and the immediacy of the threat. A dangerous suspect is, generally, an armed suspect who can inflict serious physical harm. To date, suspects armed with guns, knives, flashlights, those who use a vehicle as a weapon, or those who attempt to seize an officer's weapon have been determined by the courts to be dangerous (*Butler v. City of Detroit*, 1985; *Ealy v. City of Detroit*, 1985; *Hainze v. Allison*, 2000; *Nelson v. County of Wright*, 1998; *Pittman v. Nelms III*, 1996; *Rhiner v. City of Clive*, 1985). In each case, it was determined that the suspect was capable of inflicting serious physical harm with the weapon at hand. Courts are less willing to recognize other items as constituting a danger to police officers. In one case, a police officer shot a criminal suspect for brandishing fingernail clippers (*Zuchel v. Spinarney*, 1989; cf. *Little v. Smith*, 2000). Although the officer testified that he believed that the suspect had a knife, the court held that the jury could reasonably conclude that the officer's actions were not reasonable under the circumstances. In another case where a police officer shot a fleeing shoplifter after he allegedly attempted to strike the officer with a car, the court refused to support summary judgement for the officer because there were issues of whether the shoplifter constituted a serious threat (*Abraham v. Raso*, 1999). Therefore, the cornerstone of immediate danger requires that the target of legal force be armed, capable of, and actually presenting a threat of inflicting serious physical injury.

The second consideration is the immediacy of the threat posed by the suspect. Even if a suspect is armed and has the physical capability to inflict damage or serious injury, a police officer is not automatically legally justified in using deadly force. In one case, a federal court ruled that even though a suspect was armed and refused to heed police commands to drop his gun, "there appear[ed] to be some doubt as to whether the decedent's hand was raised in a shooting position" (*Hicks v. Woodruff*, 1999; *York v. City of San Pablo*, 1985; see also, *Sova v. Mt. Pleasant*, 1998). This factor led the court to conclude that the shooting was an act of police excessive use of force. In other cases, courts have held that "imminent danger" exists when a suspect turns and points the weapon at the officer, brandishes a weapon, is under physical assault by a number of suspects, or where a suspect has just completed an act of violence (*Boyd v. Baeppler*, 2000; *Merzon v. County of Suffolk*, 1991; *Pittman v. Nelms III*, 1996; *Rhoder v. McDannel*, 1991).

The issue of immediacy, however, has caused conflict among the courts. The case of *Hegarty v. Somerset County* (1995) illustrates how two courts considering the same set of facts can reach different conclusions about the immediacy of a physical threat to police officers. Shortly after midnight Katherine Hegarty was shot and killed in her secluded cabin by police officers attempting a warrantless arrest. Katherine Hegarty was known for her marksmanship. Several campers trespassed on Hegarty's property by setting up a campsite about 75 yards from her cabin. Hegarty confronted the campers asking who gave them the key for the gate that was supposed to block their entry onto her property. The campers thought Hegarty was either intoxicated or mentally unstable. She told the campers that they were invading her privacy. After several verbal exchanges, the campers said they would leave in the morning. Hegarty went into her cabin, got a gun, and fired shots in the air from her front porch. One of the campers asked if they could leave, and she said she would follow them so they could get through the gate. The campers called the police from a truck stop.

Reserve Deputy Giroux responded to the call. Familiar with Hegarty's reputation, he assumed that she was the person firing the shots. Deputies Guay and Crawford, Sergeant Hines, and State Trooper Wright joined Giroux. The officers collectively decided to arrest Hegarty, hoping to get her to leave the house. If these efforts failed, however, Wright warned "just because she's a woman, if things go bad, don't hesitate." When the officers arrived at the cabin, they heard music playing. Identifying himself as a police officer, Giroux yelled to Hegarty that he wanted to speak to her. There was no response. Hines knocked on the cabin door; still there was no response.

Using his flashlight, Crawford peered into Hegarty's bedroom and saw her lying on her bed with the rifle. Seeing the light, Hegarty turned the music down and asked who was at the window. Rather than informing Hegarty that she was the suspect of their investigation, the officers told her that they were investigating burglaries in the area and wanted to talk to her. Hegarty then asked them to leave her property. The officers asked Hegarty to come out of the cabin, but she refused.

About this time, Officer Guay told Hines "go." Hines then kicked in the front door, entered the cabin, and heard Guay yelling, "She's got a gun. Don't go." According to the officers, once Hines was inside,

Hegarty started to point her rifle. Guay and Wright yelled to Hegarty to put down her gun. When she did not do so, Hines, Wright, and Guay shot and killed her.

John Hegarty brought a claim in a Maine federal district court pursuant to Section 1983, alleging that the four officers violated his wife's constitutional rights under the Fourth and Fourteenth Amendments. The officer defendants moved for summary judgment asserting qualified immunity because they were fearful of personal injury. The district court concluded that Wright, Guay, Hines, Crawford, and Giroux were not entitled to qualified immunity. The court reasoned

> such fears were unreasonable under these facts. In fact, several officers have stated that, just prior to the entry, Hegarty posed no immediate danger to themselves or anyone else. Hegarty repeatedly asked the officers to leave, but she neither threatened them nor did she fire any shots while the officers were present. In fact, the officers decided to enter Hegarty's home forcibly only after it appeared that she had put down her rifle. Hegarty did not threaten injury to herself at any time, nor were there other individuals in danger. (*Hegarty v. Somerset County*, 1994, p. 257)

The defendants appealed the district court's decision, challenging the ruling that no competent police officer could have formed an objectively reasonable belief that "exigent circumstances" justified a forcible, warrantless entry for the purpose of effecting Hegarty's arrest and the subsequent use of force. Reconsidering the case, the court held that it was reasonable to believe that Hegarty "posed an imminent and unpredictable threat to their safety, and to herself" (*Hegarty v. Somerset County*, 1995, p. 1367). The court went on to note once the officers were committed to the operation they could have reasonably believed that she represented an imminent physical threat to their safety. Consequently, the court vacated summary judgment and entered judgment for the officers.

Past Dangerousness

Deadly force may be justified when officers reasonably believe that a suspect has committed a crime involving the use or threatened use of serious physical harm. Under these circumstances, officers may use deadly force in the absence of an immediate threat. Problems arise, however, in determining what crimes are dangerous. For the moment, the courts have recognized murder, bank robbery, and armed robbery (*Ford v. Childress*, 1986; *Ryder v. City of Topeka*, 1987; *Trejo v. Wattles*, 1987) as crimes that are considered dangerous enough to warrant police use of deadly force. Conversely, however, burglary and swerving at police officers during a car chase does not justify the use of deadly force (*Kibbe v. City of Springfield*, 1985; *Tennessee v. Garner*, 1985). Officers must recognize that all seemingly violent crimes do not justify the use of deadly force in the eyes of the judiciary. A simple assault would not meet the requirements of past dangerousness; therefore a police officer would not be justified in using deadly force to effect a seizure.

Past dangerousness, however, is not a simple formula from which police officers merely determine the type of crime a suspect has committed and then calculate whether they can use deadly force. The United States Court of Appeals for the Second Circuit has ruled that just because a suspect has engaged in an extremely violent crime does not render police use of deadly force reasonable (*Hemphill v. Schott*, 1998). Even if an officer thinks a suspect is armed, the officer's use of deadly force is not automatically reasonable. For example, if an officer commands a suspect to raise his hands and then shoots him after he complies, the shooting would be unreasonable.

An interesting issue, not yet directly addressed by the courts, is the idea of temporal proximity. In other words, how much time can elapse between the commission of the dangerous crime and the use of force? Can an officer use deadly force to apprehend an unarmed fleeing murder suspect who committed the crime days or even months earlier? One court came close to addressing the issue in *Wright v. Whiddon* (1990). In *Wright*, the police-shooting victim was charged with armed robbery and had been incarcerated in a county jail. Wright was transported to court for a probation revocation hearing, and the transporting officer failed to handcuff or adequately supervise the prisoner. During the court session, the officer received a call about a crime in progress and left the prisoner in the care of a seventy-year-old bailiff. Wright escaped the courthouse and dashed into the street. Officers pursued the escaping prisoner who was unarmed and made no threatening movements toward the officers or any other people. Just as the escapee was about to elude the officers on foot, one of the officers fired a single shot, mortally wounding the escapee. A Section 1983 lawsuit was filed against the officer, who argued that the escapee's past dangerousness constituted a serious threat to other persons and therefore justified the use of deadly force. Unmoved by the defendant-officer's argument, the court pointed out that several "previous attempts to apprehend Wright were successfully accomplished without the need to use force whatsoever," and in each of those incidents Wright was armed (pp. 699–700). In previous encounters after Mr. Wright had escaped, officers were able to track him down within a matter of hours and "capture him without incident" (p. 700). These facts coupled with the officer's failure to handcuff the escapee and leaving him with a seventy-year-old bailiff led the court to conclude that legal judgment for the officer was inappropriate.

Standards Governing the Use of Nondeadly Force

The *Garner* decision clarified many important issues concerning deadly force litigation. It effectively did away with common-law fleeing felon doctrines and ruled that the Fourth Amendment was the applicable standard in cases alleging the unreasonable use of deadly force by the police. The question remained as to its applicability to all circumstances in which police use force. In other words, was *Garner* applicable to cases of excessive nondeadly force? In *Graham v. Connor* (1989), the United States Supreme Court answered this question and others. There are three important conclusions from the *Graham* decision:

1. all claims of police excessive force are to be analyzed under the Fourth Amendment;
2. the proper legal standard to use in applying the Fourth Amendment is the "objective reasonableness" standard (discussed on p. 77); and,
3. four specific factors or circumstances in the act of force are to be considered when determining liability.

Graham, a diabetic, had asked a friend to drive him to a nearby convenience store to purchase some orange juice to stave off an oncoming insulin reaction. At the store, Graham decided that the lines to the cashier were too long and opted to go to a friend's house for the orange juice. A Charlotte, North Carolina, police officer observed Graham's furtive movements in the store and his hasty departure. The officer became suspicious and stopped Graham and his companion when they left the store. The officer then called for backup assistance. During this time, Graham exited the vehicle and passed out on the curbside. In the confusion of the backup arriving, Graham was handcuffed. Officers then placed him on the hood of his friend's vehicle. Graham regained consciousness and requested the officers to verify his condition with the diabetic decal he carried in his wallet. He was told to "shut up" and was then thrown headfirst into a squad car. As a result of these actions, Graham suffered a broken foot, cuts on his wrists, a bruised forehead, an injury to the shoulder, and continued to suffer from incessant ringing in his right ear. He later filed a Section 1983 suit, alleging that the officers used excessive force during the investigatory stop.

The Fourth Circuit Court of Appeals affirmed a lower court decision that the force used was not excessive. Upon appeal, however, the Supreme Court reversed the decision and ruled that the lower courts had applied the wrong legal standard—a substantive "due process" standard based on the Fourteenth Amendment—and ordered reconsideration based on the Fourth Amendment's "objective reasonableness" standard. The Court used strong language to make it clear that in the future:

all claims that law enforcement officers have used excessive force—
deadly or not—in the course of an arrest, investigatory stop, or other "seizure" of a free citizen should be analyzed under the Fourth
Amendment and its "reasonableness" standard. (p. 1871)

The objective reasonableness standard is a two-part rule. The first
consideration is a reprimand against using subjective interpretations
in excessive force cases. The Court discards the old substantive due
process standard, used by the lower courts, which required the defendant to prove that the officer acted sadistically and maliciously when
using force. In the future, decisions should be made without regard to
the officer's intent or motivation. In addition, such decisions should be
made "from the perspective of a *reasonable* officer on the scene, rather
than with the 20/20 vision of hindsight" (p. 1872 [*emphasis added*]). As
a result, future decisions are to be based only on the objective facts of
the case—no "mind reading" is allowed. This also includes consideration of information not known to the police officer at the time of the
use of force. Therefore evidence not known to the officer at the time of
the use of force is not relevant to the objective reasonableness of the
officer's decision to use force (*Palmquist v. Selvik*, 1997).

The second consideration is the reasonableness of the seizure.
Determining the reasonableness of a seizure requires "a careful balancing" of the individual's interests and those of the government. In other
words, the reasonableness standard is the balancing test of *Garner*. In
Graham, however, it appears that the conflict between individual and
governmental interests is not as dramatic as is the case in deadly force
situations. Thus, additional factors can enter into the equation when
determining liability in these cases. The Court stated that while "reasonableness . . . is not capable of precise definition or mechanical application" (p. 1871), a number of factors require careful consideration.
These factors include:

1. whether the suspect poses an *immediate* threat to the officer or
   others;
2. the *severity* of the crime;
3. whether the suspect is *actively resisting* arrest; and,
4. whether the suspect is *attempting to escape* custody (see, *Nelson v. City of Cambridge*, 2000).

In the *Garner* decision the Supreme Court noted the first two factors. If the suspect poses a threat or the crime is of sufficient severity,
it appears that the officer may use force to detain the suspect. In addition, if this type of suspect actively resists or attempts to escape, the
officer may be justified in using force. However, a cautious interpretation of these factors should be taken.

It must be noted that *Graham* involves the use of nondeadly
force. As a result, it may be imprudent to apply the four factors to sit-

uations involving deadly force. The *Garner* decision explicitly dealt with the use of deadly force; *Graham* did not. If *Graham* were applied to deadly force cases, it would seem that the Court has modified its position and now may condone the use of deadly force to prevent escape during an investigatory detention. Such a conclusion may be foolhardy, considering the facts of the case and the history of Section 1983 jurisprudence. A prudent interpretation would be that the four factors carry varying weights under specific circumstances. For example, the presence of the first three factors would normally justify the use of deadly force, whereas the presence of only the fourth factor would limit an officer's use of force to nondeadly force. Courts, however, sometimes confuse the two standards for the application of force (see, *Reynolds v. County of San Diego*, 1996). It will be interesting to note future decisions in this area of law. As mentioned earlier in the case of *Wright*, the escapee had been charged with a serious and dangerous crime, but the court felt that there was not an immediate threat posed to the officer or the general public. Therefore, courts will probably continue to base their decisions on the above-mentioned factors as well as on the totality of the circumstances surrounding the use of force by police officers.

Liability for Indirect Excessive Force

Most excessive force cases involve the direct application of force by a police officer against a citizen or suspect. In these cases a police officer intentionally uses force to control, detain, or seize a suspect. The classic case of excessive force is one in which a police officer uses direct application of force, most often by way of a firearm, to seize a citizen. There are, however, circumstances where police officers may indirectly use force to bring about a seizure. Brandishing weapons, frisking suspects, or keeping a suspect in a frisk position for an extended period of time are behaviors that can place officers at risk of liability for the excessive use of force (*Nelson v. City of Cambridge*, 2000).

Police officers may use motor vehicles to seize a suspect or they might bring about a seizure by using a roadblock to stop a fleeing suspect. Police vehicular pursuits that end in injury are "normally" not actionable under the provisions of the Fourth Amendment because the injury caused to a fleeing motorist is not the product of a seizure. If, however, an officer uses a vehicle in an unreasonable manner to effect a seizure, there is the possibility of liability (*Hockenberry v. Village of Carrollton*, 2000). Actions not designed to effect a seizure are brought under the Fourteenth Amendment's due process clause that has a higher level of culpability associated with it (see, *County of Sacramento v. Lewis*, 1998). If, however, a police officer uses a motor vehicle to bring about an unreasonable seizure, then the police may be liable for the action (*Hockenberry v. Village of Carrollton*, 2000). Indirect uses of force require plaintiffs to establish two important factors. First, plaintiffs must demonstrate that they were the targets of an official seizure. Second, plaintiffs must show that the seizure was not objectively reasonable. If these two elements can be established, then a police officer can be held liable for an indirect application of force.

In *Brower v. Inyo County*, (1989) the Supreme Court addressed the issue of police use of indirect force in the form of a roadblock. Following a 20-mile police chase, Brower was killed when the stolen car he was driving crashed into a police roadblock at a high rate of speed. Brower's heirs alleged that police intentionally placed an 18-wheel tractor-trailer across both lanes of a two-lane highway directly in the path of Brower's vehicle. Police also concealed the roadblock by placing it behind a curve and leaving the tractor-trailer without illumination. Police positioned a vehicle so that the headlights blinded Brower as he approached the roadblock.

Petitioners brought action under 42 U.S.C. 1983 in Federal District Court, claiming police violated Brower's Fourth Amendment rights by effecting an unreasonable seizure that involved excessive force. The district court dismissed the claim reasoning that the roadblock was reasonable and that the police action did not constitute a seizure. The Court of Appeals for the Ninth Circuit affirmed the district court's decision that no seizure had taken place, reasoning that prior "to his failure to stop voluntarily, his freedom of movement was never arrested or restrained" and he failed to take advantage of "a number of opportunities to stop" (*Brower v. County of Inyo*, 1987, p. 546). The case was appealed and the Supreme Court granted certiorari.

The Supreme Court began its analysis of *Brower* by revisiting its decision in *Tennessee v. Garner* where it ruled that whenever "an officer restrains the freedom of a person to walk away, he has seized that person" (p. 7). The Court reasoned that the lower court's decision that no seizure occurred when Brower collided with the police roadblock was misguided because prior "to his failure to stop voluntarily, his freedom of movement was never arrested or restrained" and because he "had a number of opportunities to stop his automobile prior to the impact" (p. 546). The Court remarked:

> Essentially the same thing, however, could have been said in *Garner*. Brower's independent decision to continue the chase can no more eliminate respondents' responsibility for the termination of his movement effected by the roadblock than Garner's independent decision to flee eliminated the Memphis police officer's responsibility for the termination of his movement effected by the bullet. (p. 1380)

Based on this reasoning, the Court held that a seizure occurs when governmental termination of a person's movement is effected *"through means intentionally applied"* (p. 1381). Because the complaint alleged that Brower was stopped by means set in motion or put in place by the police that were designed to stop him, the action was a seizure. The Court went on to explain, however, that not every seizure is actionable under Section 1983, but that the petitioner's right to recover came from the unreasonableness of the police in setting up the roadblock in such a manner as to kill Brower. The case was reversed and remanded.

Summary

Knowing when to use force is an integral part of the police officer's occupation. Although the use of deadly force is something that officers seldom confront, the use of force is a principal tool in police work. The use of force can have grave consequences both socially and legally. There are rules that control the amount of force used and the circumstances under which it can be used. When deadly force is used, the interests of the government are predicated on the potential of serious physical harm to the officer or to others. In instances where nondeadly force is used, the factors of escape or active resistance to arrest may also be considered but are not definitive.

Officers must be mindful of these rules. One way the courts enforce these rules is by imposing civil liability. Using force to detain a citizen is a seizure and is thus governed by the Fourth Amendment. Such a seizure must be reasonable regardless of whether it is the product of direct or indirect force. To be reasonable, governmental interests served by the seizure must outweigh the interests of the seized citizen.

Until recently, it appeared that the courts lacked a sense of logical consistency regarding application of varying rules. Three decisions by the United States Supreme Court—*Garner, Graham,* and *Brower*—have refined the Court's position on civil liability suits alleging excessive force. While questions regarding the use of force by police officers remain, these Supreme Court decisions have clarified many of the concerns.

Police Civil Liability for High-Risk Drug Enforcement Operations 5

For over two decades now, law enforcement has been on the front line in the "war against drugs." The federal government spends billions of dollars each year on drug enforcement efforts, and state and local police agencies spend a significant percent of their total budgets on drug enforcement activities. Law enforcement agencies have embarked on drug crop eradication programs, developed national and international interdiction strategies, and intensified street-level enforcement campaigns in the nation's urban cities.

Federal and state legislators have responded to the drug crisis by enhancing police budgets for drug enforcement, increasing the penalties for drug crimes, and mandating that courts mete out stiffer penalties to those convicted of drug possession or trafficking. The number of people imprisoned for drug-related crimes has increased. Congress has enacted legislation that permits the use of the death penalty for persons who kill law enforcement officers during the commission of a drug-related offense. Even given the extent of law enforcement's involvement in controlling drug possession and distribution, police officers are being killed at lower rates than they were two decades ago. While the number of police officers killed in the line of duty continues to decline, law enforcement may find itself taking on new casualties in the drug war—officers who are held liable for violating citizen's constitutional rights.

This chapter addresses potential liabilities of police officers involved in high-risk drug control operations—liabilities associated with planning and conducting drug raids, using force in drug operations, securing drug houses, and substance analysis. We will review recent court decisions concerning the civil liability of police officers involved in drug enforcement activities to illustrate the unique legal problems that face narcotics officers.

Search and Seizure Law in Drug Operations

The police conduct drug raids to achieve several important goals. First, officers conduct drug raids for purposes of locating evidence of a crime. Officers may conduct drug raids in hopes of collecting illegal drugs, cash, or other evidence of criminal activity. Second, officers perform drug raids for purposes of seizing suspects involved in the commission of drug-related offenses. In essence, many drug enforcement activities are missions of search and seizure.

The terms search and seizure are often used together, but they each have distinct meanings. A search is the invasion of a person's privacy for the purposes of collecting evidence for a criminal proceeding. Search not only refers to physical locations such as a residence, place of business or motor vehicle, but it also refers to the inspection of a person's clothing or body. Individuals can be the subjects of a police search when officers examine their bodies for the presence of physical evidence. Seizure, on the other hand, refers to the actual confiscation of property or evidence from a person's possession. A seizure occurs when a law enforcement officer interferes with a person's possessory interests in some meaningful manner (*Soladal v. Cook County, Illinois*, 1992). Seizures, however, are not limited to property; people can be the subject of a seizure if police officers place them in custody or curtail their freedom in some meaningful way.

All searches and seizures conducted by the police are subject to the provisions of the Fourth Amendment of the United States Constitution (see, p. 40). The Fourth Amendment requires the existence of probable cause or in limited circumstances reasonable suspicion, before a search can be conducted. Normally, this determination must be made by a judge who reviews the evidence and determines whether issuance of a search warrant would be reasonable under any given set of circumstances.

There is a substantial body of case law devoted to the topic of police search and seizure. Most police officers are trained in the legal aspects of conducting searches and applying for warrants, which give the police permission to conduct a search or seizure. While a strict interpretation of the Fourth Amendment would not allow any search or seizure without the benefit of a warrant, the courts have recognized many situations that are considered exceptions to the warrant requirement. These exceptions allow police officers to conduct limited searches without the benefit of a warrant, but require that these

searches conform to particular circumstances and be based on probable cause or reasonable suspicion that a crime has been or is being
committed. These exceptions include:

1. searches incident to arrest (*Chimel v. California*, 1969),
2. searches with consent (*Illinois v. Rodriguez*, 1990),
3. searches based on exigent circumstances (*Warden v. Hayden*, 1967),
4. stop and frisk (*Terry v. Ohio*, 1968),
5. searches of automobiles (*Carroll v. United States*, 1925; *Pennsylvania v. Lubran*, 1996),
6. search and seizure of items in plain view or open fields (*Horton
v. California*, 1990),
7. searches in correctional institutions, and
8. police protective sweeps (*Maryland v. Buie*, 1990).

The exceptions to the search warrant requirement of the Fourth
Amendment limit both the circumstances in which a lawful search can
be conducted and limit the scope or invasiveness of the search. For
example, searches justified under the stop and frisk exception would
normally be limited to weapons searches and would not allow police
officers to check the contents of a suspect's pockets for drugs or other
contraband. Similarly, most of these exceptions could not be used to
justify the use of an intrusive body cavity search.

It is important to recognize that the Supreme Court's interpretation
of the Fourth Amendment is not dependent on the officer's intentions or
the reason for the search. The Supreme Court has instructed that

> the reason why an officer might enter a house or effectuate a sei-
> zure is wholly irrelevant to the threshold question whether the
> Amendment applies. What matters is the intrusion on the people's
> security from governmental interference. Therefore, the right
> against unreasonable seizures would be no less transgressed if the
> seizure of the house was undertaken to collect evidence, verify
> compliance with a housing regulation, effect an eviction by the po-
> lice, or on a whim, for no reason at all. (*Soldal v. Cook County*, Illi-
> nois, 1992, p. 548)

In the context of drug operations, particularly drug raids, most
situations require that police officers first secure a warrant, issued by
a judge, before they conduct a drug search (*Payton v. New York*, 1980).
Securing a warrant provides officers with some insulation from liability. The case of *Williams v. City of Detroit* (1994), however, illustrates
that a warrant does not bar civil liability and that officers must use care
in obtaining drug search warrants (see also, *Dickerson v. Monroe
County Sheriff's Dept.*, 2000; *Hervey v. Estes*, 1995).

In *Williams*, Detroit police officers broke into and raided the home
of Elias and Betty Williams in search of evidence of drug trafficking.
Unfortunately, the police raided the elderly couple's home in error. The

raid yielded no evidence of drug-related activity. The search, however, was executed pursuant to a warrant obtained by Sergeant Ronald Murphy. Days before the raid, he sent an informant to make a drug buy. The informant was instructed by Murphy to attempt a purchase of narcotics. When Murphy applied for the warrant he instructed the judge that he observed the informant go directly to 2638 Buena Vista and exit a short time later. The informant told Murphy he met a seller and exchanged money for cocaine. When the court reviewed the affidavit and testimony of the informant, however, it found that several of the assertions in the affidavit were wrong. First, the house at 2638 Buena Vista was not the initial target of the drug buy as claimed. Second, the informant went down an alley that runs parallel to Buena Vista and met an individual outside, in the backyard of the house, not inside. The drug transaction apparently took place outside rather than inside a residence. Third, Murphy did not actually see the informant go inside the house or purchase the drugs; Murphy merely picked him up. Finally, the informant pointed out the house at 2638 Buena Vista as the house where he bought cocaine.

Elias and Betty Williams brought an action in a Michigan federal district court against the city of Detroit and Sergeant Murphy. The action was brought under 42 U.S.C. Section 1983 and alleged that the Detroit police and Murphy violated the Williams's constitutional rights by conducting an unreasonable search. Murphy claimed that he had secured a valid search warrant and that because the search was made pursuant to the warrant it was reasonable.

Reviewing the evidence, the court concluded "it appears that Murphy never observed the informant go inside the residence as claimed in his affidavit." Therefore the court left it to a jury to decide if Murphy "acted with reckless disregard for the truth in obtaining a search warrant for 2638 Buena Vista" and "whether the misidentification of the house resulted from defendant Murphy's reckless disregard for the truth." Accordingly, the court denied Murphy's motion for summary judgment.

In the remainder of this chapter, we look at the unique operational situations that confront drug enforcement officers. Keep in mind that the behaviors of drug enforcement officers, like all police officers, are also governed by the legal requirements for the proper use of force as discussed in chapter 4.

Emergency Response Teams

Police use of paramilitary teams has become very popular among law enforcement agencies in the last decade. Most police departments, both large and small, have developed special weapons and tactics (SWAT) teams. Since most police departments consider drug searches to be high- risk activities, many agencies use either SWAT or ERU (emergency response units) teams to conduct drug raids. The use of SWAT teams has even spilled over into the service of ordinary warrants (see, Kraska and Kappeler, 1997). These teams usually consist of officers who are trained in paramilitary operations and are equipped to respond to physical threats confronted in the process of making drug raids. Because of the potential for the abuse of force, the tactics used by these teams, and the injuries they can inflict, some litigation has surrounded the use of ERU teams for the routine service of drug-related warrants.

In *Liggins v. Morris* (1990) the court addressed two major issues confronting law enforcement officers who conduct drug raids. First, the court addressed the issue of whether ERU teams can be used to execute search warrants of suspected drug houses. Second, the court addressed the issue of acceptable conduct by officers during a drug raid. In *Liggins*, members of the Minneapolis Police Department's high-risk entry team executed a search warrant at 717 Emerson Avenue North, Apartment 102. The warrant was issued and a search was executed based on information police received from two confidential, reliable informants (CRI). The first informant was sent to apartment 204 to make a "buy" of crack but was told the residents were out and to go down to apartment 102. When the first CRI went to apartment 102, a man "answered and stated he only sold to people he knew" (p. 970). Police sent a second CRI to apartment 102. Upon the informant's return, he reported that crack had been purchased from the residents. It was later learned that the second CRI's crack was not purchased from apartment 102, but rather from another apartment. Armed with this misinformation, police obtained a search warrant and conducted a drug raid on the wrong apartment.

The police department's ERU executed the search of the plaintiffs' apartment. It was alleged that during the entry and search, officers kicked and shoved a guest they had handcuffed. One defendant-officer allegedly told plaintiffs that she knew they were in the wrong apartment but had to "go through with it and make it look right" (p. 970). Plaintiffs maintained that during the search officers destroyed items of personal property and subjected them to strip and patdown searches.

Following the drug raid, officers issued citations to the plaintiffs for operating a disorderly house. These charges were dropped when it was learned that the initial request for a search warrant and the subsequent execution of that warrant were based on misinformation. Plaintiffs claimed that the search of the apartment, strip search, and patdown searches were violations of the Fourth Amendment's reasonableness requirement. The plaintiffs also claimed that the police use of ERUs to conduct routine drug searches contributed to the unreasonable use of force.

Police moved for summary judgment, and the court held that genuine issues of fact existed as to whether the police search of the apartment and strip search of the occupants were constitutional. Therefore, the defendant-officer's motion for judgment was denied. The court did, however, find that the manner in which the police detained plaintiffs during the search was constitutional. The court noted that, "It is well-settled . . . that there is no Fourth Amendment violation for detaining individuals not mentioned in a search warrant if they are present at a premises while a search is being conducted" (p. 970). The court also found that the city of Minneapolis's mandatory policy of using ERUs to conduct raids of crack houses was constitutional and that plaintiffs failed to show how "the City's policy of using Emergency Response Units to raid crack houses could have caused these constitutional violations" (p. 972).

One should be mindful that in *Liggins*, the location searched was characterized as a "drug house." Absent such a characterization, the court may have reached a different conclusion regarding the use of ERUs. While the use of ERUs appears to enjoy some judicial acceptance (see also, *Somavia v. Las Vegas Metropolitan Police Dept.*, 1993) (at least under certain circumstances), officers must be mindful that the method in which these units are used must be strictly controlled. Several courts have questioned the assumption that drug users and drug traffickers are inevitably armed and dangerous criminals. Even the Supreme Court has questioned the assertion that all felony drug investigations are inherently dangerous for law enforcement officers (*Richards v. Wisconsin*, 1997). Many courts are not willing to accept overly aggressive police tactics just because their targets are drug traffickers or drug houses.

A suppression hearing in the case of *United States of America v. Kip R. Jones* (2000) aroused judicial concerns over the practices of police tactical teams. Kip Jones was the target of a police drug raid. Officers of the Decatur Police Department decided to execute a search warrant on Jones's residence. One officer pounded on the door and announced police. When residents did not respond, the officer checked the door and found it was unlocked. At about the same time, another officer hit the door with a battering ram and tossed a concussion grenade into the living room. One member of the police tactical team instructed the unarmed Jones to "get down." When Jones failed to comply he was tackled, struck on the neck, and handcuffed. The subsequent search of the apartment uncovered marijuana, cocaine, and equipment for weighing drugs, but no weapons were found. Jones was convicted of possession of cocaine.

Jones did not challenge the warrant or the fact that the officers did not give sufficient notice before using the battering ram. Rather he argued that the evidence against him should be suppressed because the police method of entry was unreasonable. Specifically, he argued that to use a battering ram on a door already open, to throw an explosive device into the apartment when officers knew a child was present, and to tackle him while he was stunned were unreasonable actions.

The district court held that the officers' actions were reasonable in all aspects. The case was appealed to the United States Court of Appeals for the Seventh Circuit. Reviewing the facts of the case, the court expressed concern over the police tactics. The court rejected the

> argument that drug dealers are invariably so dangerous that no-knock entries are proper; by the same token, police cannot automatically throw bombs into drug dealers' houses, even if the bomb goes by the euphemism "flash-bang device." The police did not believe that Jones was an unusually dangerous drug dealer. . . Police had little reason to apply a battering ram to a door that was already ajar, and using the concussion grenade created a risk that people close to the detonation point would be injured. Children are especially vulnerable, and the officers knew that one was in the apartment. . . . If this were a damages action seeking compensation for injury to the occupants or the door, the claim would be a serious one. (p. 29)

The use of a tactical team or paramilitary operation can, in fact, compound problems. The case of *Hervey v. Estes* (1995), illustrates how police deception and the subsequent use of an ERU expose a department to civil liability.

In *Hervey*, the Tahoma Narcotics Enforcement Team and a Washington State Police Detective, Coral Estes, began an investigation into a suspected methamphetamine laboratory. After completing the investigation, Estes secured a warrant to search for drugs in Michael Hervey's rural home, based on alleged tips from informants. The warrant was issued because of Estes' testimony that informants had advised her that they detected the strong odor of the chemical acetone on the property, that United Parcel Service made frequent deliveries to the residence, that Hervey was armed, and that he used vehicles to block his driveway. Further supporting the affidavit was Estes' claim that in an unrelated call, members of sheriff's department went to Hervey's home and heard the sound of a portable generator running. Michael Hervey was alleged to have approached the deputies with white powder on his lips, nostrils, and hair. According to Estes, one of the deputies (trained in drug detection) could smell the odor of P2P on Hervey and that the odor of acetone was detected coming from vehicles parked in the driveway.

Based on this information, law enforcement officers secured a search warrant and conducted a surprise military-style raid to uncover the methamphetamine laboratory. Officers were armed with submachine guns equipped with muzzle suppressors; they wore black fire retardant Nomex suits, boots, gloves, hoods, heavy ballistic vests, and full-face respirator masks. The raid's element of surprise was lost, however, when two children and two adults spotted the ERU and began screaming. ERU members threw all the home's occupants on the ground in a violent fashion, but no methamphetamine laboratory was discovered.

The Herveys and others brought a Section 1983 action against the various police officers alleging that Estes obtained the search warrant through an affidavit containing false and misleading information. The Herveys contended that sheriff's deputies did not tell Estes that they smelled P2P or acetone; that Estes had misled the court about how qualified those officers who conducted the raid were in narcotics detection; and that the officers used excessive force.

The district court granted summary judgment in favor of the officers on all claims stating that, "I think this warrant application, while not a hundred percent accurate, was not substantially misleading or unfairly misleading." (p. 787). The case was appealed.

After reviewing the evidence, the circuit court concluded,

> We have no doubt that Hervey has made the required substantial showing that Estes made deliberately false statements or recklessly disregarded the truth in the affidavit. Hervey specified precisely what portions of the affidavit were false, and supported her claim with documentation. . . . More importantly, the deputy did not tell Estes that he smelled acetone or P2P when he was on the Hervey property; indeed he stated that he had no knowledge of the smell of these chemicals . . . the deliberately false or reckless inclusion of those perceptions is unforgivable. (p. 788)

The court found that the damage caused by the police deception had been compounded by use of an ERU.

> Courts must be exceptionally vigilant when officers fabricate these perceptions. Estes' conduct is even more outrageous in this case, where the warrant issued was used to conduct a full-scale assault on the Hervey's property. Such a dramatic intrusion on property and privacy must not be tainted by such material falsehoods as those included by Estes in the affidavit. (p. 788)

Accordingly, the court reversed summary judgment in favor of Estes, remanding the case for trial with the instruction that Estes was not to be granted qualified immunity because her conduct was unreasonable and thoroughly unprofessional.

The deployment of an ERU for conducting a drug-related search does not excuse officers from obtaining search warrants based on factual information—nor does it allow officers to use unreasonable force. While police may view drug suspects as dangerous, courts view aggressive police tactical operations with suspicion.

Securing Drug Houses

While the service of every drug-related search warrant does not entail a violent threat to police officers, there is always the potential that an officer will confront some form of resistance to the search. Drug enforcement officers conducting raids are often faced with unique situations that call for judgment in determining how best to secure the scene of a search. Offenders may attempt to resist apprehension and may impede the searching officer. The case law in this area is quite clear. Police departments that do not adequately train, equip, control, and screen their SWAT teams risk the possibility of civil liability for the damages or injuries they cause during tactical operations.

In *Murray v. Leyshock* (1990), the court addressed a situation where a suspect used a guard dog in an attempt to avoid arrest. Several police officers executed a search warrant for drug-related activity at a house in St. Louis, Missouri. When the officers arrived at the house they observed a man through a window but received no response when they knocked on the door. With weapons drawn the officers forced their way through the door and entered the home. One of the officers entering the residence saw the plaintiff and ordered him to place his hands against the refrigerator and "assume the position." Within a few seconds a "large, extremely dangerous, half-wolf, half-Belgian shepherd dog charged out of a dark hallway into the room and attacked" the officers (p. 1198). The guard dog rushed the officers and bit one of them on the thigh. The officer responded by firing his gun once at the attacking dog and it retreated. The dog then lunged a second time; again, the officer responded by discharging his gun. This time one of the shots grazed the dog's muzzle and struck the plaintiff. The officer fired a third shot at the dog as it fled down the hallway.

The plaintiff brought suit against the officer claiming that his actions constituted excessive force as well as negligence under Missouri state law. The jury found against the plaintiff on his federal claim but found in his favor based on his state law negligence claim. The officer moved for summary judgment, arguing that the judge erred in refusing his initial motion for a directed verdict in the officer's favor. The appeals court held that the officer was entitled to judgment on both claims because he was engaged in a discretionary function when he shot at the guard dog and injured the plaintiff. The decision, however, drew sharp dissent from one of the judges.

Officers conducting drug raids must be mindful of the possibility that using force may later be determined to be unnecessary or even unconstitutional. In the above-mentioned case, the officer was granted judgment because of the discretionary function doctrine—not because his actions were necessarily justifiable or reasonable under the circumstances. In other cases, officers have been held liable for shooting household pets during a drug raid. This was the outcome in *Erwin v. County of Manitowoc* (1989) where sheriff's deputies obtained a search warrant in an attempt to locate a stolen pressure cooker and four ounces of marijuana.

Upon entering the residence, a deputy encountered one of several family dogs. In an alleged act of self-defense, the officer shot and killed the pet. At trial, plaintiffs alleged that the county was grossly negligent in failing to train its deputy sheriffs about the proper execution of drug-related search warrants. The jury found that the county sheriff department's operation was not unreasonable but that the officer was liable for damages in shooting the dog. They also found that there was a link between the failure to train the officers properly in executing drug raids and the damages sustained by the plaintiff.

Threats to the physical safety of police officers conducting drug raids come not only from suspects and their attempts to prevent apprehension but also from fellow officers who engage in negligent conduct during a raid (recall *Jensen v. City of Oxnard* in chapter 3). Police officers who negligently conduct raids and injure their coworkers can be held liable for their actions. Such was the case of *City of Winter Haven v. Allen* (1989) where a Polk County sheriff's deputy procured a search warrant for a boarding house.

Deputy Allen contacted the Winter Haven Police Department and requested that several city police officers assist him in the execution of the warrant. On the afternoon of the drug raid, officers held a briefing to plan the execution of the raid. The city of Winter Haven sent two officers to the briefing, and a deputy from the sheriff's department acted as operational supervisor. As part of the operation, a confidential informant was selected to make a drug buy and to inform the officers of the presence of other people in the house. The confidential informant advised that the suspect had a female friend with him in the boarding house.

At the briefing the deputies had established the order in which they would enter the boarding house. Despite the plan, Deputy Allen entered "first without waiting to verify if the two city officers were in position at the rear of the house. As Allen entered the house, a man began to run down the hall toward the rear of the house and was pursued by sheriff's officers" (pp. 129–30). Allen indicated that the door to the suspect's room in the house opened immediately after a deputy began pursuing the other fleeing man.

> The suspect waved what appeared to be a long stick at Allen. Allen shot his revolver twice at the suspect. Another deputy, who was behind Allen, testified that he did not know what caused Allen to fire his weapon. The suspect retreated back into his room. . . . [Another deputy] advanced up the hall toward the suspect's room and asked who was doing the firing. He received no answer, but heard three more shots. Allen later stated that he fired these shots without being in visual contact with the suspect. (p. 130)

Meanwhile, the two city officers approached the house from a side street, but they were not yet in their planned position when they heard the gunshots. The city officers entered the house in an attempt to assist and saw a deputy running, dodging, and weaving down the hall toward the rear of the house. Because of the deputy's actions, the city officers thought that he had either been shot or was dodging bullets. One city officer grabbed the deputy, forced him to the ground and, to protect himself and the others, fired his shotgun down the hall. The shot struck Deputy Allen, who died months later of the gunshot wound. His estate brought a claim of wrongful death against the City of Winter Haven and the city police officer. The jury found for the estate and awarded $600,000 in damages against the city police (see also, *Carlin v. Blanchard*, 1988).

Officers conducting drug raids must be careful in planning their execution. Drug raids are potentially dangerous situations, and they can result in legal liability if officers are negligent in planning or carrying out the operation. Ironically, suspected drug offenders are perceived as a serious physical threat to law enforcement officers, yet police officers themselves may present the greatest potential for injury and civil liability.

Detentions and Searches of Drug Suspects

After the scene of a drug raid has been secured, the next issue often raised is whether police officers can detain and search all the occupants of the residence. While the courts have generally ruled that police officers can legally detain people found at the scene of a drug raid, the nature of that detention and the types of searches conducted have been the focus of litigation. In the case of *Orozco v. County of Yolo* (1993), officers of the Yolo County, California, Narcotics Enforcement Team (YONET) conducted a drug raid at the Madison, California, home of the plaintiffs. With guns drawn, officers ran toward the house and came across Luis Orozco, Jr., on the front lawn. One officer covered Luis with a shotgun, handcuffed him, and forced him prone on the lawn. Four other officers went to the front door and announced that they were police officers serving a warrant. Twelve-year-old Rosa Orozco answered the door. Seventy-year-old Maria Orozco, who did not speak or understand English, asked the officers in Spanish what crime they had committed. The officers ignored the question.

Police searched the house room by room. As officers moved toward one room, they observed eighteen-year-old Lucy Orozco, dressed in her nightclothes. An officer shoved Lucy down the hall where she joined Maria and Rosa Orozco who were being detained in the living room. When the officers reached the bedroom of Luis Orozco, Sr., he barricaded himself behind the door. When officers tried to push open the door, Luis, mentally ill, fired gunshots through the door, killing one officer and wounding another. Officers returned fire, killing Luis. After the shooting the female occupants attempted to leave the house, but the police forced them to return at gunpoint.

Because of the homicides, control of the crime scene was turned over to the Yolo County Sheriff's Department. Sheriff's deputies decided that the Orozcos should be detained and interviewed away from the scene. The Orozcos were taken from their home and transported to the sheriff's department. Lucy Orozco was still wearing only her bedclothes, yet officers refused to allow her to change. Luis, Jr., still handcuffed, was also transported to the sheriff's department.

Upon arrival at the sheriff's department, the Orozcos were placed in an empty office were they were kept overnight. Officers reasoned that because the homicide investigation and drug search had not been completed, the Orozcos were not free to leave. Officers admitted, and the court concluded, that nothing in the record established probable cause for the arrests of the Orozcos.

The officers of YONET completed the search of the house pursuant to the warrant, finishing late the next morning. No evidence of a drug-related crime was uncovered, no criminal charges were filed against the Orozcos, and they were released and returned to their home.

The Orozcos brought a Section 1983 action in a California Federal District Court alleging that they were illegally arrested in violation of their Fourth Amendment constitutional rights and that their arrests were not supported by a warrant or probable cause. Since the officers had admitted they lacked probable cause for the arrests, the court considered only whether the detentions rose to the level of an arrest. The court viewed the detentions in three stages: (1) the detention at the house; (2) the transportation to the sheriff's department; and (3) the interrogation and continued detention following questioning.

The court concluded that the detention of the Orozcos while police were executing a search warrant was justified. The transportation of the Orozcos, however, was not supported. This detention, instructed the court, was "so coercive as to be indistinguishable from a full-scale arrest when the officers transported the Orozcos to the sheriff's station without their consent" (p. 817). Likewise the court concluded that the interrogation and continued detention at the conclusion of questioning by the police "had already ripened" into a full-scale arrest. "The coerciveness of the detention increased significantly when the officers questioned each Orozco separately in a small, windowless, internal interrogation room" (p. 817). The court found that the coerciveness of the interrogations and the intrusiveness of the overnight detention clearly demonstrated that the Orozcos were under arrest. Accordingly the court denied the officers' motion for summary judgment.

The case of *Burns v. Loranger* (1990) further illustrates the complexity of the issues surrounding the detention and search of drug suspects. In this case, members of a county drug task force conducted two controlled drug buys from a residence. Because of the illegal sale, officers secured a search warrant for the suspect's residence. Before executing the search warrant, officers observed the suspect's vehicle and home and noted that the suspect's girlfriend had accompanied him in his vehicle. Upon entering the residence, officers saw two suspects. One passed a small plastic baggie of cocaine to the other in the presence of the girlfriend. The ensuing searches disclosed approximately $6,000 in cash, some cocaine and hashish, drug records, and drug paraphernalia. While conducting the search, the suspect's girlfriend asked twice if she could use the rest room. Both requests were refused and officers called a female officer to search the plaintiff. The female officer took the plaintiff to a private bedroom where she conducted a visual strip search, which failed to uncover drugs.

As a result of the strip search, the plaintiff filed a Section 1983 action against the officer claiming a violation of the Fourth Amendment's prohibition against unreasonable searches. In reviewing the case, the court found that the officer's actions were reasonable in that she had "witnessed the commission of a felony offense in the plaintiff's immediate presence" and that the plaintiff had asked on two occasions for access to the rest room (p. 237). Given these circumstances, the officer had sufficient information to "reasonably believe that there was a fair probability she [the plaintiff] had readily disposable evidence that could be found on her person" (p. 237). Thus, the police officer could conclude that the plaintiff might try to conceal evidence and, thereby, was permitted to conduct the strip search without a warrant. Under different circumstances, however, the courts may find that an officer's strip search of a suspected drug offender may not be reasonable (*Sims v. Forehand,* 2000; *Kelleher v. New York State Trooper Fearon,* 2000).

Figure 5.1

A Ten-Point Guideline for Conducting Defensible Strip Searches

---

1. Whenever possible, strip searches should be conducted after obtaining a warrant authorizing the search.
2. All strip searches should be made based on probable cause, not merely on suspicion of a crime.
3. In the absence of a search warrant, officers should attempt to gain the suspect's consent to search.
4. Whenever possible, in the absence of a realistic safety threat or danger of destruction of critical evidence, officers should wait to conduct the strip search until the offender is at a correctional facility.
5. Strip searches are serious invasions of privacy and officers should conduct them in a professional manner.
6. Strip searches should be conducted by an officer of the same sex as the suspect. Male officers should search only male suspects and female officers should search only female suspects.

7. Strip searches should be done at a private location and, whenever possible, in the presence of two officers of the same sex as the suspect. Officers not participating in the strip search should not be allowed to view the search.

8. Officers should not touch the suspect or make any unnecessary remarks during the search.

9. If during the course of the search, the officer's suspicion is alleviated and the search becomes no longer reasonable, the strip search should be discontinued.

10. Officers should document every incident of strip search. Such documentation should include the justification for the search, its location and results as well as any statements or actions made by the suspect.

The possibility of civil liability for the search of suspected drug traffickers was amply demonstrated in the case of *Marriott v. Smith* (1991). The *Marriott* decision addressed the issue of strip searching a jail visitor suspected of introducing contraband into a correctional environment. One of the recognized exceptions to the Fourth Amendment's requirement of a search warrant based on probable cause is a search in the confines of a detention center. Courts reason that the correctional environment must be controlled, and states have a high interest in limiting the introduction of contraband into these facilities. This exception, however, does not give law enforcement officers carte blanche in the use of searches not supported by warrant.

In the *Marriott* case, the plaintiff regularly visited her brother, an inmate at the county jail. The jailer learned that some of the inmates had been smoking marijuana and that the plaintiff had supplied her brother with marijuana. In an attempt to intervene in the drug trafficking, law enforcement officers arranged to record conversations between the plaintiff and her brother in the visiting area. Although the quality was poor, the tape revealed something to the effect that the plaintiff had been smoking all afternoon and that she was sorry that she did not bring him his "stuff" because she had smoked it all. The plaintiff then advised that she would bring some "stuff" on her next visit to the facility.

During the plaintiff's next visit, law enforcement officers posted watch in an attempt to observe the passing of contraband. Although the officers were unable to observe any contraband, they detained the plaintiff as she was leaving the jail and took her to a private room where she was strip-searched. The officer failed to obtain a search warrant. As a result the plaintiff brought a Section 1983 action against the law enforcement personnel for violating her Fourth Amendment right to be free from an unreasonable search. The district court entered summary judgment for the plaintiff against the officers who had detained and searched her. On appeal, the circuit court held that since the plaintiff was leaving the facility at the time she was stopped and searched she could no longer have presented a threat of introducing drugs into the jail environment. Therefore, the officers' actions in detaining and searching the plaintiff were not reasonable and could not be supported by an exception to the Fourth Amendment's warrant requirement.

Drug enforcement activities are not limited to residences or extreme searches. A substantial number of search and seizures involving drugs result from traffic enforcement activities, which far outnumber police drug raids. These activities are another source of potential civil liability if officers do not carry them out within the confines of the Fourth Amendment's search and seizure requirements. In *Chatman v. Slagle* (1997), Ohio State Highway Patrol Troopers James Slagle and Richard Unger stopped Ronnie Chatman for speeding. The two troopers noticed the odor of beer coming from the car and asked Chatman and his passenger, David Clay, to exit the vehicle. Chatman stepped out of the car, but Clay remained in the vehicle and placed his hand in his coat pocket. After repeatedly asking Clay to get out of the car and to take his hand out of his pocket, Trooper Slagle became concerned that Clay was armed. The trooper grabbed Clay and forced his hand from his pocket discovering 15 grams of crack cocaine. Clay was arrested and searched. During the search, one of the troopers found $1,340 in his pocket.

Trooper Unger then began to frisk Chatman. He took Chatman's wallet, opened it, and found one gram of powder cocaine. Unger handcuffed Chatman, pushed him, told him to "shut up," and said, "I am tired of you people." One of the troopers searched Chatman's vehicle and discovered a loaded firearm and a number of small plastic bags.

Chatman and Clay were charged with drug offenses. Clay was convicted of aggravated drug trafficking and sentenced to a year in prison. At a suppression hearing it was determined that the cocaine found in Chatman's wallet was the product of an illegal search. The drug charges were dismissed, and Chatman was never charged with speeding, an alcohol offense, or possession of a weapon.

Chatman sued Unger and Slagle under Section 1983 claiming that the troopers violated his Fourth Amendment right to be secure from unreasonable searches and seizures. During the trial, the troopers argued for summary judgment claiming that if they had searched the car after arresting Clay, they would have discovered the gun and would then have arrested Chatman at that point in time. They claimed this sequence of events would have resulted in an inventory search of Chatman's wallet, and the cocaine would have been found inevitably. The court accepted the troopers' claim but left the inevitable discovery issue to the jury. The jury found in favor of the plaintiff, and Unger was ordered to pay $8,500 in damages. The case was appealed to the United States Court of Appeals for the Sixth Circuit.

On appeal, Unger argued that Chatman's evidence of injury was insufficient and the doctrine of inevitable discovery barred recovery. The circuit court disposed of the trooper's inevitable discovery argument in short order stating that, "it is clear to us that the inevitable discovery doctrine is no bar to a § 1983 suit . . . Moreover, the reasoning which supports the use of the Fourth Amendment exclusionary rule and the related inevitable discovery doctrine in criminal cases does not apply in civil rights actions" (p. 67). To hold otherwise, the court reasoned, would "both eliminate an important disincentive to police misconduct and leave victims of unreasonable police action without any remedy." On the issues of injury and the sufficiency of evidence the court held that under Section 1983 there is "no requirement that the defendant's conduct be outrageous or that plaintiff's injury be extreme. To the contrary, we have often upheld damages under § 1983 without requiring any such showing . . . Where any harm is shown, then, damages proportionate to that harm should be awarded . . ." (p. 70). The court concluded that although the district court erred on its jury instruction concerning the inevitable discovery doctrine in a civil lawsuit, plaintiff's evidence was sufficient to support the jury award under § 1983 standards.

The *Chatman* case is important for law enforcement officers because it illustrates a number of important lessons. First, legal liability under Section 1983 can attach to actions that officers might perceive as being minor violations that do not result in serious injury. Second, doctrines of criminal procedure like the exclusionary rule or the inevitable discovery doctrine provide officers with no insulation from liability. Finally, by following proper search and seizure procedures this trooper would have secured a conviction for the drug offense and escaped civil liability.

Confiscation of Property

Officers conducting drug raids must be sensitive to the property rights of persons subjected to searches and seizures. Although a search warrant can authorize the seizure of contraband and other instruments of a crime, officers cannot exceed the scope and authority of the search warrant and must be mindful that seemingly incriminating items are not always subject to seizure. Frequently a large amount of cash that may have played a role in some drug-related offense is seized. Under certain circumstances, the seizure of cash or property may constitute a violation of the Fourth Amendment and may provide the basis for police civil liability.

In *Hernandez v. Maxell* (1990) the United States Fifth Circuit Court of Appeals addressed such a seizure of cash during the service of a drug-related search warrant. In the *Hernandez* case, police officers conducted a residential search pursuant to a warrant, which authorized officers to search for and seize heroin believed to be on the premises. During the search, officers were unable to locate any heroin. Police officers did, however, confiscate $2,311 from Hernandez's person and property and failed to provide him with a receipt for the cash. The plaintiff's property was not returned, even after the charge of possession of a controlled substance was dismissed due to lack of evidence.

Defendant-officers moved for and were granted summary judgment by the district court, and the plaintiff appealed the judgment. The circuit court found Hernandez had a viable claim under Section 1983: that officers, while executing an invalid search warrant for heroin, took cash from his person and bedroom. The circuit court was not persuaded by the lower court's reasoning that "significant amounts of cash are often associated with drug trafficking, and . . . the cash in question was found in 'plain view' scattered on the bedroom floor and upon Hernandez's person after his arrest" (p. 96). The circuit court concluded that Hernandez adequately "alleged a violation of his constitutional right under the Fourth Amendment to be free of unreasonable searches and seizures, as well as his Fourteenth Amendment right not to be deprived of his property except pursuant to due process of law" (p. 96).

Confiscation of property should be limited to illegal substances and evidence directly related to the commission of a crime. In the absence of discovery of a controlled substance or other direct evidence of a crime, personal property should not be confiscated by police officers. Even though money could be used as indirect evidence of drug trafficking, officers should leave the money alone—absent the finding of controlled substances. In the alternative, officers should, at the very least, provide the suspect with a receipt for all property seized and return the property following a dismissal of the charges.

Although drug enforcement officers may develop strong suspicions that a person is involved in illegal drug trafficking, suspicion alone does not allow officers to seize property. Consider the case of *Lindsey v. Storey* (1991) where an officer seized personal items from motorists. Following a traffic accident, a Georgia state patrolman conducted a driver's license check on the drivers involved in the accident. After learning of a suspended license, the patrolman arrested the plaintiff for various traffic offenses. The driver of the other vehicle told the patrolman that the plaintiff had offered him $2,500 in cash not to report the accident. All plaintiffs denied knowledge of the $2,500 bribe and offered conflicting responses about the purpose and destination of their trip. The patrolman then searched the plaintiffs for weapons and placed them in his patrol car while he conducted a search of their automobile. The body searches revealed more than $2,600 in cash on one of the plaintiffs, and the patrolman seized the money along with some jewelry. In addition to seizing property from this plaintiff, the patrolman seized $457 in cash and more than $89,000 worth of jewelry found on a second plaintiff.

While searching the trunk, the patrolman discovered "a compartment with such a large amount of cash that the money was visible without opening the compartment" (p. 557). The patrolman seized more than $50,000 in cash from the trunk of the automobile and collected what he thought to be handwritten notes in a narcotics-related code. All three occupants of the vehicle were transported to the county sheriff's office and turned over to a county narcotics investigator. The county narcotics investigator claimed at trial that the suspects matched photographs, which had been circulated by the Georgia Intelligence Network, of the "Miami Boys in Georgia"—a drug-trafficking network. The investigator kept the cash and jewelry seized by the state patrolman after agents of the Drug Enforcement Administration said they planned to begin a forfeiture proceeding.

A Section 1983 action was brought against the Georgia state patrolman and the county narcotics investigator. The district court granted a motion to dismiss several of the claims against the investigator and later granted summary judgment on the remaining claims. The case was appealed and the court ruled that the gold jewelry seized by the Georgia State Police was seized based on the offer of $2,500 to the other driver not to call the police and on the conflicting stories the plaintiffs gave about their travel plans. The court instructed that although the patrolman claimed "he immediately suspected the occupants of the car were involved in some narcotics-related crime, mere suspicion of drug dealing was not 'particularized' enough to justify the seizure of property with no apparent connection to drug trafficking." The patrolman's "seizure of the jewelry clearly failed to establish the reasonable suspicion necessary" (p. 560). The court, therefore, ruled that the district court's granting of summary judgment to the officers was improper (cf. *Conrod v. Missouri State Highway Patrol*, 1991; *Mills v. Graves*, 1991).

Drug Detection and Probable Cause

Just as searches are limited by the requirements of the Fourth Amendment of the United States Constitution, so are "seizures" and "arrests" of persons. Officers are permitted to detain people when there is reasonable suspicion that they are engaged in criminal activity. However, unless the circumstances surrounding the detention evidences probable cause, a police officer cannot effect an arrest. As discussed in chapter 2, a false arrest does not require that a person be physically restrained or taken to jail. As we shall see in the cases that follow, a meaningful restriction on a person's freedom may constitute a seizure.

For liability purposes, there are a number of unique problems that drug enforcement officers face when they attempt to detect and identify drugs and drug offenders. First, officers use a number of techniques to detect the presence of controlled substances. These methods can range from simply noticing the odors of a drug-manufacturing lab to an officer's use of trained sniffer-dogs to ferret out drugs. Second, officers use several methods to detect drug traffickers. These methods can range from tips received from informants to the use of elaborate drug courier profiles to identify people who might be transporting drugs. Finally, once officers have uncovered what they suspect to be a controlled substance, some verification process is necessary to establish that the substance found is in fact illegal. These problems and the methods police officers employ to detect drugs and to identify drug traffickers go to the heart of developing probable cause to arrest.

Detection of Drugs and Drug Traffickers

If a police officer receives a tip that a person may be trafficking in a controlled substance, this information alone does not establish probable cause for an arrest. Officers must investigate to develop independent knowledge of a crime and to verify the reliability of the information they receive from an informant. Placing too much stock in information received from an informant can provide the basis for legal liability. In the case of *Buffkins v. City of Omaha* (1990), police officers received a tip that cocaine would be imported into the city of Omaha on a specific date. The tip received by the officer indicated that a black person or persons would be arriving with drugs on a commercial flight originating out of Denver, Colorado. Two officers from the Omaha police department planned to meet at the Omaha airport to investigate the information. The DEA had used "drug courier profiles" to train the officers. They had also been instructed on the proper way to intercept drug traffickers at airports.

The officers arrived at the airport and observed a single black woman exiting the plane that had just arrived from Denver. Her sister met her at the gate. The officers claimed that the deplaning plaintiff behaved nervously and observed that she was carrying a teddy bear with seams that appeared to have been resewn. One of the officers approached the plaintiff and identified himself as a police officer conducting a narcotics investigation. The officer requested the plaintiff's identification and asked her to come to an office for questioning. The officers picked up two of the plaintiff's suitcases and escorted her to the office. The plaintiff loudly protested the officers' actions as being racist and unconstitutional. After arriving at the office, one of the officers examined the teddy bear but failed to find any indication that it contained drugs. The officer then requested that she allow them access to her baggage. She refused and, after a heated exchange, was arrested for disorderly conduct. The officers told the plaintiff that they were going to confiscate her luggage and inventory it. The officer then

allowed the sister to go through the luggage while the officer watched.
No drugs or other illegal substances were uncovered during the search.

The plaintiff sued the officers under Section 1983 claiming that
her detention was a violation of the Fourth Amendment. The district
court, however, entered a directed verdict for the officers, finding that
her detention was based on a reasonable and articulable suspicion of
criminal activity. The case was appealed and the circuit court held that
the detention was illegal and violated the plaintiff's constitutional right
to be free from an unreasonable search and seizure. The court
instructed that what was once a consensual encounter became a seizure when the officers requested that the plaintiff accompany them to
the office. The officers, at that time, had seized both the plaintiff and
her baggage. The court instructed that "although a seizure does not
automatically occur if an officer does not inform a detainee that he or
she is free to leave, the absence of such notice may imply that the
detainee is being restrained" (p. 469). Under these circumstances, that
court found that the encounter was totally:

> devoid of any facts or circumstances that would permit a finding that
> the officers possessed a reasonable articulable suspicion that the
> [plaintiff] was carrying drugs into the Omaha area. Both officers tes-
> tified that Buffkins did not have any of the characteristics common to
> drug couriers. The officers stopped [plaintiff] solely because her race
> fit the racial description of the person described in the tip. . . . (p. 469).

The court went on to instruct that innocent travelers cannot:

> be subject to virtually random seizures merely because of their
> race. . . . The officers could not have narrowed their suspicion to a
> particular individual based on the tip alone. The tip was very indefi-
> nite in that it did not state how many individuals on the flight were
> involved in the illicit activity or give a physical description of the sex,
> height, weight, clothing, or other characteristics of the person[s] who
> would be carrying the drugs. In order to constitute a reasonable artic-
> ulable suspicion the known facts must reasonably relate to the per-
> son about to be stopped and demonstrate a reasonable suspicion that
> the person has engaged or will engage in criminal activity. (p. 470)

Courts generally have been lenient with the police use of dogs to
detect the presence of drugs in public areas (*United States v. Place*,
1983). The use of dogs in public places is not for the most part considered a search, but it is considered evidence suggestive of probable
cause to suspect drug possession. "Warrantless sniffing has therefore
been given the seal of approval by the courts" (del Carmen and Saucier,
1985, p. 50). The detection of drugs by a sniffer-dog does not, however,
remove the requirement of a search warrant following an alert. As one
court has instructed, "the mere fact that a dog alerts to a suitcase, even
where there is founded suspicion to allow the dog to sniff, is not necessarily grounds for probable cause to open and inspect [the] suitcase"
(*United States v. Beale*, 1982, p. 1327).

In *Jennings v. Joshua Independent School District* (1989) the issue of police civil liability for the use of dogs to detect the presence of drugs was brought before the courts. The Joshua Independent School District adopted a program to educate students about the dangers of drugs. As part of their deterrence effort, the school contracted with a private company to have drug-sniffing dogs patrol certain parts of the school property to detect the presence of drugs as well as alcohol, firearms, ammunition, and other substances that are prohibited from the school grounds. On occasion, these dogs would patrol the school's parking lot. If a dog detected contraband, school officials would contact the student responsible for the vehicle and ask for consent to conduct a search of the vehicle. If the student refused consent, the school would contact the student's parent(s) for consent. If the parent(s) also refused, then school officials would contact the police.

While patrolling the parking lot, the private service's drug detection dog alerted its trainer to a parked vehicle. The student-plaintiff was called out of class and was asked for permission to search the vehicle. The plaintiff, whose father was a former law enforcement official, had been instructed to refuse permission. The plaintiff's father was then contacted and he also refused consent to search the motor vehicle. The police were then notified, and an officer arrived on the scene to investigate. The officer inquired as to the reliability of the dog and was provided with a demonstration of the dog's ability. The officer then contacted the district attorney for advice and was instructed that there was sufficient probable cause to seek a search warrant. The evidence was presented before a county judge and a search warrant for the vehicle was issued. The subsequent search, however, failed to unearth any drugs or other substance prohibited by the school.

As a result of the search, the student's father brought a Section 1983 action against the officer. The district court denied the officer motion for summary judgment, but a jury found for the police officer. The reviewing court noted that the officer's "belief in the existence of probable cause was not objectively unreasonable given the proven reliability of the dog on the day in question in detecting the presence of trace amounts of alcoholic beverages, pyrotechnics and controlled substances in vehicles in the school parking lot" and that the officer acted reasonably when he sought the advice of the county attorney in seeking the warrant (p. 318).

Although the court supported the use of drug-sniffing dogs to establish probable cause for the issuance of the warrant, a different conclusion may have resulted had the officers failed to seek a judicial determination of probable cause to search. Additionally, the officer in this case did not effect an arrest of either the student or the parent. Had the officer arrested the plaintiff based solely on the dog's alert, it would be doubtful that the courts would have recognized such an arrest as being based on probable cause.

Kimberly Kingston (1989), a special agent assigned to the FBI's Legal Counsel Division, suggests that officers using drug-sniffing dogs must be careful to limit their use to the boundaries of the Fourth Amendment. She summarized these boundaries as follows:

1. If the dog is used to sniff an area where the defendant has an extremely high expectation of privacy, then a warrant based on probable cause or an exception to the warrant requirement is a prerequisite;

2. If the sniff is to occur in an area of reduced expectation of privacy, then a mere showing of reasonable suspicion is all that is required; and

3. If the dog is used to sniff an item located in a public place or a place controlled by a third party, then no search will occur and Fourth Amendment proscriptions regarding searches need not be of concern (pp. 31–32).

She cautions, however, that "other constitutional considerations may arise, such as the level of suspicion needed to seize luggage from a traveler or the amount of time an item may be detained prior to conducting a sniff test" (p. 32).

This may well have been good advice considering that just a few years later a federal circuit court addressed these concerns in the case of *Karnes v. Skrutski* (1995). In this case, George Karnes was driving his car on an interstate in Pennsylvania when Trooper Skrutski stopped him for a speeding violation. Skrutski requested a Canine Drug Enforcement Unit be sent to assist him. Skrutski claimed he asked for the unit after observing factors that made him suspect Karnes was involved in drug trafficking. While waiting for the K-9 unit to arrive, Skrutski asked to search Karnes's camera bag, film canister, and an envelope. Karnes allowed the search, but refused consent to a search of his luggage and car. Meanwhile another trooper arrived with a dog trained in narcotics detection. Both troopers repeatedly asked to search the car but Karnes refused. Eventually, the troopers used the dog to sniff the car and searched the vehicle's interior and trunk. After detaining Karnes for two and a half hours, nothing illegal was uncovered, and he was cited for speeding.

Karnes filed suit under Section 1983 alleging the troopers violated his rights under the Fourth and Fourteenth Amendments to the United States Constitution. The district court denied Karnes's motion and granted qualified immunity to the troopers, finding reasonable suspicion for the initial and continued detention. Karnes appealed the district court's judgments arguing that the investigatory stop was made without reasonable suspicion and that he was unconstitutionally detained following the stop.

On appeal, the troopers maintained that use of the dog did not violate the Fourth Amendment because they had reasonable suspicion to continue the detention of Karnes to investigate drug trafficking. The troopers attempted to justify their detention by asserting that Karnes was argumentative and questioned their tactics. The troopers further claimed that because the dog jumped into the car it signaled the presence of drugs, thus providing them with probable cause to conduct a full search of the vehicle.

Attempting to bolster justification for the detention and search, the troopers argued that Karnes fit a drug-trafficker profile. Apparently using indicators established by the Pennsylvania State Police Department's Operation Whiteline, the troopers noted that the car had high mileage, was equipped with a two-way band radio, had a radar detector and antenna, and bore Florida license plates. This, combined with the fact that Karnes had maps, had brown and green "vegetable matter," in the car, and was traveling near a "regional center" for drug trafficking, provided reasonable suspicion for the detention.

The appeals court, however, disagreed that these factors provided the troopers with reasonable suspicion to continue the detention. The court stated, "We find the factors here insufficient as a matter of law to provide reasonable suspicion for defendants to have detained Karnes beyond the point needed to issue the speeding citation, and that there was no objectively reasonable basis for defendants to have believed they did have reasonable suspicion." The court went on to note that the factors did "not provide any basis for the police to distinguish Karnes from the vast majority of innocent drivers on our interstate highways." The court went on to note that the troopers:

> used much of the period between the arrival and use of the dog to attempt to cajole Karnes into granting them consent. The fact that defendants did not accept Karnes's refusal to consent, in combination with their attempt to use his refusal as a factor in creating reasonable suspicion shows a misunderstanding about the purposes of the Fourth Amendment. Karnes does not bear the burden of justifying his refusal to allow police to invade his privacy; it is rather the government official who must meet the constitutional requirements before he can encroach upon an individual's privacy. The district court's grant of qualified immunity to defendants on the length of detention issue was improper. (p. 487)

Substance Identification and Analysis

An officer may develop probable cause to search or may be given consent to search by a suspect. However, if the officer does not take reasonable measures to determine whether the evidence uncovered is in fact a controlled substance, liability may result if an arrest is made. One such situation arose in the case of *Jeffers v. Heavrin* (1991). The plaintiff and several of his friends arrived at Churchill Downs in Louisville, Kentucky, to attend the annual running of the Kentucky Derby.

The plaintiff and his friends brought a cooler, blankets, sleeping bags, and groceries. Derby officials must attempt to control the rather large crowds that attend this event; therefore, certain items are prohibited from entering the racetrack. To control the introduction of weapons and other contraband at the track, officers conduct limited consent searches of the patrons. The plaintiffs were aware of this fact, and the track officials posted a notice to this effect for the patrons.

When the plaintiff arrived at the gate, he consented to a search of his cooler and grocery bag. The police officer working the gate came across an opened canister of Pringles potato chips. When she picked up the can, she noticed that it was too heavy to contain just the potato chips. "Upon opening the container, she found plastic eating utensils, chewing gum, napkins, and a small amber bottle containing pills. There was no label on the outside of the bottle, but inside was an unattached prescription label and several pills" (p. 1162). The officer inquired about the pills, and the plaintiff replied that they were his allergy medication. Assuming the plaintiff was lying, the defendant-officer made brief inquiries among other officers about the identification of the pills. Based partly on these inquiries, the officer concluded that the pills were probably Valium and arrested the plaintiff for having medication in an improper container.

The evidence was sent out for lab analysis, but as the trial date approached the officer made no further inquiry and simply notified the court that the lab report was not ready. "Had she read the report, she would have learned that it confirmed the pills were allergy medication . . ." (p. 1162). A new trial date was set and the officer learned that the lab report was negative, "but she took no action and discussed it with no one" (p. 1162). The officer failed to appear in court on the second trial date and the criminal charge against the plaintiff was dismissed.

The plaintiff brought a Section 1983 action against the officer claiming a violation of his Fourth Amendment rights. The district court found that the initial search of the plaintiff was based on consent and, as such, could not form the basis of liability. The court, however, determined that, "Although voluntary consent is the substitute for probable cause as to the initial search, when it comes to the arrest, the officer must have independent probable cause. We simply cannot find probable cause in the 'totality of the circumstances' presented here" (p. 1163). The court reasoned that the pill bottle contained no substance that the officer recognized as a prohibited substance and that the plaintiff had offered an adequate explanation about the medication "nor were there any other indications in . . . appearance or decorum to suggest illegal drug involvement. . . . Under these circumstances, we are forced to conclude that the requisite probable cause for an arrest was lacking" (p. 1163; see also, *Lewis v. McDorman*, 1992).

Summary

Drug enforcement operations are high-risk police activities in both the contexts of potential injury as well as civil liability. To avoid becoming a civil liability casualty in the war on drugs, police officers must realize that the provisions of the Fourth Amendment of the United States Constitution, which requires that all searches and seizure be reasonable, control most of their actions. Regardless of the operational nature of a drug enforcement activity, it is always advisable to secure a warrant before embarking on a drug operation. The possession of a warrant by a police officer greatly reduces the chances that an officer's actions will later be determined unreasonable. Although warrants provide a measure of insulation for police officers conducting drug operations, the provisions of the Fourth Amendment also apply to the manner in which these warrants or orders are executed (*Cortez v. Close*, 2000). Being armed with a search warrant does not guarantee that an officer who exceeds the scope and authority of that warrant will not be held liable. If police officers exceed their authority by using excessive force, conducting intrusive searches, or confiscating personal property that does not evidence criminality, courts are more than willing to hold officers liable for these actions.

Just as important as conforming to the requirements of reasonableness and probable cause is the need to conduct drug operations in a non-negligent fashion. While police officers perceive drug offenders as being serious sources of potential injury and litigation, fellow officers can also be a source of substantial danger. Police drug operations must be carefully planned and executed if officers are to prevent injury and civil liability for any harm they may inadvertently inflict on each other. One of the best ways to prevent such problems is to develop well-planned operations, to use experienced and well-trained officers, and to obtain a warrant before embarking on a drug operation.

Police Liability for Abandoning Citizens in Dangerous Places and Situations

6

Law enforcement officials and researchers alike have long recognized that certain urban locations are particularly prone to violence and crime. For decades researchers have explored the relationships among urban growth, structural change, population density, industrialization, and crime. Recently, research has focused on changing community structures and has increasingly used terms such as "high crime areas," (Trickett, Osborn, Seymour, and Pease, 1992) "disorderly places," (Koper, 1995; Skogan, 1990; Warner and Pierce, 1993) "deviant or dangerous people," (Green, 1995) and "hot spots" (Sherman, Gartin, and Buerger, 1989; Sherman and Weisburd, 1995).

The increased interest in "hot spots" spawned applied research showing that certain parts of cities produce more police work and consume a significant amount of police resources. Not only are certain urban locations prone to a disproportionate amount of crime, but police perceive these areas as being so fraught with danger that they require special police responses. Accordingly, many police departments developed special tactics to address urban hot spots. Some departments have replaced random patrol with directed patrol. Under this police strategy, officers are directed to spend more of their patrol time in hot spots watching for certain types of criminal activity. Other police departments have adopted variants of the directed patrol strategy—saturation patrol, split-force patrol, and street sweeps—in attempts to make hot spots safer. Despite the variety of tactical responses, researchers report that hot spots are still characterized by victimization of individuals. This is perhaps the most prevalent trait of hot spots compared to low crime areas.

One issue researchers have failed to address adequately in their examination of hot spots is that certain urban areas also exhibit a heightened risk of police civil liability. Police officers who provide services in hot spots are particularly vulnerable to civil lawsuits. It is the increased likelihood of citizen victimization coupled with increased police contact with persons at risk that make hot spots fertile ground for civil litigation (Vaughn, 1994).

This chapter discusses police civil liability for abandoning citizens in hot spot areas characterized by crime and dangerousness. It examines how the common-law public duty doctrine has been incorporated into constitutional jurisprudence through the Fourteenth Amendment's due process clause under the theory of "special relationships." The chapter specifically focuses on how police–citizen contacts in hot spots might create special relationships, requiring a heightened duty of police to protect citizens from victimization. The chapter analyzes judicial decisions in this developing area of civil liability.

Governmental Liability for Third-Party Criminal Victimization

As discussed in chapter 2, the police generally are not liable for the criminal victimization of citizens because of the public duty doctrine. Derived from common law, the public duty doctrine holds that police have no duty to protect the general public from harm, absent a "special relationship." The Supreme Court crafted the public duty doctrine in its 1856 decision in *South v. Maryland*, where a sheriff was sued for refusing to protect a citizen from injuries inflicted by a violent crowd. Failing to find the sheriff liable for the plaintiff's injuries, the Court said that peace officers protect the general public, not specific individuals. Since *South*, the public duty doctrine has been widely adopted into American jurisprudence at both the state and federal levels, with most courts ruling that the state is not required to provide police services (see, *Reiff v. City of Philadelphia*, 1979).

The contemporary interpretation of the public duty doctrine holds that where a duty is owed to the general public and not to any particular person, there can exist no cause of action or subsequent liability for failure to protect individuals from injuries caused by a third party. Recent years, however, have seen a growing trend toward exceptions to the public duty doctrine for police failure to protect citizens from criminal victimization. One such exception recognized at the federal level is when a "governmental entity [has] a constitutional obligation to provide such protection, either because of a 'special relationship' with an individual or because the governmental entity itself has created or increased the danger to the individual" (*Ketcham v. Alameda County*, 1987; *Ying Jing Gan v. City of New York*, 1993, p. 553). Although the "parameters of what constitutes a 'special relationship' are hazy and indistinct" (*Ying Jing Gan v. City of New York*, 1993, p. 535), the police may be liable for abandoning citizens in danger of criminal victimization or injury. This is particularly relevant in hot spots, if police abandon citizens under circumstances that heighten the possibility of criminal victimization.

The brutal victimization to which citizens are frequently subject and the concomitant poor judgment exhibited by some law enforcement officers have made it difficult for courts to define the parameters of federally protected rights under Section 1983 in abandonment cases. The dilemma for courts usually revolves around whether police insensitivity and callousness are evidence of "deliberate indifference" or "mere negligence" (Gotham, 1992).

While the Supreme Court has yet to decide a police abandonment case, it has twice handed down decisions pertaining to governmental liability for third-party victimization. The Court first addressed the issue in *Martinez v. California* (1980). In *Martinez*, the Court refused to hold members of a California parole board liable for the murder of a fifteen-year-old girl by a dangerous parolee released five months earlier. The Court said that the parole board did not violate the girl's constitutional rights because she was victimized solely by the parolee and the parole board did not have knowledge that the girl faced any more danger than the public at large. The Court in effect used the reasoning underlying the public duty doctrine to reach its decision and pointed to the need for plaintiffs to establish that governmental officials had special knowledge of an impending criminal victimization.

The Supreme Court revisited the issue of governmental liability for third-party criminal victimization in *DeShaney v. Winnebago County Department of Social Services* (1989). In that case, a four-year-old child was severely beaten and injured by his father, who had custody following a divorce proceeding. Local social workers knew the boy was abused on at least five previous occasions but did not remove the child from the father's custody. Pursuant to the Fourteenth Amendment, the boy and his mother brought a Section 1983 claim against the county social service agency. The United States District Court for the Eastern District of Wisconsin granted the agency summary judgment, which was ultimately affirmed by the Supreme Court. The Court held that the Fourteenth Amendment's due process clause does not require the government to protect citizens against private injury. The due process clause only applies to limit the government's power or to "protect the people from the state" (p. 1003). The Court also rejected the plaintiff's special relationship theory, holding that the agency did not create or enhance the danger to the boy; hence, no "special relationship." Although the

Court rejected DeShaney's special relationship theory, it acknowledged that "in certain limited circumstances the Constitution imposes upon the state affirmative duties of care and protection with respect to particular individuals" (pp. 1004-5). The Court concluded that the state owed no special duty to protect the boy because he was not in custody. Yet, as the Seventh Circuit recently pointed out, "DeShaney . . . leaves the door open for liability in situations where the state creates a dangerous situation or renders citizens more vulnerable to danger" (*Reed v. Gardner*, 1993, p. 1125).

While the Supreme Court has failed to develop a clear formula for determining when governmental liability should attach, a reading of these two cases as well as the Seventh Circuit's interpretation of DeShaney indicates that there are three primary requirements lower courts are to consider when making determinations of liability for third-party criminal victimizations. These requirements include whether public officials: (1) created the danger to which plaintiffs were exposed; (2) had knowledge of the impending danger; and (3) had custody of plaintiffs. The Supreme Court left it to the lower courts to define the contours of these requirements. Likewise, because both the *Martinez* and *DeShaney* cases involved serious physical injuries, the Supreme Court was silent as to the weight that the injury should carry when lower courts make determinations of governmental liability for third-party criminal victimization.

Abandoning Vehicle Occupants and Qualified Immunity

Establishing the requirements necessary for litigating a successful case of governmental liability for third-party victimization is a formidable task. Police officers traditionally have prevailed in abandonment cases because of qualified immunity. Under the Supreme Court's *Harlow v. Fitzgerald* (1982) precedent, police are not liable under Section 1983 for performing discretionary functions unless their actions violate a "clearly established constitutional or statutory right" (p. 818). In abandonment cases, the problem for most plaintiffs is showing that the police had a constitutional duty not to abandon them. This is difficult to show because the "contours of the right must be sufficiently clear that a reasonable official would understand that what he is doing violates the law" (*Anderson v. Creighton*, 1987). In essence, if the law is not clearly established and settled at the time of the alleged police deprivation of civil rights, then the officers are to be afforded qualified immunity from liability.

In *Hilliard v. City and County of Denver* (1991), police were held immune from Section 1983 liability when they abandoned a person who was subsequently victimized in a hot spot. The facts of the *Hilliard* case show that the plaintiff was a passenger in a vehicle involved in a minor traffic mishap. When police arrived to investigate the accident, the driver was arrested for drunken driving, and the plaintiff was told she was too drunk to drive, thus the automobile was impounded. The police then left the accident scene, abandoning the passenger alone in a high crime area. The woman failed to secure transportation after walking to a nearby store and phoning for help. When the plaintiff returned to the impounded automobile, she was robbed, raped, and left for dead.

The plaintiff brought suit pursuant to Section 1983, alleging the police violated her Fourteenth Amendment rights to "life, liberty, travel, and personal integrity" by "failing to take her into protective custody pursuant to Colorado's emergency commitment statute" (p. 1518). The United States District Court for the District of Colorado granted the defendant's motion to dismiss under Section 1983 but denied the officer's motion under state tort law because of his "reckless disregard of the state emergency commitment statute" (p. 1519). The United States Court of Appeals for the Tenth Circuit reversed, maintaining that although the police acted in an appalling and unprofessional manner, a "liberty interest in personal security protected by the Fourteenth Amendment . . . was not clearly established in the law" in 1988 when the police abandoned the plaintiff in a high crime area (p. 1519). The court invoked the custody requirement announced in DeShaney, holding that only those persons under "some degree of physical control by the state" possessed a clearly established constitutional right to protection of personal security (p. 1520).

In another qualified immunity case, *Courson v. McMillian* (1991), the driver of an automobile was arrested for drunken driving and the car was impounded. A female passenger was detained for over 30 minutes at the scene but ultimately was told to leave. The passenger did not request transportation, did not suffer physical injuries, and did not miss any work. Despite the lack of physical injury, plaintiff filed a Section 1983 claim, alleging that the roadside abandonment violated her Fourteenth Amendment rights because she experienced "permanent and definite mistrust and fear of police officers" (p. 1485). The United States District Court for the Northern District of Florida denied the officer's motion for summary judgment based on qualified immunity, and the officer appealed. The United States Court of Appeals for the Eleventh Circuit reversed, saying that as of May 1985 it was not clearly established that the officer had a constitutional duty under the Fourteenth Amendment not to leave an "unarrested passenger" (p. 1486) ". . . alone at the side of a highway late at night without transportation home" (p. 1496). The fact that the plaintiff suffered no serious physical injury perhaps made the qualified immunity defense more palpable to the court.

In any event, the court concluded that there were no Supreme Court or Eleventh Circuit precedents that mandated a law enforcement officer to provide transportation to a passenger in a vehicle that was subsequently impounded and the other vehicle occupants were arrested; hence, the officer was entitled to qualified immunity.

In a more recent case, *Pinder v. Johnson* (1995) the court considered the contours of qualified immunity under 42 U.S.C. Section 1983 when a plaintiff alleged an affirmative duty on the part of police to protect citizens from the actions of third parties. The lawsuit arose out of a violent domestic relationship between the plaintiff, Carol Pinder, and her former boyfriend. Pinder sought to impose civil liability against an officer of the Cambridge (Maryland) Police Department for his failure to safeguard her children from the boyfriend's violence. Pinder alleged that the officer's express promises of protection created a special relationship that gave rise to an affirmative duty to protect her under the due process clause of the Fourteenth Amendment. The United States Court of Appeals for the Fourth Circuit held that the due process right to protection, as clearly established in DeShaney, does not require the government to protect citizens against private injury and therefore the officer was entitled to qualified immunity.

While the absence of a clearly established right to police protection from third-party victimization has hampered plaintiffs' ability to sue, contemporary findings of liability for police abandonment are eroding the immunity defense. The examples of abandonment cases included below illustrate the changing judicial view of police liability for third-party victimization. Police may be liable, for example, when they take a drunken driver into custody and abandon an obviously intoxicated passenger to operate the vehicle.

This form of police abandonment arose in *Reed v. Gardner* (1993). Police arrested an individual for drunken driving, leaving behind an intoxicated passenger. Two hours later, the passenger became a drunken driver, killing and severely injuring several members of a family. The *Reed* court held that similar to abandoning citizens in high crime areas where chances of victimization increase, police "who remove sober drivers and leave drunk passengers with keys may be said to create a danger or at least render others on the road more vulnerable" (p. 1125; *Ross v. United States*, 1990).

The Seventh Circuit in *Reed* concluded that police may be held liable when they create a specific danger even if they do not have particularized knowledge of who will be injured by that danger. This case is potentially significant in litigation involving abandonment and subsequent criminal victimization in hot spots because at the time of most abandonments, police rarely have particularized knowledge of impending victimizations or assaults. What the Seventh Circuit said in *Reed*, however, might be interpreted as meaning that if abandonment itself creates a specific and heightened danger of victimization it may trigger a constitutional duty to protect—a duty that if breached, may result in police liability.

Wood v. Ostrander (1989) is another case in which the police arrested some occupants of a vehicle and abandoned others in a hot spot. A police officer stopped a car, placed the driver under arrest for drunken driving, and impounded the vehicle. A female passenger of the vehicle asked the arresting officer how she was going to get home. Saying that he was sorry, the officer returned to his car and drove away, leaving the plaintiff at the scene of the traffic stop five miles from home in a part of the county with "the highest aggravated crime rate" (p. 586). The time was 2:30 A.M., the temperature was 50 degrees, and the plaintiff, who had no money, was wearing only a blouse and jeans. After first declining "rides offered by three or four strangers, she accepted a ride with an unknown man" who drove to a remote location and sexually assaulted her (p. 586). The woman brought a civil rights action against the officer pursuant to Section 1983 for violating her Fourteenth Amendment guarantee of due process. The plaintiff alleged that the officer acted with "'deliberate indifference' to [her] interest in personal security" (p. 588). The United States District Court for the Western District of Washington granted summary judgment for the defendant, and the plaintiff appealed. The United States Circuit Court of Appeals for the Ninth Circuit reversed, holding that summary judgment for the defendant was inappropriate because the officer's conduct showed a "disregard for [the victim's] safety, amounting to 'deliberate indifference'" (p. 588). The court concluded that the facts should be presented for a jury to decide, saying that it was inappropriate to dispose of the issue on summary judgment.

Abandoning Children and Severity of Injury

Courts have recognized that certain individuals, particularly children, are vulnerable to victimization and injury. Thus, the chances of police liability increase if children are abandoned in hot spots or dangerous areas and they suffer physical injury or victimization. This situation arose in *White v. Rockford* (1979) where police officers arrested an adult for drag racing on a freeway. When the adult was taken into custody, the officers abandoned three children on the side of the road. The adult "pleaded with the officers" to secure transportation for the children or to take the children into protective custody—the officers refused (p. 382). Consequently, the children were stranded at night in an automobile on an eight-lane expressway. After an hour in the cold weather, the children exited the car and crossed several lanes of traffic to find a telephone. Although a neighbor finally picked up thie children, one child with asthma was hospitalized for a week due to exposure, and the other children experienced emotional pain and trauma. The United States District Court for the Northern District of Illinois granted the officers' motion to dismiss the plaintiffs' Section 1983 claim. The United States Court of Appeals for the Seventh Circuit reversed, holding that the police had an affirmative duty to protect the children once they took their adult protector into custody. According to the Seventh Circuit, the act of abandoning children in a highly dangerous situation violated due process guarantees of personal and bodily integrity.

The *White* case is important because it shows that the police increase liability risks when they arrest an adult supervisor of children and then abandon the children, without adult protectors, in a crime-prone or victimization-prone situation. This case is a reminder that an increased duty may arise, where no previous duty existed. If police action places individuals in increased danger of injury, harm, or victimization, a special relationship may have been created. The case also illustrated that the custody requirement announced in DeShaney may not require the police to have formal custody of the person victimized. Constructive custody or taking a parent into custody and abandoning children may be sufficient to satisfy the custody requirement for a successful civil liability case.

Another case of child abandonment was *Walton v. City of Southfield* (1993). In that case a police officer stopped a woman for not having a child in a safety seat as required by Michigan law. After the officer discovered that the woman's license was suspended and had expired, the woman was placed under arrest, and the automobile was impounded. The officer then refused to take the woman's fifteen-year-old daughter and two-year-old granddaughter into protective custody and denied the woman's request to reach into her purse and give the fifteen-year-old some money. Although the officer did not secure transportation for the girls, he watched them enter an adjacent office building before leaving the scene. The girls had difficulty securing a ride home. The two-year-old went for six hours without food or clean diapers, and the fifteen-year-old suffered severe abdominal pain.

The girls brought a Section 1983 claim of abandonment under the Fourteenth Amendment, and the United States District Court for the Eastern District of Michigan denied the officer's motion for summary judgment. The United States Court of Appeals for the Sixth Circuit reversed, opining that the police were not liable because they had not abandoned the children in a dangerous situation. In finding for the police, the Sixth Circuit distinguished *Walton* from the Seventh Circuit's decision in *White v. Rockford*, noting that the children were not subject to as much danger as the children in *White*, suggesting that exposing children to a truly dangerous or crime-prone situation would be a necessary component in establishing liability.

Moore v. Marketplace Restaurant, Inc. (1985) is another case in which the Seventh Circuit refused to hold the police liable for abandonment because the minor suffered no physical injury. In *Moore*, after her parents were arrested, a fifteen-year-old minor was stranded in a camper that had heat, electricity, and locks. The minor alleged in a Section 1983 action that being abandoned in the camper resulted in psychological and mental anguish. The United States District Court for the Northern District of Illinois granted the officer's motion for summary judgment. The United States Court of Appeals for the Seventh Circuit affirmed, saying that although the police "should have been more sensitive to the needs of the minor," the constitutional guarantee of liberty under the Fourteenth Amendment was not violated (p. 1336).

White, *Moore*, and *Walton* show that the lower courts frequently look at the physical harm caused by police abandonment in determining liability. Although the Supreme Court has held that serious physical injury is not required to trigger constitutional protections (*Hudson v. McMillian*, 1992), lower courts are reluctant to impose police liability if minors are abandoned and suffer no physical injury or if abandoned minors are not placed in a vulnerable situation. One of the reasons the police were liable in *White* was because the abandonment exposed a five-year-old with asthma to cold weather, resulting in a week of hospitalization. Although significant injury to the children was absent in *Moore* and *Walton*, it appears that the police may have been liable if the children had suffered serious physical injury.

Abandoning Assault Victims and Knowledge of Impending Victimization

Regardless of whether a hot spot area is inside or outside a building, law enforcement officers and their agencies may be liable if officers abandon individuals in the process of being assaulted. The risk of liability increases substantially if police are present during an assault and turn a blind eye to it (*Horton v. Flenory*, 1989). It also increases if police have information that a specific person is being assaulted and fail to render assistance to the victim or to protect the specific victim from further injury. In *White v. Humbert* (1994), the police were dispatched at 12:30 A.M. to the decedent's home for emergency assistance after two neighbors witnessed the decedent being attacked through a window and heard her screaming for help. Although the witnesses conveyed the information to the officers when they arrived at 1:30 A.M., the officers "circled the building, and left without knocking on decedent's door or otherwise attempting to make contact with decedent to determine if she, in fact, was being or had been attacked" (p. 1). At 4:15 A.M., the decedent's husband called the 911 operator, saying that he had just stabbed his wife to death. A subsequent autopsy placed the time of death at 4:50 A.M.; the cause of death was said to be from loss of blood from multiple stab wounds. The decedent's estate sued the police for abandoning her in a dangerous situation despite having knowledge that a violent crime had occurred or was occurring. Ruling on a motion for summary disposition, the Court of Appeals of Michigan held that

> where an officer is responding to a call that a specific crime is occurring or has occurred, the specific nature of that police activity is sufficient to give rise to the special relationship between the officer and the victim so as to impose a duty upon the officer to render assistance to the victim or to protect the specific victim from further injury. (p. 3)

The operative question on remand will be whether the officers' behavior was appropriate given the nature of the emergency dispatch and the information they obtained from eyewitnesses at the scene. The court concluded that the appropriateness of the officers' behavior should be determined by considering "whether there was a likelihood that there was a victim in need of assistance, whether the apartment should be approached, and whether the facts would justify their entry into the apartment to determine whether the victim was in need of assistance" (p. 3). *Humbert* shows that a hot spot may be defined very narrowly and consist of an area within a building that possesses heightened danger to a potential crime victim.

In a similar case that involved a dangerous area inside a building, the United States Court of Appeals for the Third Circuit required the police to protect a known crime victim from harm. In *Horton v. Flenory* (1989), the police witnessed an assault, but abandoned an individual who was suffering a fatal beating at the hands of a retired police officer. The assault occurred at a private club (known for violent altercations) that served alcoholic beverages; it was owned by the retired police officer. The police officer who responded to the disturbance abandoned the assault victim pursuant to a departmental policy, relegating "law enforcement in private clubs to the proprietors of those clubs" (p. 458). Evidence showed that the officer who abandoned the decedent possessed a 14-year working relationship with the retired officer. At trial the officer said that he believed the decedent was in "good hands," although the decedent was pleading for the officer not to abandon him (p. 456). The decedent's estate filed a Section 1983 claim against the city and the officer, alleging that the abandonment resulted in a Fourteenth Amendment violation. A federal jury in the Western District of Pennsylvania awarded the plaintiff $65,899, and the police appealed. The United States Court of Appeals for the Third Circuit affirmed the judgment in a post-DeShaney opinion, holding that an unconstitutional policy mandating abandonment in the face of a life-and-death beating violates the due process guarantee of bodily integrity and liberty embodied in the Fourteenth Amendment.

In *Dwares v. City of New York* (1993) police permitted a group of skinheads to beat an individual severely who was exercising his First Amendment right to burn the American flag. Officers at the scene of the flag burning told the skinheads "that unless they got completely out of control they would neither interfere with their assaults nor arrest them" (p. 97). This agreement was formed despite officers' knowledge that the skinheads possessed a "history of racism [in which they perpetrated] violent attacks on individuals engaged in lawfully protected First Amendment activity" (p. 98). The United States District Court for the Southern District of New York dismissed the plaintiff's Section 1983 claim, saying that the police had no affirmative duty to protect citizens from assault. The United States Court of Appeals for the Second Circuit reversed, holding that the police owed a special duty to protect because they created or enhanced the victim's danger of assault. In distinguishing *Dwares* from *DeShaney*, the Second Circuit said that the police actively conspired to permit the skinheads to beat the flag burners. Thus, the Fourteenth Amendment's guarantee of liberty is violated when the police with knowledge of an impending assault, abandon likely victims by conspiring with potential assailants.

Dwares has broad implications for the police in high crime areas, particularly where public events are held. Although the case rested on a unique set of circumstances that rendered the police liable when they conspired or enticed victimization, the principle of law may be applicable to a wide range of police work. If the police are liable when they enhance or contribute to victimization, then risks of liability increase when the police have knowledge of potential disturbances and do not act to quell the disturbances at parades, sporting events, political campaigns, and public ceremonies or at protests over abortion clinics, wars, and other governmental actions. The police would not normally be liable for injuries inflicted on persons who attend a political rally that ends in violent disturbance. However, if the police were forewarned in specific detail about the potential for violence and allowed it to occur, then police inaction might have enhanced or contributed to the risk of victimization.

Case Analysis

Cases in which police were held liable for abandonment show that affirmative police actions that place individuals in danger are just as likely to trigger liability as police inaction in which individuals are exposed to potentially dangerous situations. The Supreme Court's decision in *DeShaney* distinguished circumstances in which officials "played no part" in establishing dangers to personal security versus leaving a victim in a high crime area. Following that reasoning, the *White* and *Wood* courts said that a special duty to protect attaches when a law enforcement officer's "affirmative" conduct places a citizen in danger. The *Horton*, *Dwares*, and *Humbert* cases also show that police inaction in abandoning a crime victim might invoke liability if that inaction increases or enhances the victim's exposure to assault. In essence, these cases have begun to define the contours of the "creation of danger" standard required to hold the police liable for third-party victimization.

Liability may attach if a law enforcement officer acts with reckless disregard to the safety needs of an abandoned citizen in a high crime area, thus violating the victim's interest in personal security and liberty under the Fourteenth Amendment. When deciding abandonment cases, courts examine the age and mental capacity of the plaintiff and whether the abandoned individual was subject to physical injury or psychological distress. As a general rule, *Moore* and *Walton* instruct that liability only attaches when the police abandon minors who are physically harmed. As a matter of sound public policy, however, the police should not abandon children if their adult-protectors are taken into custody. Although law enforcement officials eventually may prevail in these cases, they increase the risk of liability if they arrest adults and then leave children without adult supervision. While the Supreme Court has been ambiguous as to the necessity of establishing serious physical injury in third-party victimization cases, law enforcement officials should take little comfort since the Court has held in other governmental liability cases that a serious physical injury is not required to establish a constitutional violation.

In abandonment claims, courts consider different tiers of foreseeability of danger and the offending police conduct. Drawing on the knowledge requirement announced in *Martinez*, lower courts have begun to define the contours of this consideration and its effects on police liability. The first and perhaps lowest level of requisite knowledge is when police are aware of the general dangerousness of a situation or location. This type of knowledge addresses whether the police know or should have known that an area in which a victim is abandoned is a "hot spot" or a "dangerous or deviant place."

For the police to be held liable under this tier, they must be aware or possess constructive knowledge that the situation in which the potential victim is abandoned is truly dangerous. The Seventh Circuit's decision in *Reed*, however, may reduce this requisite level of knowledge because it found that abandonment that creates a specific danger may alone trigger liability regardless of the degree of dangerousness known to the police. According to at least the Seventh Circuit, police creation of a danger may be a viable replacement for the requirement of knowledge.

A second tier of analysis focuses on the level of culpability necessary to bring a constitutional tort claim pursuant to Section 1983. As a general rule, "negligence," "carelessness," or "bad judgment" by the police is not sufficient to invoke liability. As the Ninth Circuit said in *Wood*, to be liable the police must demonstrate a "reckless disregard" or a "deliberate indifference" to the safety of abandoned citizens. This type of analysis focuses more on police conduct than on police knowledge of the dangerousness of the situation or location. Knowledge, however, may be inferred from the level of police culpability. Thus, this tier of analysis invokes both the creation of danger requirement announced in *DeShaney* and the knowledge requirement advanced in *Martinez*.

A third tier of analysis focuses on police possession of actual knowledge of specific danger faced by an identified crime victim. While both the second and third tiers incorporate the "danger creation" and "knowledge" concepts, the third tier differs because it focuses on both specific knowledge and conduct, while the second focuses more on police conduct alone. In these types of cases, what the officers knew, when they knew it, and their actions after becoming aware of the specific danger to an identifiable victim is critical to court analysis. Both the *Humbert* and *Horton* courts instruct that when police officers have knowledge that a specific crime is occurring and know that a specific victim is being injured, it does not matter if the knowledge was obtained directly by the officer as was the case in *Horton* or by eyewitnesses as was the case in *Humbert*.

The fourth tier of analysis focuses on the general degree of dangerousness combined with an aggravating factor that indicates culpability of the police. The *Dwares* court held that, although a general level of knowledge of potential dangerousness was not enough to trigger liability, the police are liable when a general knowledge of potential dangerousness is coupled with a police conspiracy to harm the plaintiffs. The fourth tier of analysis is perhaps the most difficult to establish in that it requires plaintiffs to show the requisite level of knowledge of danger, an element of police custody or control, affirmative police conduct tantamount to a conspiracy, and physical injury of the plaintiff.

Summary

Given the perception that the number of dangerous places and urban hot spots are increasing, it is reasonably foreseeable that citizens will continue to have contact with police officers in high-crime areas. It is also reasonable to assume that the current trend toward allowing police liability for abandonment will continue and that law enforcement agencies will remain viable targets of civil litigation. Because law enforcement officers perform high-risk activities, personal injuries and economic loss cannot be completely avoided. There are, however, several measures that police administrators can take to minimize the risk of civil liability for abandonment. Police agencies can develop policies that prohibit abandonment of citizens in dangerous situations and hot spots. This is not to say that police executives must anticipate every conceivable abandonment scenario that might potentially develop. Rather, policies should be developed that are broad enough to afford individual police officers wide discretion in performing their day-to-day duties—but restrictive enough to provide proper guidance for officers who operate in complex urban environments. Abandonment policies should focus on young children; intoxicated or mentally incapacitated individuals; persons engaged in fights, disputes, or confrontations; and victims of spousal abuse. These persons seem particularly vulnerable to third-party victimization, and courts seem receptive to their claims that affirmative police conduct leads to constitutional deprivation.

While abandonment policies should sensitize officers to the unique vulnerability of certain citizens and prohibit the abandonment of individuals at risk of criminal victimization or injury, policies and procedures should provide individual officers with practical alternatives to abandonment. Policies should direct officers to referral resources like public and private agencies in the medical, religious, and social service communities. Use of dispositional referrals could be an important resource for law enforcement agents faced with an individual at risk of danger or criminal victimization. In these ways, police executives can minimize civil liability by identifying high-risk persons, activities, and places and by adopting policies that ensure that citizens are not abandoned in hot spots or high crime areas. Strong leadership, appropriate training, and constitutional policies should protect police from hidden dangers harbored in urban hot spots.

Legal Issues in Police Negligent Operation of Vehicles in Emergency Situations

7

Law enforcement agencies historically have applied new technologies and innovations to control criminal behavior. The automobile was one of the more significant technological innovations adopted by the police. We can trace the use of motor vehicles by the police to the early twentieth century. In 1905, the St. Louis Police Department developed one of the nation's first traffic control units—in response to a growing number of citizen complaints about speeding automobiles. That same year the department also reported its first police vehicular accident. Two St. Louis police officers, in pursuit of a speeding automobile, were forced to jump from their vehicle to avoid injury. The vehicle was left to collide where it would (*St. Louis Globe*, 1904; 1905).

The automobile has become an important part of police work—its use being justified by the need to apprehend suspected law violators. Over time, this justification has changed. One observer stated (emphasis added) "the main reason law enforcement began to use motor vehicles was to pursue *serious offenders* who used vehicles to effect their escape" (Cunningham, 1986). Others maintain "law enforcement administrators in policy-making positions have justified the use of high-speed chases to effect the arrest of any actual or suspected felony offenders" (Zevitz, 1987). These rationalizations for the use of vehicular pursuit do not encompass what we currently know about the use of motor vehicles by the police—many negligence cases brought against the police result from attempts to apprehend minor traffic violators.

Besides the obvious costs associated with injury and loss of life, this police practice often results in legal liability. Courts attempt to balance criminal apprehension and the potential dangers of police pursuit. In doing so, a number of lawsuits have resulted in six- or seven-figure awards, and several have brought some municipalities and townships to near bankruptcy. Litigation has provided a substantial body of case law governing the operation of police emergency vehicles.

This chapter analyzes state court decisions on the issue of police liability for the negligent operation of emergency vehicles, focusing on cases where innocent third parties are injured during police pursuits. The theory of negligence provides the framework from which the analysis is made; deviations from historical precedent and emerging judicial concepts of police negligence are noted: we will review the development of a duty of care and analyze its judicial interpretation.

Statutory Immunities

The operation of motor vehicles by the police can be classified into two categories. First, police officers operate motor vehicles under routine conditions while performing patrol duties. When motor vehicles are operated under normal conditions, any accident or injury leading to a claim of negligence is litigated under the general theory of negligence. Police officers are afforded no special privileges or immunities in the routine operation of motor vehicles (*Brown v. Tate*, 1994). Police officers driving on public streets in nonemergency situations do not have immunity for their negligence. Accordingly, police officers are held to the same standard of reasonable conduct required of private citizens operating motor vehicles (*Anderson v. Jones*, 1995). Allegations of negligence must show that a law existed to prevent the damage inflicted. In addition, the law must have been designed to protect a specific class of persons (*Baum v. Ohio State Hwy. Patrol*, 1995). If these factors are established, most jurisdictions recognize the violation of a state or municipal traffic regulation as prima facie proof of negligent conduct. Both citizens and police officers are liable for damages from the violation of state or municipal traffic regulations that result in injury or damage.

The second type of operation involves the use of motor vehicles in emergency situations. Police officers are often called to respond to emergencies, render assistance, and apprehend suspected law violators. Due to the dangers involved in emergency responses by the police, all states have enacted statutes that govern the operation of emergency vehicles (Silver, 2000). Most jurisdictions grant drivers of emergency vehicles limited statutory immunity for violations of state and municipal traffic regulations while responding to an emergency. Therefore, when police officers are operating vehicles under emergency circumstances they are afforded some legal protection that citizens would not enjoy. Police officers are permitted to take greater risks that could amount to negligence if they were undertaken by private citizens (*Baum v. Ohio State Hwy. Patrol*, 1995).

What constitutes an emergency is a question of fact to be determined by the courts based on situational factors and the officer's perception. An officer must be involved in emergency use of the vehicle, and the officer must reasonably believe that an actual emergency exists (*Keating v. Holston's Ambulance Serv., Inc.*, 1989). In *Lakoduk v. Cruger* (1956) the Washington Supreme Court said:

> The test for determining whether a publicly owned motor vehicle is at a given time responding to an emergency call is not whether an emergency in fact exists at the time, but rather whether the vehicle is being used in responding to an emergency call. Whether the vehicle is being so used depends upon the nature of the call that is received and the situation as then perceived to the mind of the driver. (p. 699)

The officer's perception of an emergency, however, must be grounded in fact. For example, if a police officer's claim that he was chasing a speeder and therefore operating his vehicle in an emergency situation were refuted by evidence at trial, the officer would not be extended any of the immunities afforded operators of emergency vehicles. Mere assertions by police officers that they were involved in emergency responses are not sufficient to bring them under a less stringent standard of negligence or to invoke other immunizing principles used by the courts (*Anderson v. Jones*, 1995).

For purposes of immunity, some courts hold that a chase in an attempt to apprehend violators of the law (or persons suspected of violating the law) is not always an emergency. Accordingly, a police officer's negligence in violating a traffic regulation is determined by the circumstances surrounding the use of the motor vehicle and the seriousness of the law violator's conduct. In *Fiser v. City of Ann Arbor* (1983) the Michigan Supreme Court emphasized that "in order for [statutory immunity] to apply, defendants must show that the officers reasonably believed an emergency existed. The chase or apprehension of violators of the law does not necessarily constitute an emergency situation" (p. 417; see also, *Ewing v. City of Detroit*, 1995).

In jurisdictions granting limited statutory immunity, liability does not attach when an officer violates a state or municipal traffic regulation while responding to an emergency. The violation of a traffic regulation resulting in injury is not conclusive proof of an officer's negligence. Plaintiffs wanting to establish the negligent operation of an emergency vehicle must identify factors beyond the violation of a traffic regulation to support a claim of negligence. This limited statutory immunity varies from state to state and is restricted to the operation of a motor vehicle in actual emergency situations. These statutes provide law enforcement officers with a limited shield from claims of negligence based solely on the violation of a traffic regulation.

Some jurisdictions hold that statutes immunizing police officers from liability bar findings of police negligence in the emergency operation of motor vehicles. These statutes usually immunize officers from liability when they attempt to apprehend escaping law violators. In *Kisbey v. California* (1984) the California Supreme Court interpreted such a statute:

> The purpose of the legislation was to immunize public entities and employees from the entire spectrum of potential injuries caused by persons actually or about to be deprived of their freedom who take physical measures of one kind or another to avoid the constraint or escape from it. (p. 1096)

More recently, the Ohio Supreme Court expressed its reasoning for extending statutory immunity to highway patrol officers:

> A finding that patrol troopers are immune from liability in the absence of willful or wanton misconduct also serves a vital public interest. Patrol troopers have the duty to preserve the public peace, safety, and welfare. Patrol troopers are expected to act promptly in emergency situations in order to protect the public. If troopers were held to a higher standard of care . . . they might hesitate for fear that the pursuit could result in potential liability. Thus, the goal of promoting patrol troopers' prompt action in emergency situations will be furthered by a finding that the State Highway Patrol is immune from liability. (*Baum v. Ohio State Hwy. Patrol*, 1995, p. 1351)

These courts have interpreted their statutes to mean that negligent police pursuits are immune from liability.

Traditional Barriers to Liability

Other legal barriers, established by statute or judicial decision, preclude findings of police liability for the negligent operation of emergency vehicles. In some jurisdictions, findings of police liability are limited by an adoption of the ministerial/discretionary function distinction (*Johnson v. State*, 1968). Ministerial functions are those behaviors that are considered line or operational functions, similar to the routine operation of motor vehicles discussed earlier. The duties include day-to-day tasks police officers must perform. Discretionary functions, on the other hand, entail policy development or planning tasks, similar to the use of motor vehicles in emergency situations. The arrest of an intoxicated person would normally be considered a ministerial function, whereas the assignment of an officer to patrol a selected area of the community for alcohol-related crime would be a discretionary function.

The courts are, however, very much divided on the issue of which are ministerial and which are discretionary. Under this dichotomy, some other courts have ruled that the emergency operation of a motor vehicle is a discretionary function; hence, they have precluded police liability for negligent operation of motor vehicles. Conversely, other jurisdictions have determined that a police pursuit is a ministerial function and thus allow liability to be imposed (*Gibson v. Pasadena*, 1978; *Young v. Woodall*, 1995). Courts using the ministerial/discretionary dichotomy often hold that an officer's decision to pursue or engage in a chase is discretionary, but the physical operation of the motor vehicle is ministerial. Therefore an officer's decision is not a source of liability, but the officer's method of vehicle operation may be.

Jurisdictions retaining the vestiges of sovereign immunity, such as Virginia, consider police pursuit as a conduct within the scope of official employment and therefore bar negligence actions. The problem with using sweeping immunization of the police is that the social goal of compensating persons injured by acts of negligence becomes impossible.

Negligence Principles and Police Pursuit

In jurisdictions where negligence action is not barred by sovereign, discretionary, or statutory immunity, state courts use the general theory of negligence to determine liability. The principles of duty, breach of duty, and proximate cause are applied to situations where actual injury or damage occurs.

The Duty of Care

Courts universally recognize the existence of a duty of care by police officers operating emergency vehicles. This requires the operator of an emergency vehicle to drive with due care for the safety of all persons using the public roadways (*Fitzpatrick v. City of Chicago*, 1987). This standard of care is based either on interpretations of state statute or on common law. In jurisdictions where the standard is not specified in the statute, the courts have either adopted the standard from common law or have carved out the duty in the process of judicial decision making (*Miami v. Horne*, 1967). Under this standard, police officers are not immune from liability when their actions reflect carelessness, recklessness, or a wanton disregard for the safety of other persons using public roadways. The level of culpability required to establish police liability in these situations depends on the jurisdiction (see, *Peak v. Ratliff*, 1991).

Figure 7.1

Some Key Factors to Consider in Developing Police Pursuit Policies

1. ***Use of Force:***
    deadly force
    ramming
    blocking
    roadblocks: stationary and rolling
    spikes
    boxing in

2. ***Roles and Responsibilities:***
    supervisor
    dispatcher
    driver of primary car
    driver of secondary car
    drivers of support cars

3. ***Communications Responsibilities:***
    for pursuing cars
    for supervisors
    for support vehicles

4. ***Environmental Conditions:***
    time of day
    night/day
    road conditions
    traffic: pedestrian and vehicular
    location and neighborhoods
    weather

5. ***Reasons for Initiation of Pursuit:***
    identify offense
    seriousness of offense

6. ***Reasons for Termination of Pursuit:***
    environmental conditions
    general safety considerations
    seriousness of offense

7. ***Interjurisdictional Pursuits:***
    who's in charge?
    reporting requirements for initiating agency
    reporting requirements for assisting agency
    pursuits out of your jurisdiction
    hot pursuits into your jurisdiction
    conditions under which assistance is requested/given

8. *Vehicles:*
    marked vs. unmarked
    use of motorcycles
    condition of vehicles
    officer's driving records/previous performance in pursuits
    number of cars for misdemeanor offense/for felony offense

9. *Use of Emergency Warning Devices:*
    citation from state statutes
    reinforcement to utilize both audible and visual warning devices
    following of stricter standard even if state statute does not require either
        (New York) or both (Florida)
    support vehicles and the use of emergency warning devices if they are
        allowed to parallel chase

Source: Gallagher, G. P. (1989).

Courts operationalize the duty of care based on the reasonable and prudent man test. Courts have adopted this test from common law and have modified it to fit the situational context of police emergency vehicle use. The doctrine has been construed to require that an officer's conduct must meet that of a reasonable and prudent emergency vehicle operator or a breach of duty may be found. Application of this test does not require that the officer make the best decision (*Dillenback v. City of Los Angeles*, 1968); rather, the standard merely requires the officer's conduct to be reasonable under the totality of circumstances (*DeWald v. State*, 1986).

Many courts have decided that the standard of care and the reasonableness of an officer's conduct is a question of fact to be determined by a jury, taking into account the totality of the circumstances surrounding an injury. The behaviors that establish a breach of the standard of care and reasonableness test are varied; some courts hold that an officer's conduct can be unreasonable even if the officer is acting within the law. To determine the boundaries of the standard of care expected of police officers, an examination of breaches of reasonable behavior is necessary.

Breaches of Reasonableness

Negligence is a question of fact and law. Proving the existence of a duty and then observing a behavior that constitutes a breach of that duty establishes negligence. Since courts universally accept the duty of care standard and hold that this duty extends to all persons using the public roadways, in essence the existence of a duty is assumed. The courts then must consider what behavior constitutes a breach of duty.

The traditional approach taken by the courts is to group certain types of behavior and exclude them from the realm of negligence. Rather than considering all possible behaviors that breach the responsibleness standard, the courts develop principles of law that exclude certain types of behavior from constituting a breach of duty. The result is that courts are freed from considering the total spectrum of police behavior that may arise in every situation. Theoretically, this practice lends consistency in judicial decision making because the application of general principles to like situations should result in similar outcomes.

These negating principles of law are derived from two distinctions. First, the courts distinguish between the actual operation of an emergency vehicle and the initial decision-making process of the pursuing officer. Applying this, some courts have held that the duty of care standard and reasonableness test are triggered only by the actual operation of the vehicle and not by the officer's decision to pursue a suspected law violator. The decision of an officer to pursue a suspected law violator generally cannot form the basis of negligence. Officers, therefore, are shielded from liability associated with decision making at the initial stages of a pursuit. This principle is sometimes extended to the decision whether or not to discontinue a pursuit (*Day v. Willis*, 1995). In some jurisdictions the courts not only refuse to consider the decision to begin a pursuit as a basis for negligence but hold that, "When police observe 'erratic and dangerous driving . . . [they are] duty-bound to investigate, using all reasonable means, including pursuit, to stop the lawless vehicle's forward progress'" (citations omitted, *Cavigliano v. County of Livingston*, 1998, p. 187). Some courts have held that failure to discontinue a high-speed pursuit that results in the injury of a third party or fleeing motorist is not necessarily a violation of the reasonableness test of the due care standard (cf. *Jones v. Chieffo*, 1995).

The second distinction deals with the actual physical operation of emergency vehicles. Courts isolate certain types of conduct and remove them from those that constitute conclusive proof of negligence. For example, the courts have held that the driver of an authorized emergency vehicle exceeding the speed limit in pursuit of a suspected law violator is not negligent per se (*Brown v. City of New Orleans*, 1985; *Riggs v. State*, 1986). Other courts have held that an officer's failure to use emergency equipment alone is not sufficient to cause liability (*Hudson v. Carton*, 1929). These distinctions are based on a totality of the circumstances approach to assess reasonableness. Under these principles, a plaintiff must establish that an officer's conduct, determined in the totality of the circumstances, was a breach of reasonableness. A single factor, such as excessive speed or failure to use all available emergency equipment, is generally not conclusive proof of negligence. Nor is violation of a departmental policy or state statute, even if it speaks in mandatory terms, automatically proof of negligence, because the violated policy or statute may be rebutted with evidence that the officer's actions were reasonable under the circumstances (see, *Norton v. City of Chicago*, 1997) The courts consider the officer's conduct, along with all the situational factors surrounding the accident, to determine negligence. State courts consider a variety of factors in determining negligence in the operation of police emergency vehicles. These factors can be classified into four zones of negligence: justifications for pursuit, actual vehicle operation, circumstances of operation, and external factors.

Justification and decision-making factors considered by the courts include whether:

1. a real or apparent emergency existed (*Day v. Willis*, 1995; *Ewing v. City of Detroit*, 1995; *Hamilton v. Town of Palo*, 1976; *Keating v. Holston's Ambulance Serv., Inc.*, 1989);

2. the offender's conduct was serious (*Ewing v. City of Detroit*, 1995; *Gibson v. Pasadena*, 1978);

3. alternatives to pursuit were available to the officer; and (*Mason v. Britton*, 1975);

4. apprehension of the suspect was feasible.

Factors in the actual physical operation of the vehicle considered by the courts include the:

1. speed at which the vehicle is operated (*Ewing v. City of Detroit*, 1995; *Helseth v. Burch*, 2000);

2. use of emergency equipment (*Fowler v. North Carolina Dept. of Crime Control*, 1989; *Jones v. Chieffo*, 1995; *Norton v. City of Chicago*, 1997);

3. violation of traffic regulations or statues (*Sansonetti v. City of St. Joseph*, 1998);

4. violation of departmental policies, rules, or regulations (*Sansonetti v. City of St. Joseph*, 1998); and

5. disregard of traffic control devices (*Brown v. City of Pinellas Park*, 1990).

Factors in the circumstances of operation considered by the courts include the:

1. physical conditions of the roadway (*Ewing v. City of Detroit*, 1995);

2. weather and road conditions (*Bickel v. City of Downey*, 1987; *Day v. Willis*, 1995; *Ewing v. City of Detroit*, 1995; cf. *Cavigliano v. County of Livingston*, 1998);

3. density of traffic (*Brown v. City of Pinellas Park*, 1990);

4. presence of pedestrians (*Ewing v. City of Detroit*, 1995);

5. presence of audio or visual warning devices (*Jones v. Chieffo*, 1995); and

6. area of pursuit (*Brown v. City of Pinellas Park*, 1990; *Ewing v. City of Detroit*, 1995; *Helseth v. Burch*, 2000).

External factors considered by the courts include the:

1. existence and adequacy of a department's pursuit policy (*Cavigliano v. County of Livingston*, 1998; *Costello v. City of Ellisville*, 1996);
2. violation of departmental policy regarding police pursuits;
3. officer's training in pursuit driving (*Jones v. Chieffo*, 1995; *West v. United States*, 1985); and
4. physical and visual condition of the police vehicle.

The presence of a single factor alone is usually insufficient to establish unreasonable behavior, but as the number of factors increase, the probability of a finding of unreasonable behavior also increases. An examination of over 275 state court appellate cases on police liability for the negligent operation of emergency vehicles shows that the courts are more likely to support a finding of police liability where multiple factors are present. By way of example, an officer's decision not to discontinue a high-speed pursuit in dense traffic may not provide conclusive proof of unreasonable behavior; however, an officer's decision not to discontinue a high-speed pursuit, coupled with a department policy requiring the termination of such pursuits in dense traffic situations, may establish unreasonable behavior (*Mason v. Britton*, 1975; *Tetro v. Town of Stratford*, 1983). One must be careful, however, in assuming that these factors can only be used to indicate the negligence of a police officer's actions. Some courts have used these factors to justify a police pursuit. For example, in *Cavigliano v. County of Livingston* (1998) while considering the fatal consequence of a police pursuit, the court held, "While wet road conditions . . . increased the risk, they also 'increased the need for . . . immediate apprehension'" (citations omitted, p. 187).

Judicial Constructions of Causation

Even if unreasonable behavior is established and a breach of duty is proved, a plaintiff must show that the pursuing officer's conduct was the proximate cause of the damage or injury. This element in the theory of negligence has led to conflicting principles of law and judicial opinions on proximate cause and police pursuit liability. Police pursuit cases involving the injury of innocent third parties illustrate the disagreement among the courts when determining proximate cause issues.

State courts have adopted three approaches to proximate cause in the litigation of third-party police pursuit cases: (1) proximate cause as a doctrinal barrier to findings of police liability, (2) proximate cause as a function of police conduct in a particular situation, or (3) foreseeability analysis. In adopting a particular approach, the courts create differ-ent "zones of risk" for proximate cause.

Courts operating under the first approach (doctrinal barrier) take the position that the conduct of a pursuing police officer cannot be the proximate cause of an injury sustained by an innocent third party or fleeing motorist (*Sansonetti v. City of St. Joseph*, 1998). These courts are reluctant to find liability when an officer's vehicle is not directly involved in a collision with the injured third party (*Dennis v. City of Philadelphia*, 1993; *Ewing v. City of Detroit*, 1995) or where a fleeing motorist becomes injured in a pursuit (*Urban v. Village of Lincolnshire*, 1995). Some courts are so convinced that liability for third-party injury should not be extended to the police that they only reluctantly follow the precedent established by their own Supreme Court. Consider the following remarks made by the Michigan Court of Appeals:

> Reluctantly, we also find that a question of material fact existed re-garding whether defendants' actions were a proximate cause of plaintiff's injuries. In *Fiser*, the Supreme Court held that the police officers' pursuit of the third-party defendant caused him to drive recklessly in an effort to evade them. Therefore, the police were a proximate cause of the plaintiff's injuries when her car was hit by the fleeing third-party defendant. Because this case also involved a high-speed pursuit in which McGuigan was attempting to escape from the pursuing police officers and hit plaintiff as a result, we are bound to follow *Fiser*. . . .
>
> When a situation occurs. . . where an officer performs his legal duty by attempting to catch a fleeing lawbreaker, conducts the pursuit in what one may minimally call a negligent manner, and does not strike any vehicle with his vehicle, it is a remarkable legal principle that he can be said to have "caused" the resultant accident. To pre-vent this accident, all the fleeing driver need have done is stop. (*Ewing v. City of Detroit*, 1995, p. 3)

Courts often refuse to extend the zone of proximate cause beyond the actual collision of a police vehicle and a third party or to the injuries sustained by a fleeing suspect. This position is achieved on the follow-ing rationale:

1. Police officers have a duty to pursue, apprehend, and arrest law violators. The courts deem this duty so important that it out-weighs any other policy concern. From this position, the duty of care becomes subordinate to the duty to apprehend (see, *de Koning v. Mellema*, 1995).
2. Police officers and public entities should not become the ensur-ers of the negligence damage caused by law violators.
3. The actions of a fleeing law violator are an intervening cause that negates the possibility of an officer's conduct constituting the proximate cause of injury.

These courts assume that a police officer cannot be the proximate cause of a collision where the suspect's vehicle, and not the police officer's, strikes an innocent third party (*Ewing v. City of Detroit*, 1995). An intervening cause, not reasonably foreseeable, becomes the sole cause of the liability (*Angle v. Miller*, 1993). This approach can be attributed to the common-law concepts of proximate cause, contributory negligence, and a desire to limit police liability. A fleeing suspect, however, becomes part of the causal chain of events at the onset of a pursuit. Since an intervening cause is presumed to come after the defendant-officer's initial negligence, the logic in this position is questionable. Court decisions using this approach come with little explanation and do not represent a reflective application of the concept of proximate cause.

The second approach reflects the growing trend among state courts. In applying the concept of proximate cause, courts examine the situational factors surrounding the conduct that led to an injury (*Cavigliano v. County of Livingston*, 1998). Rather than making a pronouncement that police conduct in a third-party pursuit situation cannot be the proximate cause of injury, these courts adopt a case-by-case approach (*Norton v. City of Chicago*, 1997). In doing so, the courts do not automatically confine proximate cause to the zone of physical contact between the police vehicle and the injured third party, holding instead that the conduct of a pursuing police officer may be the proximate cause of injuries sustained in an accident even where the police vehicle did not directly become involved in the collision. This allows for findings of police liability based on proximate cause by examining the extent to which an officer's behavior and the situational factors surrounding the accident contributed to the injury or damage. This judicial approach to proximate cause is based on the following rationales:

1. a refusal to recognize an absolute duty to apprehend suspect law violators (*Estate of Aten v. City of Tucson*, 1991);
2. a refusal to relegate the duty of care to the duty to apprehend;
3. an acceptance of the possibility of a concurring cause modification of proximate cause doctrine;
4. deference to subjective jury decision making; and
5. application of a failure to warn doctrine (see chapter 9, pp. 155–159).

Expansion of the zone of proximate cause, however, is not without problems. Seldom are circumstances surrounding a police pursuit easily isolated, nor are their contributory influences easily discerned. Courts operating in this zone of proximate cause may use a simplistic construction of proximate cause that seems to be based on determining whether the officer's conduct was close in time and space to the injury. After this determination is made, the court addresses the issue of whether or not the actions contributed to the injury in a meaningful way. For example, in the case of *Norton v. City of Chicago* (1997) an Illinois Court of Appeals held that where a police pursuit vehicle was nearly two blocks away from the third-party injury and where the police failed to use their siren, such a situation could not establish proximate cause.

Courts using the third approach base findings of proximate cause on the "foreseeability" of injury or damage. This analysis is less stringent than strict proximate cause and allows more flexibility in judicial decision making. Nonetheless, the approach is at odds with several basic principles of law previously established by the courts when examining what behaviors and circumstances establish breach of duty in the emergency operation of police vehicles.

Some courts have taken the doctrinal position that an officer's decision to pursue or to discontinue a pursuit cannot constitute unreasonable behavior. Foreseeability has no application in such decisions. Further clouding the foreseeability analysis is the time-honored concept of negligence as unintentional conduct not requiring a specific mental state. If foreseeability becomes the requisite for negligence litigation, then the theory will begin to resemble intentional tort. Under this formulation of proximate cause, emphasis is placed on the mental state of the officer-defendant and the extent to which the danger of injury was foreseeable at the time of pursuit. Foreseeability analysis, in this area of law, has been given little attention by the courts and is only recently beginning to generate a viable doctrine or unifying principle of law.

Courts that accept the notion that a police officer's decision to pursue or discontinue a pursuit can form the basis of a breach of duty (*Jones v. Chieffo*, 1995) are combining an intervening substantial cause conception of causation with foreseeability analysis. In this construct, immunity would be extended to police officers only if the intervening criminal acts of a third person are so extraordinary or unforeseeable that they nullify any underlying police negligence as being a substantial contributing factor in causing the accident (*Black v. Shrewsbury Borough*, 1996). Therefore, if initiating and continuing a pursuit was negligent and amounted to a substantial contributing factor in causing the victims' injury, liability may be imposed. This construction of causation is based on the following reasons and rationales:

1. police defendants should not be afforded blanket immunity in every tort claim where the victim's injuries were caused in part by intervening criminal conduct;
2. criminal conduct or third-party behaviors merely form a link in the chain of causation;
3. regardless of the intervening conduct, police negligence may still be a substantial contributing factor in causing victims' injuries; and
4. deference should be given to juries to make decisions of whether intervening criminal conduct of third parties is so

extraordinary as not to be reasonably foreseeable by police because it was a superseding cause precluding liability.

Defenses to Negligent Operation

If a plaintiff can establish that the defendant-officer's conduct during a pursuit was the proximate cause of injury or damage, redress of that damage may still be avoided. Recovery may be forestalled under two legal defenses. In police pursuit litigation, defenses to claims of negligence take the form of contributory or comparative negligence. Depending on the prevailing theory in a jurisdiction, proof of the plaintiff's negligence can either totally bar or severely limit recovery. Contributory negligence is a defense that is pleaded and established by the defendant, and the burden of proof lies with the defendant.

The defense of contributory negligence, as discussed in chapter 2, holds that if a plaintiff's conduct contributed to the injury or damage, recovery is barred. Under a strict application of the doctrine, any contributing negligence by the plaintiff, no matter how slight, bars recovery of damage and therefore negates liability. Because of the possible inequity of this defense, a majority of states moved to the more equitable defense of comparative negligence.

The defense of comparative negligence (see chapter 2) also requires a showing that the plaintiff's conduct contributed to the damage or injury. As in the contributory negligence defense, defendants must show that the plaintiff's conduct had a contributory effect on the damage or injury. After a showing of the plaintiff's contributory conduct, the court weighs the negligence of the plaintiff with that of the defendant and assesses a portion of negligence to each litigant. The defendant is only liable for a portion of the damage commensurate with the percentage of the blame. If negligence is determined to be split 75/25 between the plaintiff and the defendant respectively, and the total damage count is $1,000, the defendant would be liable for $250. The main distinction between contributory and comparative negligence is the extent to which recovery is mitigated. Contributory negligence bars recovery totally, whereas comparative negligence only limits it.

Courts construe contributory conduct as a mixed question of fact and law to be determined by either a jury or the court. Contributory negligence often takes the form of statutory violations. In police pursuit, certain statutes mandate the behavior of citizens using the roadways. Since there are a variety of traffic regulations, and a violation of each can lead to a determination of contributory negligence, the range of behaviors that constitute contributory negligence is vast. Violations of these statutes often establish contributory negligence and become an affirmative defense for the defendant-officer. For example, courts have determined that the drivers of motor vehicles have a duty to yield the right of way to law enforcement officers operating vehicles under emergency circumstances. A plaintiff's violation of this duty can establish contributory negligence and mitigate recovery, even in the face of evidence of an officer's previous negligence.

Court rulings on contributory negligence have not always been based on statutory violations. Several decisions have held that a plaintiff's behavior, even if it is not a statutory violation, can constitute contributory negligence. In *Maple v. City of Omaha* (1986) the Nebraska Supreme Court ruled that a driver's failure to hear a police siren could be considered contributory negligence. Further extending the boundaries of behaviors that constitute contributory negligence is a decision of the Alabama Supreme Court. In *Smith v. Bradford* (1985) a thirteen-year-old boy was riding his bicycle along the side of a highway. An Alabama state trooper pursued a speeding motorist along the same highway, reaching speeds of more than 90 miles per hour. The trooper's vehicle struck the child, who died four days later. The court held that although there was support for the trooper's wanton conduct, the child "may be shown to be capable of contributory negligence by a showing that he possessed that discretion, intelligence, and sensitivity to danger which an ordinary thirteen-year-old child possesses." Such a determination would bar damage recovery.

Contributory and comparative negligence defenses indicate that there is a broad range of behaviors that provide proof of negligence. Case law, however, has yet to yield a uniform doctrine or principle of law as to what behaviors establish contributory negligence in vehicular cases. What the courts have done instead is to lay out broad boundaries of behavior that run from statutory violations to a lack of awareness or diligence by plaintiffs. An analysis of these cases suggests that as a plaintiff's behavior moves toward statutory violation, the likelihood of a finding of contributory negligence increases.

Summary

A duty of care by police officers when operating emergency vehicles is universally recognized. This duty requires the operator of an emergency vehicle to drive with due care for the safety of all persons using the public roadways. Breaches of duty are determined by assessing the reasonableness of an officer's conduct. In doing so, courts use a totality of circumstances approach and examine four zones of negligence. These zones include justifications for pursuit, actual vehicle operation, circumstances of operation, and external factors. The presence or absence of a single factor within a zone is not sufficient for a finding of police negligence.

Proximate cause in police emergency vehicle operation is also determined by a totality of circumstances approach. Conflict exists between jurisdictions on the issue of proximate cause in third-party litigation. Some courts take the position that the conduct of a pursuing police officer *cannot* be the proximate cause of an injury sustained by an innocent third party. Other courts have moved toward allowing liability in third-party cases. That is, the conduct of a pursuing police officer may be the proximate cause of injuries even where the police vehicle did not directly become involved in the collision. Determinations of proximate cause are made from the totality of circumstances surrounding a damage or injury or by the foreseeability of damage.

Specific defenses to claims of negligence in the police operation of motor vehicles may bar or limit a damage recovery. These defenses take the form of contributory and comparative negligence. Courts have determined that drivers of motor vehicles have a duty to yield the right of way to law enforcement officers operating vehicles under emergency circumstances. Violation of this duty is conclusive proof of contributory negligence. The boundary of contributory negligence has recently been extended to include behaviors by plaintiffs that do not involve statutory violation. Behaviors such as inattention or lack of diligence may establish contributory negligence, determinations being made on a case-by-case basis.

Police Civil Liability for Failure to Arrest Intoxicated Drivers

8

There is a growing public concern in the United States about the dangers associated with drunk driving. This concern may be well-founded; research has indicated that drunken drivers kill approximately 23,000 persons each year. Arrests for DWI have increased tremendously over the last two decades. In any given year between 7 and 10 percent of those confined in local jails are charged with DWI. Estimates indicate that about 50 percent of all the fatal traffic accidents in the United States involve intoxicated drivers. While the percentage of alcohol-related deaths has declined slightly in recent years, the numbers are still disturbingly high.

The political response to this social problem has been swift and certain. State legislators in many states have increased the sanctions for alcohol-related traffic offenses, raised the legal drinking age, and enacted legislation prohibiting the possession of open containers of alcohol in motor vehicles. Although the dangers of drunk driving are compelling, the response to the problem is perhaps more of a political reaction to public outcry than a rational consideration of viable policy alternatives. The lobbying activities of Mothers Against Drunk Drivers (MADD) and enhanced coverage of drunk driving by the media have led to greater public awareness and concern with police enforcement of drunk-driving statutes.

This chapter analyzes recent state court decisions on police liability for failure to restrain drunk drivers. It focuses on jurisdictions that either reject the public duty doctrine or have reinterpreted the special relationship/discretionary function doctrine to allow for causes of action and, ultimately, determination of police liability. The chapter considers the legal theories used by the courts to establish a cause of

action and the types of police conduct in drunk-driving situations that
lead to police liability, focusing on cases in which intoxicated drivers
have injured innocent third parties. After analyzing the development
of the public duty doctrine and its exceptions, the chapter concludes
with an extrapolation and restatement of contemporary principles of
law on police liability for failure to arrest intoxicated drivers.

Traditional Barriers to Liability

There are two primary barriers to negligence claims against the police
for failure to arrest drunk drivers who are involved in accidents that
result in injury to innocent third parties. These barriers are the sovereign immunity doctrine (see chapters 2 and 7) and the ministerial/dis-
cretionary distinction (see chapter 7).

The Sovereign Immunity Doctrine

Federal and state voluntary legislative waivers or waivers forced by
judicial decisions have eroded the protection against liability through
sovereign immunity. In jurisdictions where immunity is waived, these
waivers most often include cases arising out of motor vehicle incidents.
If a state or municipal entity contracts for insurance coverage for damages incurred while performing governmental functions, the courts
have construed such behavior as a voluntary and limited waiver of
immunity. The rapid change in doctrines on police negligence has led to
increased agency vulnerability to lawsuits involving police failure to
arrest intoxicated drivers.

Ministerial/Discretionary Distinction

The ministerial/discretionary function distinction originated in
early case law on governmental liability (*Dalehite v. United States*,
1953). It has acted as a shield against liability of governmental entities
by establishing a legal dichotomy between governmental functions that
are considered "discretionary" and those deemed "ministerial" (*Whitney v. Worcester*, 1977). Discretionary acts are characterized by the
high degree of discretion and judgment involved in weighing alternatives and making choices in public policy and planning (*Adams v. State*,
1976). These acts are immune from liability. Ministerial acts, on the
other hand, are operational functions—the actual carrying out of established plans and policies. As operational functions, ministerial acts do
not enjoy immunity (*Chambers-Castaner v. King County*, 1983). Courts
applying the ministerial/discretionary function distinction examine a
number of factors to determine whether an act or function is ministerial or discretionary. The factors considered most important are:

1. Does the act involve high-level discretionary decisions executed at the executive level of government?
2. Does the function involve governmental policy or its development?
3. Is the act or omission critical to attaining or accomplishing governmental policy, as opposed to acts that would not change the course of policy intent?
4. Does the act require the exercise of policy evaluation, judgment, and special expertise on the part of a governmental entity?
5. Is the agency vested with the required legal authority to either carry out or omit the act?
6. Is the act carried out at the operational level?

The extent to which these criteria are used varies from court to court. This lack of consistency, coupled with judicial vagueness as to the actual meaning of the terms "ministerial" and "discretionary," has led to conflicting interpretations about whether the decision to arrest an intoxicated driver constitutes a ministerial or a discretionary act.

In several cases, courts have held that the duty to arrest an intoxicated motorist is a mandatory function. An officer's breach of this duty, resulting in injury, leads to officer and municipality liability for damages. For example in *Landis v. Rockdale County* (1992), the Georgia Court of Appeals addressed the issue of whether law enforcement officers owe a duty to members of the general public injured by drunk drivers. In this case a minor was operating her vehicle under the influence of alcohol. During the course of driving to a party she drove her vehicle off the roadway, returned to the roadway, and crossed the centerline into the path of an oncoming car. The resulting accident killed Landis. It was learned afterwards that less than two hours earlier an on-duty deputy sheriff observed the minor operating her vehicle while noticeably intoxicated and failed to arrest her because her father had allowed the deputy to play golf for free at a club he owned.

Before trial, the deputy moved for summary judgment by arguing that his duty to arrest, if any, was owed to the public at large and did not extend to an individual member of that public. The trial court sustained his motion, and the case was appealed. Considering the issue of a law enforcement officer's duty to arrest intoxicated drivers, the appeals court held that duty in these situations arises because of the General Assembly's efforts to control drunk driving for the protection of all drivers on the highways not the general public. The court noted that law enforcement officers have the duty, authority, and opportunity to prevent noticeably intoxicated drivers from continuing to drive based on the statutory prohibition against alcohol-influenced driving. This coupled with law enforcement's unique awareness of the dangers of drunk driving and the ability to prevent this behavior creates a duty to third parties. Summary judgement was overturned.

The issue of liability for failure to arrest drunk drivers, however, is often more complex than the announcement that there exists a duty to arrest. This was illustrated in the 1984 case *Irwin v. Ware*. A Massachusetts resident brought suit against the city police for the negligent release of an intoxicated driver who subsequently was involved in a vehicular accident that seriously injured the plaintiff and her son and killed her husband and two daughters. Minutes before the accident, two police officers had stopped the driver for a speeding violation. During questioning by the police, the driver told the officers that he had been drinking a "couple of beers." The officers reportedly smelled an intoxicating beverage on the subject's breath but failed to administer a field sobriety test. After making other routine checks, the officers released the driver who later became involved in the fatal accident that led to the plaintiff's suit. The jury awarded the plaintiff $873,697 in damages. On appeal to the Massachusetts Supreme Judicial Court, the town of Ware argued that the police officers' duty to arrest the intoxicated motorist was a discretionary act precluding liability. The court, relying on a distinction between mandatory and discretionary functions, noted that although the officers were engaged in an exercise of judgment when determining whether to arrest the intoxicated driver, they were not "carrying out previously established policies or plans" (*Irwin v. Ware*, 1984, p. 16). The court said that there was no "reasonable basis for arguing that a police officer is making a policy or planning judgment in deciding whether to remove from the roadways a driver who he knows is intoxicated" (p. 16). The court then concluded that a municipality may be held liable for the negligent failure of its police officers to remove from the highways intoxicated motorists who cause injury to innocent third parties (see also, *Blea v. City of Espanola*, 1994). The court added, however, that making this distinction does not imply that in every case in which a peace officer fails to arrest an intoxicated driver, liability necessarily follows. The court applied many of the six criteria mentioned earlier in analyzing the facts of this case to determine if the town of Ware could claim discretionary immunity.

In a Colorado case, *Cain v. Leake* (1984), police officers were summoned to investigate a large outdoor party. When they arrived, the officers directed the teenagers to disperse. A guest at the party had been drinking, became disruptive, and attempted to strike one of the officers, forcing the police to restrain him physically. Shortly thereafter, the guest's juvenile brother approached the officers and requested the subject's release. After ascertaining the younger brother's identity and sobriety, the officers released the intoxicated subject with the understanding that the younger brother would drive him home. A chain of events led to the intoxicated brother driving the motor vehicle, resulting in a collision that killed two pedestrians. The Colorado Court of Appeals reversed the trial court's summary judgment in favor of the defendant-officers and the city, citing as precedent the *Irwin* case in Massachusetts. The court reasoned that "a decision by a police officer to release a disputatious, intoxicated person from custody, and to send that person onto the roadway" (*Cain v. Leake*, 1984, p. 796) is not a discretionary act; therefore, the plaintiffs did have a cause of action, and police officials were not to be afforded blanket immunity under the discretionary function doctrine. On appeal, the Colorado Supreme Court reversed the appellate court decision (*Leake v. Cain*, 1986), ruling that the decision of a police officer to arrest an intoxicated "subject" was a discretionary governmental function that enjoyed official immunity.

Although the Colorado high court's decision appears to have been based on rejection of the precedent set in *Irwin*, the facts in the two cases were markedly different. In *Cain*, the intoxicated person the police failed to arrest was not operating a motor vehicle, and the police had every reason to assume that he would not drive the vehicle. The Colorado court noted this, stating that the "potent harm resulting from the release . . . was far less foreseeable than the release of the intoxicated driver in *Irwin v. Ware*" (*Leake v. Cain*, 1986, pp. 163–64). The Colorado court distinguished these two cases by saying that when an officer stops an intoxicated driver, the officer has no discretion but to arrest that driver, but when the officer stops an intoxicated person, the officer is required to have probable cause to believe the person presents a danger to himself or to another before an arrest can be made. The court declined to state whether a similar verdict would have been rendered in a situation akin to *Irwin* and refused to determine whether a police officer's decision to arrest or detain a drunken driver is a discretionary or ministerial act. Thus, the court left the door open for future considerations of the issues involving the release of intoxicated drivers.

A traditional ministerial/discretionary function approach would have excluded foreseeability from consideration and left the court with no alternative but to find that the decision to arrest an intoxicated person is a ministerial function. In *Cain* the court established a line of argument that involved foreseeability and a connection between the intoxicated person, the defendant-officer, and the ensuing damage or injury. Thus, if the injury or damage is foreseeable and the contact between the officer and the intoxicated person is close, a finding of ministerial function is likely. Conversely, if foreseeability is questionable and the officer's intervention is remote from the actual damage, spatially or temporally, a finding of discretionary function is likely.

In a situation analogous to *Irwin*, the Florida Supreme Court ruled in *Everton v. Willard* (1985) that a peace officer's decision to arrest an intoxicated motorist is a discretionary function; hence, governmental entities could not be held liable for damages. The court, in a cursory decision using a rationale contrary to both *Irwin* and *Leake*, stated "discretionary power is considered basic to the police power function of governmental entities and is recognized as critical to a law enforcement officer's ability to carry out his duties" (*Everton v. Willard*, 1985, p. 938). The court gave scant heed to the ministerial/discretionary distinction noted by other courts and opted for an extremely broad definition of discretion stating that "merely because an activity is operational, it should not necessarily be removed from the category of governmental activity which involves broad policy or planning decisions" (p. 937).

The discretionary function defense is but one barrier in police liability cases based on the public duty doctrine. The disagreement among courts about whether the decision to arrest or release an intoxicated motorist constitutes a discretionary or ministerial function has stemmed in part from the ambiguity of the term discretionary and what appears to be a conscious effort to support a preferred position. Courts taking the position that the decision of a police officer to arrest or release an intoxicated motorist is a discretionary function, such as the Florida court in *Everton*, have relied on a definition of discretion as denoting the need to make a judgment or choice between alternatives in the enforcement of law (see also, *Makris v. City of Gross Pointe Park*, 1989). This definition implies that the authority of police officers to decide whether to arrest or release a subject is critical to law enforcement and that police officers cannot function effectively without protection in making judgment calls. Although that position has some merit, interpretations based on it confuse police discretion—the selection of alternatives in dealing with violations of criminal law—with discretionary function. Discretionary function pertains to the distinction between levels and types of decision making by municipalities. For example, an operational function such as a decision made by a police officer in the street between arresting a drunk driver or taking that person home is not akin to the decision made by a city official to reduce the number of patrol officers assigned to enforce drunk-driving statutes. The latter is a policy function that enjoys immunity, while the former is an operational function to which immunity does not extend.

Although police discretion may very well be, as the *Everton* court stated, "critical" to law enforcement, the decision to arrest or release a drunk driver is clearly an operational-level decision and should not fall under the discretionary act defense umbrella. Judge Shaw, in a dissenting opinion, ruled the effect of the position taken by the *Everton* court: "Given the sweep of discretionary [function] . . . I suggest that there is very little, if anything, left in the way of government action on which a tort victim could sue" (*Everton v. Willard*, 1985, p. 942). Judge Shaw said, as did the California Supreme Court in *Johnson v. State*, that virtually all human endeavors carry with them some form of discretion—even the "driving of a nail" (*Johnson v. State*, 1968, p. 357).

The *Everton* court established a third line of reasoning that focuses on the consequences of imposing civil suit liability on governmental units. A semantical approach enabled the court to bypass the traditional arguments and to focus on the possible adverse consequence of a liability ruling. Under this approach, a decision of immunity is almost inevitable. The Florida Supreme Court faced a conflict four years after the *Everton* decision because of its confusing precedent. In the case of *Kaisner v. Kolb* (1989) the court decided "that acts by law enforcement officers in respect to persons whom they have detained, other than whether to arrest or detain those persons, were operational acts not protected by sovereign immunity" (p. 537). The court stated that it has consistently "held that liability may exist when the act of the government or its agent is not discretionary, but operational in nature" (p. 537). In essence the court modified its position to circumstances outside the decision to detain or arrest. Having modified its construction of the ministerial/discretionary distinction, it was only a matter of time before the court faced a case of police liability for failure to protect an intoxicated driver.

Fourteen years after the *Everton* decision, Isaac Bowden and Luna Dell Archie Haywood brought a wrongful death suit in the state of Florida when two of their sons were killed after a roadside detention by sheriff's deputies of Hillsborough County. One of the deputies, Gary Herman, stopped a vehicle for driving 74 miles per hour and arrested the driver, Jimmy Bowden. There were three passengers in the car: Lyons and Damon and Robert Bowden. Lyons said that the deputy directed him to drive to a nearby Circle K convenience store. The deputy allegedly told Lyons that he would follow him to the store. Lyons drove to the Circle K and waited. After a while, Lyons decided to drive away from the parking lot. Deputy Garcia arrived at the store and saw Lyons's vehicle leaving the parking lot at a high rate of speed. Lyons subsequently collided with a cluster of trees, killing Damon and Robert.

The court, in *Henderson v. Bowden* (1999), distinguished this case from its earlier decisions. It concluded that "the sheriff's deputies placed the passengers of Lyons's vehicle in danger by directing an intoxicated Lyons to drive to the Circle K store and that this direction, more likely than not, created a foreseeable zone of risk, thereby giving rise to a legal duty." The court went on to remark that, "While the act in question in this case certainly involved a degree of discretion, we cannot say that it was the type of discretion that needs to be insulated from suit." The court concluded "that the alleged actions of the sheriff's deputies during the roadside detention of the Lyons vehicle are not the type of actions which are insulated from suit" (pp. 538-39). The court in effect modified its construction of the ministerial/discretionary functions distinction to bring it more in line with Irwin and Leake.

The Idaho Supreme Court in *Sterling v. Bloom* (1986) espoused a more defensible legal position. The court in this case found that a probation officer had breached his duty to motorists by negligently per-

mitting his client to operate a motor vehicle in violation of the proba-
tioner's conditions of release. The court upheld the ministerial/discre-
tionary dichotomy as a useful tool but recognized only qualified
immunity in the governmental performance of operational functions.
The court ruled that in instances of planning functions "the government is immune even where the planning was negligent" but that
immunity in carrying out operational functions is "contingent upon the
use of due or ordinary care" (*Sterling v. Bloom*, 1986, p. 774).

Conflicting judicial decisions on the issue of whether a police
officer's decision to arrest an intoxicated driver is a ministerial or discretionary function have resulted from differing judicial approaches to
the issue and from differing methods of analysis. Some courts have used
a traditional approach to decision making (*Chambers-Castaner v. King
County*, 1983). Under this approach, the court considers the issue apart
from considerations of proximate cause and foreseeability, and the min-
isterial/discretionary function distinction is viewed as a threshold question. Issues bearing on the traditional principles of negligence, such as
foreseeability and proximate cause, are not addressed until the threshold issue is settled. Courts adopting this approach have held that the
police officer's decision is ministerial and thus susceptible to liability.

Other courts have adopted a semantical approach (*Everton v. Willard*, 1985; *Makris v. City of Grosse Pointe Park*, 1989) in which the
objective criterion as to what constitutes a discretionary function is
disregarded and the courts develop a particularistic interpretation of
the term "discretionary," based on consequential factors. Such an
approach focuses on the potential impact of a ministerial function ruling on the governmental service. In the case of police failure to arrest
intoxicated drivers, courts using this approach have held that the decision to arrest is a discretionary function that cannot form the basis for
a claim of negligence.

Alternatively, courts have confused discretionary/ministerial
analysis in an examination of statutes (*Irwin v. Ware*, 1984) and in an
introduction of traditional negligence principles (*Cain v. Leake*, 1984).
Reliance on existing statutes has led to conflicting opinions, based on
wording. Similarly, the inclusion of foreseeability and proximate cause
at this stage of the decision-making process has led to conflicting opinions as to whether the decision to arrest is ministerial or discretionary.

The Public Duty Doctrine

Even if a plaintiff overcomes the discretionary function barrier to governmental liability, liability may still be denied under the concept of
public duty, which we introduced in chapter 2. Based on this concept,
the courts have traditionally rejected police liability for failure to arrest
drunk drivers and failure to protect citizens.

Recall that the public duty doctrine (of common-law origin) holds that governmental functions, such as police protection, are owed to the general public and not to specific individuals. Where a duty is owed to the general public and not to any particular person, there can be no cause of action or subsequent liability for failure to protect individuals from injuries caused by third parties. Since 1856, when the United States Supreme Court first formulated the public duty doctrine, most state courts have adopted it in government negligence cases. Several state supreme court cases illustrate the use of the doctrine.

In *Massengill v. Yuma County* (1969) the Arizona Supreme Court held that the duty to arrest an intoxicated driver was a duty owed to the general public and that individual third parties injured by intoxicated drivers who are released by police officers are denied recovery. In *Massengill*, the plaintiff brought action against a sheriff, his deputy, and the county for failure to arrest two traffic violators who subsequently became involved in a head-on collision. The accident resulted in the death of five persons and the total disability of a sixth individual. Before the accident, a sheriff who was on duty observed two vehicles leaving the parking lot of a local bar. Both vehicles then proceeded, at a high rate of speed, down a dangerous and heavily traveled highway.

One of the sheriff's deputies, who had been parked along the highway, observed and followed the vehicles as they were driving side by side erratically down the road. The deputy knew or should have known that the drivers were intoxicated, but he failed to take any action until after the accident had occurred. The Arizona Supreme Court ruled that the circumstances of the case did not demonstrate any greater duty to the injured individuals than that owed to the general public, adding that if the damage was to be redressed at all, a public criminal prosecution would be required.

In a similar case, *Fusilier v. Russell* (1977), the plaintiff brought criminal action against two deputy sheriffs in Louisiana for failure to restrain an intoxicated subject who later became involved in an automobile accident that left the plaintiff-victim severely burned. Before the accident, deputy sheriffs were called to a nightclub to evict a disorderly customer. When they arrived, the officers observed an intoxicated person in the parking lot. Even though the officers saw the subject staggering around the lot for several minutes, they failed to take the individual into custody. Without the officers' knowledge, the subject left the parking lot in a motor vehicle. Subsequently, the officers followed the suspect; ten minutes later, the deputies saw two vehicles on fire. The drunk driver had struck the plaintiff's vehicle, causing the serious accident. The trial court dismissed the plaintiff's action against the sheriff and his deputies. On appeal, the Court of Appeals of Louisiana affirmed the dismissal, holding that the duty to arrest is a duty owed to the general public and that a special relationship was absent. The court sympathized with the officers' dilemma and cited Justice Warren's remarks in *Pierson v. Ray* (1967), that "[a] policeman's lot is not so unhappy that he must choose between being charged with dereliction of duty if he does not arrest when he has probable cause, and being mulcted in damages if he does" (p. 555).

A third case that applies to the public duty doctrine is *Crosby v. Town of Bethlehem* (1982), a New York decision. In *Crosby* the mother of a pedestrian killed by an intoxicated operator of a motorcycle brought action against a police officer and a municipality for the alleged negligent failure to restrain an intoxicated driver. Before the accident, an off-duty police officer who resided next door to the site of a large lawn party had a conversation with and later observed an intoxicated person mounting his motorcycle. The officer failed to intervene; instead she allegedly called the police department and reported the violation. Neither the officer nor other members of the police department took action to prevent the driver from operating the motorcycle, and no record of the defendant-officer's call could be produced. The driver subsequently became involved in the fatal accident that led to the death of the plaintiff's daughter.

The New York Supreme Court, affirming the summary judgment granted the defendant-officer by the trial court, failed to find a breach of duty, saying that although the "ultimate tragedy was entirely foreseeable . . . foreseeability is not to be confused with duty and foreseeability may not be used to create a duty where none existed before" (p. 619).

Courts adopting the public duty doctrine have justified its use on several grounds. The first is the need to preserve governmental entities. To impose liability for the negligent behavior of governmental units creates great economic hardship and depletes government resources. Thus, the individual's loss is subordinate to the compelling need to protect the government and its limited resources. The second justification is use and tradition. That is, the public duty doctrine is a traditional principle of legal theory derived from common law, and deviation from it, after all this time, is undesirable. Perhaps the clearest accounting for the public duty doctrine is provided by Supreme Court of Tennessee when it explained that a

> number of public policy considerations have been advanced to explain and support adoption of the public duty doctrine. One policy consideration frequently expressed is that individuals, juries and courts are ill-equipped to judge governmental decisions as to how particular community resources should be or should have been allocated to protect individual members of the public. Some courts have theorized that severe depletion of those resources could well result if every oversight or omission of a police official resulted in civil liability. They have also observed that such a rule would place police officials in the untenable position of insuring the personal

safety of every member of the public, or facing a civil suit for damages, and that the public duty doctrine eliminates that dilemma. . . .

Another policy consideration justifying recognition of the public duty doctrine is that police officials often act and react in the milieu of criminal activity where every decision is fraught with uncertainty. . . .

Finally, many courts subscribing to the public duty doctrine have emphasized that mechanisms, other than civil negligence actions, exist wherein individual officials may be held accountable for dereliction of duty, for instance, internal disciplinary proceedings or formal criminal prosecutions. (citations omitted; *Ezell v. Cockrell*, 1995, pp. 397–98; *Holsten v. Massey*, 1997)

Regardless of these rationales the public duty doctrine has come under attack from several state supreme courts.

Demise of the Public Duty Doctrine

Some state courts have simply rejected the concept of public duty. The rejection is based on the realization that "duty to all" amounts to "duty to no-one" (*Adams v. State*, 1976, p. 235) and that the doctrine amounts to another form of sovereign immunity, which these state courts have rejected. Where this has happened, state courts have abolished the concept of public duty in favor of general tort principles; governmental entities and their agents are treated as private individuals. In these cases, the courts apply the essential elements of negligence tort—duty, breach of a duty, proximate cause, and injury.

Rejecting the public duty doctrine in drunk-driving cases in favor of general negligence tort is a growing trend that began in the mid-1980s. Several state supreme court cases from that decade exemplify this trend. Thirteen years after the Arizona Supreme Court decision in *Massengill*, that court reversed its position in *Ryan v. State* (1982). In *Ryan* the court stated "we shall no longer engage in the speculative exercise of determining whether the tort-feasor has a general duty to the injured party, which spells no recovery, or if he had a specific individual duty which means recovery" (p. 599). The court declined to adopt the discretionary acts approach in favor of an ad hoc decision-making process. It sought to avoid the semantic legerdemain involved in applying a "discretionary acts" exception in the liability litigation and to steer the development of case law accordingly.

In 1986 the Wyoming Supreme Court rejected the public duty doctrine in *DeWald v. State* (1986). In *DeWald*, state highway patrol officers were involved in the pursuit of an intoxicated driver. Having been informed by a complainant that an intoxicated driver was operating a motor vehicle, the officers obtained a description of the vehicle and went out to locate it. The officer later spotted a vehicle matching the description given him by the complainant, and he observed it crossing the centerline of the roadway several times. The officer activated his emergency equipment and attempted to stop the motorist, but the motorist failed to obey the officer's directive. The officer then followed the vehicle to a nearby town and repeatedly directed the driver to pull his vehicle to the side of the road. At one point the officer pulled alongside the intoxicated driver and signaled the driver to stop; the vehicle then left the intersection at a high rate of speed and traveled through the town at approximately fifty-five miles per hour. The officer followed the vehicle for several blocks before discontinuing the chase. Shortly thereafter, the intoxicated driver struck another vehicle that had stopped at a traffic control device. The driver of the stopped vehicle was killed in the collision and suit was brought against the state and the officer.

The trial court entered summary judgment in favor of the state and defendant-officer, and the judgment was appealed. The Wyoming Supreme Court rejected the defendant's contention that under the public duty doctrine the officer could not be held liable for the injuries to individuals and ruled that the public duty doctrine could no longer be invoked, in view of the state's abolition of sovereign immunity. The court reasoned, as did the New Mexico Supreme Court in the case of *Schear v. Board of County Commissioners of Bernalillo County* (1984), that:

> The trend in this area is toward liability. The "public duty" doctrine has lost support in four of the eight jurisdictions relied upon by the city [for its argument that it owed no duty of ordinary care to an individual citizen]. These courts have demonstrated a reasoned reluctance to apply a doctrine that results in a duty to none where there is a duty to all. (p. 731)

Generally, courts rejecting the public duty doctrine have determined that regardless of its origin in the common law, the doctrine serves the same function as sovereign immunity, which has been rejected in the vast majority of states. In contrast to outright rejection, other courts have retained the doctrine but have allowed exceptions. These exceptions come under the general rubric of special relationships.

Special Relationship

The term *special relationship* lacks a precise legal definition, but in the context of legal liability cases it implies the presence of factors that transcend the usual police-public relationship (see chapter 2). In police liability cases, these factors may involve: (1) the intent of state legislation to create a duty peculiar to a class of individuals, or (2) the peculiar circumstances surrounding the incident and the behaviors of the parties involved. The presence of either may give rise to a cause of action and the potential for government liability (*Irwin v. Ware*, 1984).

Statutorily Established Special Relationships

After addressing the threshold question of discretionary function, the court in the *Irwin* case found that a cause of action existed due to the special relationship between the police and the plaintiff. Such a special relationship existed, not just based on the circumstances of the case, but also because of the legislative intent evident in the state statute prohibiting drunken driving. The court stated "Statutes which establish police responsibility in such circumstances evidence a legislative intent to protect both intoxicated persons and users of the highway" (*Irwin v. Ware*, 1984, pp. 1303–4). While relying on the statute, the court also noted that the most critical factor in these determinations is the "foreseeability" of the harm resulting from the behaviors involved—the absence of which might have led the court to a different finding.

In *Bailey v. Town of Forks* (1985), the Court of Appeals of the State of Washington took a position contrary to *Irwin*. In *Bailey*, a police officer investigated an altercation at a local lounge. During his investigation, the officer observed and had "contact" with an intoxicated person. The subject left the area driving a pickup truck; the officer chose not to intervene. The pickup truck collided with a motorcycle on which the plaintiff was a passenger. The driver of the motorcycle was killed in the accident, and the plaintiff was seriously injured. The plaintiff brought suit against the police officer and the city for negligent failure to restrain an intoxicated driver.

The Court of Appeals ruled that there existed no cause of action based upon state statutes: "The Legislature has not seen fit to impose for the benefit of particular individuals as opposed to the general public—any duty on police officers to arrest, detain or otherwise prevent even obviously intoxicated persons from driving their vehicles" (p. 531).

The court refused to establish an exception to the general-duty doctrine based upon statute and failed to find a special relationship between the police and the victim, leaving plaintiff to "seek redress elsewhere" (p. 531). The implication is clear—that the court would have decided differently had legislative intent to impose been evident.

In a similar case from the same state, the Ninth Circuit Court of Appeals supported the state court's position in *Bailey*. The court found that the conduct of military police officers in releasing an intoxicated person, who later operated a motor vehicle that struck and killed an innocent third party, did not create a special relationship (*Louie v. United States*, 1985). The court noted that under Washington state law, state officials who observe intoxicated persons owe no duty to motorists who are injured in vehicular accidents; therefore, the court refused to find a special relationship between federal government personnel (military police) and the plaintiff. Echoing *Bailey*, the federal appellate court reiterated the Washington requirement for an exception to the public duty doctrine, which called for "a clear statement of legislative intent to identify and protect a particular and circumscribed class of persons [and] a member of that class has an individual claim for violation of the ordinance or statute or creating duty" (p. 826).

A similar verdict was reached in *Barratt v. Burlingham* (1985), a case decided by the Rhode Island Supreme Court. In *Barratt* a police officer who was on duty encountered a drunken driver who was attempting to leave a restaurant parking lot. The officer, observing the driver's impaired condition, advised him to park the vehicle where it was. Ensuing traffic congestion, due to the vehicle's position, motivated the officer to allow a sober passenger to move the vehicle off the lot. Later events led to the switching of drivers and a subsequent accident that left the passenger-plaintiff a quadriplegic. Plaintiff brought action against both the officer and the municipality for the negligent release of an intoxicated motorist. Plaintiff argued that once the officer had taken action to protect the parties by instructing them to remain in the parking lot, a special relationship had developed; hence a breach occurred when the parties were later allowed to leave the parking lot. The Supreme Court of Rhode Island rejected plaintiff's theory, saying that statutes prohibiting driving while intoxicated were intended for the protection of the general public and that the nature of the contact between the defendant-officer and plaintiff did not constitute a special relationship or an individual duty to protect that was any greater than that owed to the general public.

The above cases illustrate that courts can either find a special relationship based on statute or reject the notion entirely (*Hoffman v. Warden*, 1990). In this approach, the circumstances surrounding the injury have little if any impact on the court's determination of whether a special relationship exists between the police and the injured party.

Circumstances and Special Relationships

Despite the above cases, most courts have been reluctant to recognize exceptions to the public duty doctrine based on a finding of a special relationship through statutory intent. In contrast to the statutory approach, some courts directly examine the circumstances surrounding an injury or damage (*Townley v. City Of Iowa*, 1997). Consideration of these factors has led some of these courts to reject application of the public duty doctrine and its special relationship exception. Instead, they have scrutinized closely the behavior of the police and the circumstances surrounding the release of intoxicated motorists to determine liability.

Despite the imposition of liability in the *Irwin* and *Ryan* cases, most state courts have rejected liability even when the factual circumstances have been worse than those in *Irwin*, *Ryan*, or *DeWald*. An example is *Burchins v. State* (1974). In *Burchins*, a New York state trooper had stopped a vehicle for driving on the wrong side of the road. The trooper issued the driver a summons, but then arrested the driver when he was unable to pro-duce a valid operator's license. The trooper then ordered a passenger of the vehicle to drive the vehicle and follow the squad car to the jail. The pas-senger-plaintiff advised the trooper that he was sick and intoxicated; the trooper responded saying "drive or walk." Minutes later the plaintiff was involved in an accident. The New York Supreme Court Appellate Division held that the state could not be held liable in the absence of proof that the accident was caused by a breach of a duty owed by the state.

Shore v. Stonington (1982), a Connecticut case, led to a similar decision. A Stonington police officer, while on routine patrol, observed a motor vehicle being driven erratically and at a high rate of speed. After the vehicle crossed the centerline of the roadway several times, the officer followed it until it was stopped in a parking lot. After a brief investigation, in which the officer failed to conduct a sobriety test, the driver was released with a warning. Subsequent events led to the intox-icated driver's involvement in a traffic accident, in which a member of the plaintiff's family suffered from injuries that resulted in her death. The Connecticut Supreme Court found no error in the trial court's grant of summary judgment to the defendant and refused to find a spe-cial relationship between the town and the victim. The court noted the need for law enforcement officers to exercise discretionary judgment in these situations, saying: "we do not think that the public interest is served by allowing a jury of laymen the benefit of 20/20 hindsight to second-guess the exercise of a policeman's discretionary professional duty. Such discretion is no discretion at all" (p. 1381).

Thirteen years later, the opportunity to revisit the *Shore* decision was presented to the Connecticut Supreme Court. In *Sarno v. Whalen* (1995), the plaintiff, Dagmar Sarno, asked the court to reconsider the *Shore* decision. In her complaint, Sarno alleged that police officers, John Whalen and Alfonso Sneed, negligently failed to detain a drunk driver who caused Tracy Sarno to sustain injuries in a collision. The trial court granted a motion for summary judgment filed by the defen-dant officers and the city of Bridgeport. The decision was appealed and transferred to the Connecticut Supreme Court.

Reviewing the record, the Connecticut Supreme Court found that Whalen saw a van about three feet from a street curb. He spoke to the driver and detected the odor of alcohol. The driver informed the officer that the previous evening he had a couple of beers. Whalen concluded that the driver was possibly impaired, but when the driver's wife appeared at the vehicle and told Whalen she would drive, he let them go. A short time later, Sarno was injured in an automobile accident in which her car was hit by a van driven by the released driver.

The court distinguished *Sarno* from *Shore* noting that unlike *Shore*, Officer Whalen did not observe the drunk driver operating his van and did not leave the scene without first directing someone else to drive. Given these facts the court refused to revisit the merits of *Shore v. Stonington.*

In cases in which the courts have rejected plaintiffs' claims that special relationships existed between them and the government, the rejection has been based on a narrow interpretation of the special relationship and of the individual duty requirement of the public duty doctrine. This view of individual duty and special relationships requires that a foreseeable danger exists to an identifiable member of the public. That particular individual must, by the nature of the government's behavior, be set apart and distinct from the general public to create an individual duty.

Conversely and more rationally, the *Irwin* court found that a special relationship existed between police officers and the innocent third-party victim through both the foreseeability of the consequences of the behavior and the legislative intent to protect an entire segment of the population. Prosser wrote that "liability in tort is based upon the relations of persons with others; and those relations may arise generally, with large groups or classes of persons, or singly, with an individual" (Prosser and Keeton, 1984).

The Idaho Supreme Court, in accord with Prosser's view, stated in *Sterling v. Bloom* (1986) "a duty can be owed to more than single individuals . . . a case like the instant one, the duty is owed to a class rather than a single individual. With a drunk driver on the highways it is strictly a matter of chance who may become his victim" (p. 769).

Even greater judicial skepticism was expressed in the Arizona Supreme Court's position in *Ryan*, in which the justices refused to engage further in such "speculative" deliberations of individual versus public duties.

There has been very little uniformity in court decisions on special relationships in which the courts have focused on consideration circumstances. However, some semantical factors are identifiable. The language used by the courts provides clues for determining what type of relationship might be considered "special" enough to allow liability. Courts applying this approach—while generally unwilling to find a special relationship in drunk-driving cases—have characterized such relationships in a number ways. According to court decisions, a special relationship can be based on:

1. whether the defendant could have foreseen that he/she was expected to take action in a given situation to prevent injury;
2. departmental policy or guidelines that proscribe or prohibit a certain course of action (*Fudge v. City of Kansas City*, 1986);
3. unique knowledge possessed by an individual defendant-officer;
4. affirmative conduct on the part of a defendant-officer (*Ashburn v. Anne Arundel County*, 1986);

   5. the spatial and temporal proximity of the defendant-officer behavior to the injury damage (*Kendrick v. City of Lake Charles*, 1986).

Many courts have further constructed a special relationship finding to require some, if not all, of the following factors:

1. that the defendant-officer created the peril that led to injury or damage (*Lehto v. City of Oxnard*, 1985);
2. the assumption of an affirmative duty to act by the defendant-officer (*Holsten v. Massey*, 1997);
3. that there was imminent harm known to a foreseeable victim and that this knowledge was possessed by the defendant-officer (*Holsten v. Massey*, 1997; *Shore v. Stonington*, 1982);
4. reliance by the injured party on defendant-officer (*Ashburn v. Anne Arundel County*, 1986; *Holsten v. Massey*, 1997);
5. the manifestation or exertion of control by the defendant-officer over the injured individual.

Summary

The public duty doctrine, although it continues to be invoked in cases of police liability for failure to arrest drunk drivers, is starting to erode. The erosion has taken the form of outright rejection of the doctrine or carving out exceptions to its application. Concomitant with the doctrine's erosion, there has been confusion on the state level about the meaning and application of the concepts associated with governmental liability for failure to restrain drunken drivers. The discretionary/ministerial dichotomy has been confused in many jurisdictions, while others have downplayed the distinction with discussions of the need for police discretion in law enforcement and the specter of municipal bankruptcy from a predicted tidal wave of litigation. Other jurisdictions have refused to lower the special relationship/individual duty barrier to litigation, failing to recognize that duty can be owed to classes of individuals based upon legislative intent to protect certain segments of society. All these doctrines have made it difficult for plaintiffs to succeed in civil litigation.

   Some courts, however, have begun to reject artificial barriers to litigation of governmental negligence. Courts taking this route have been imposing liability based upon the duty-as-a-mandatory-function and the special relationship exception to the public duty doctrine. It remains to be seen whether other exceptions will emerge. Although only a few states thus far have used these exceptions, they are nonetheless worthy of attention and analysis—they may presage a legal development that may impact significantly the way the police deal with drunk-driving cases in the future.

The Liability of Traffic Officers 9
Negligence at Accident Scenes

Police officers routinely provide an array of traffic services to the public. Some of these services include maintaining safe conditions on public roadways; others arise as a result of traffic accidents. Police officers provide warning to motorists concerning safety hazards, assist persons injured in traffic accidents, investigate accidents, and secure the scene of an accident so that it does not present a danger to other drivers. When police officers fail to perform these duties or perform them in a negligent or careless fashion, civil liability can often result.

Determining what legal duties police officers have in these circumstances raises challenging issues for state courts. Even though case law is growing, there is confusion and lack of uniformity in court decisions. This is likely the result of different judicial approaches to issues of police liability and the myriad situational contexts in which the police provide public service involving traffic.

This chapter addresses four areas of potential police liability at accident scenes and explores judicial concepts of negligence relating to a variety of police functions. The chapter illustrates how the use of several theories of liability can either create a police duty where none has existed before or bar recovery by plaintiffs. Specifically discussed is the conduct of police officers before an accident, at the scene of an accident, and following an accident. We will examine four legal aspects of police duty: (1) the duty to warn and protect, (2) the duty to render assistance, (3) the duty to investigate traffic accidents, and (4) the duty to secure accident scenes.

The Duty to Warn and Protect

States and municipalities have a duty to use reasonable care in maintaining roadways for public safety (*Drawbridge v. Douglas City*, 1981;

Naylor v. Louisiana Dept. of Public Highways, 1982; *Wingerter v. State of New York*, 1984; cf. *Gregory v. Cardenaz*, 1991). This duty includes maintaining the physical condition of a roadway and the removal of obstructions and other road hazards. Sometimes this duty of care is extended to police officers and law enforcement agencies when they become aware of a particular traffic hazard.

Where a police officer or agency has actual or constructive knowledge of a potentially dangerous condition and that officer fails to take reasonable action to correct the existing hazard, civil liability may be imposed (*Spotts v. City of Kansas City*, 1987; cf. *Gregory v. Cardenaz*, 1991; *Trull v. Town of Conway*, 1995; *Wells v. Stephenson*, 1990). Where a police officer takes control of a hazardous situation (a traffic accident scene, for example), the duty to warn can extend to third parties not directly involved in the initial accident (*Coco v. State*, 1984). One scholar has stated there may be "liability when the police [leave] the scene of an accident aware of the dangerous condition without properly warning later arriving cars of the problem" (Silver, 2000, 7.1).

A variety of conditions—oil spills, malfunctioning traffic control devices, stray cattle, smoke, or disabled vehicles—may be considered hazardous and create police or municipal liability if an officer fails to act (*Coco v. State*, 1984; *Comm. of Pa. Dept. of Trans. v. Philips*, 1985; *Duvernay v. State*, 1983; *Foremost Dairies v. State*, 1986; *Napolitano v. County of Suffolk*, 1983). Courts apply different theories of negligence to these situations.

In *Naylor v. Louisiana Department of Public Highways* (1982), state troopers responded to the scene of a single-car accident. The accident was caused by an oil spill on a dangerous portion of the roadway. The troopers asked the department of transportation to cover the spill with sand and then ignited flares to warn oncoming motorists of the danger. After securing the scene, the officers returned to their normal patrol activities.

Several hours later, one of the troopers returned to the scene of the accident and found traffic having trouble on the curve because of the oil spill. The officer saw that the oil had absorbed the sand and the flares had expired. The trooper ignited additional flares and called for more sand. Remaining near the accident scene, the trooper parked his vehicle and activated his emergency lights. Meanwhile, the flares went out, and the trooper failed to replace them. Within a few minutes, an unsuspecting motorcyclist approached the oil slick. Upon entering the oil-covered portion of the roadway, the driver lost control of his motorcycle. The vehicle left the roadway, went over an embankment, and struck a tree. The driver suffered brain damage and later died from the injuries.

Wrongful death action was brought against the department of transportation and the state police for negligent failure to warn. The trial court decided for the plaintiff, ruling that the presence of oil, sand,

and gravel on a curve created a hazard that the departments should have removed. The trial court further held that the state police have a duty to provide for the physical safety of motorists when they are aware of potential danger. This includes the duty to warn and to take adequate measure to prevent injury and damage. The police officer breached his duty when he failed to have the oil removed, failed to replace the flares, and improperly positioned his own vehicle. An award of $4,036,535.00 was granted to the plaintiff.

On appeal, the Louisiana appellate court held that the state police had a duty to provide advance warning to drivers of existing highway dangers and that this duty was breached when the officer failed to "replace flares prior to the accident" (p. 674) and position his vehicle to alert motorists of the danger. These breaches of duty, according to the court, were the proximate cause of the injury in that, absent the officer's breach, the plaintiff may have avoided the injuries. The court interpreted the officer's breach of duty as "a substantial factor in causing the accident" (p. 674) and affirmed the ruling of the trial court.

The court in *Naylor* applied the traditional theory of negligence to the issue of police liability for failure to warn drivers of traffic hazards. The court distinguished the duty to warn from the police duty to protect members of the public. Other courts, however, have deviated from this traditional conception of negligence and have applied the public duty/special duty doctrine to similar situations.

In *Gary Police Department v. Loera* (1992) an appeals court relied on the special relationship requirement to render its decision in a negligence action. Robert Halko was traveling an icy highway and had an accident. An officer from the Gary police department, who had been investigating another accident nearby, stopped and talked to Halko. He told Halko that his tour of duty was over, but that he would have another officer dispatched to the accident scene. Moments after the officer left, the plaintiff, Robert Loera, tried to maneuver around the scene of yet another accident but his vehicle began to slide, collided with the stopped car, crossed the highway, and hit another car. Following Loera's accident another officer arrived at the scene, called a salt truck, and began directing traffic around the accidents. Even after the officer began directing traffic, several more accidents occurred.

Because of the injuries Loera sustained in the accident, he brought a negligence action against the police department alleging that the police failed to protect the accident scene adequately. The trial court denied the city's motion for a directed verdict based on immunity and found the city owed a special duty to Loera when the police first arrived at the scene. A jury found for Loera and awarded him $25,000, but the case was appealed.

On appeal the city argued that it did not owe a private duty to protect and warn Loera of dangerous conditions on the roadway. Loera maintained that once police arrived at the scene the city owed him a duty to
warn and protect him from vehicles and debris on the roadway. The
appeals court, however, noted that an unknown police officer had
stopped at the Halko's accident prior to Loera's accident. While the
officer spoke to Halko, he never spoke to Loera. Given this fact the court
refused to find duty on the part of the city to secure the accident scene
and reversed the decision. As *Naylor* and *Gary Police Department* illustrate, some courts do not recognize the distinction between a duty to
warn and a duty to provide police protection.

The California case of *Westbrooks v. State* (1985) illustrates the
distinction between the duty to warn and the duty to protect. In that
case, a violent rainstorm washed away a bridge located on a well-travelled portion of roadway. State and county police were notified and
responded to the call. Before notification, fire department officials in
the area placed flares at the site to warn motorists of the hazard. State
police officers diverted traffic on one side of the bridge, and a sheriff's
department official diverted traffic on the other side. Two vehicles
passed the sheriff's post. The officer stopped the first vehicle, but the
second vehicle ignored the flares and the officer's physical attempt to
halt the vehicle. It reached the spot where the bridge had been and
plummeted into the water below, killing the driver.

The widow and sons of the victim brought suit against the state,
county, and a deputy sheriff, claiming that the officer breached a duty
to warn motorists of existing road hazards. The jury found that the
sheriff had assumed the duty to protect motorists at the scene of a
traffic hazard and concluded that the county was negligent in failing
to warn of the hazardous road conditions. Judgment was entered for
the plaintiff.

On appeal, the county and other defendants maintained that they
voluntarily came to the aid of others and that in doing so they neither
increased the risk of harm nor created a relationship of reliance with
the plaintiff. In effect, the defendants argued that no special relationship existed between the sheriff's department official and the plaintiff
and that police officers had no duty to render aid or assistance. The
California appellate court agreed and held that, "as a general rule, persons, including employees of public entities, have no duty to come to
the aid of others unless there is a special relationship between them
which gives rise to a duty to act" (p. 677). The court reversed the judgment against the county and remanded the case.

In *Westbrooks*, the court rejected the plaintiff's theory that police
officers owe a duty to warn drivers of existing dangers. Without discussion, the court rejected the plaintiff's failure to warn argument and
considered the case an issue of failure to render aid and protection.

This allowed the court to apply the public duty/special duty rule rather than using traditional tort principles, thus precluding county liability by requiring a special relationship between the plaintiff and the defendant-county before liability would attach.

The above discussion and case analyses show that there are two approaches to police liability for failure to warn motorists of traffic dangers. First, a duty to warn can arise when a municipality or a police agency creates a danger to the public. Second, a duty to warn can arise when the municipality or police agency has knowledge of a dangerous situation but does not take precautionary measures to prevent injury or damage (Silver, 2000). Under this latter conception of duty, many courts have held that police officers must take precautions to prevent and avoid dangerous situations on the public roadways even when the officer or municipality did not create the danger or peril (*Commonwealth of Pa. Dept. of Trans. v. Philips*, 1985).

Courts are free to take one of the above approaches to determine whether police officers breach a duty to warn. Under the second approach, although police officers have a general duty to take precautionary measures to prevent injuries on the roadway, liability cannot attach without the presence of factors that show a breach of duty to an individual. Courts can apply the public duty doctrine and require the existence of a special relationship between the police or municipality and the injured individual before liability will be found. For example, in a case where a police officer observes icy conditions on a roadway, stops, and notifies the department of transportation about the condition and leaves the scene, a court may rule that police did not voluntarily undertake specific duties for a special class of citizens so as to induce reliance on those services to form a special relationship (*Trull v. Town of Conway*, 1995).

In contrast to this approach, some courts maintain that a police officer's conduct in maintaining the safety of public roadways is distinguishable from police protection cases. These courts apply ordinary tort principles rather than the public duty/special duty rule (*Napolitano v. County of Suffolk*, 1983). Under this approach, plaintiffs are required to show the elements normally associated with negligence theory—duty, breach, proximate cause, and damage. This position assumes the existence of a duty to warn by police officers. Recently, the duty to warn has been further extended in some jurisdictions to the actions or behaviors of third parties. Police officers may also be held to a duty to warn unsuspecting motorists of the hazardous behaviors of other drivers. Where a police officer fails to warn oncoming traffic of a hazard and injury results, negligence may be found (cf. *Jones v. Maryland-National Capital*, 1990; *Trull v. Town of Conway*, 1995).

The Duty to Render Assistance

As a general rule, there is no common-law duty to aid strangers in distress even if aid can be provided without any cost or risk to the would-be rescuer (*Jackson v. City of Joliet*, 1983; *Williams v. State of California*, 1983). This common-law position is based largely on the notion that liability should not attach where an individual does not engage in affirmative conduct that increases danger or risk. Omissions in these situations are not considered a source of liability; therefore, police officers are not liable for failing to aid or assist endangered individuals. Even though it has been argued that a police officer's official function may be to protect and aid persons, this fact alone is not sufficient to establish liability. Failure of a police officer to render aid or assistance is not tortious conduct just because the defendant is a police officer whose employment function includes rescuing persons in distress (*Williams v. State of California*, 1983).

There are, however, exceptions to this position that require consideration. Some courts have held that police officers have a duty to render aid and save lives at accident scenes (*Battista v. Olson*, 1986; *Caldwell v. City of Philadelphia*, 1986). While this is a minority view, such a finding of duty requires officers to exercise reasonable care in rendering aid or assistance (*Ramundo v. Town of Guiderland, Albany City*, 1984). Depending on a court's position, unique circumstances can create a duty to rescue persons in distress for which a breach may constitute negligence and, ultimately, liability.

These courts base liability findings on the general rule that a municipality is not liable for failure to provide service but allow exceptions where there is a special relationship extending to a particular individual (*Long v. Soderquist*, 1984). The courts, therefore, apply the public duty/special duty doctrine rather than the common-law position. Courts using this theory of duty have determined that the mere arrival of a police officer at the scene of an accident does not create a special relationship (*Messico v. City of Amsterdam*, 1983). Factors beyond a police officer's presence must exist to establish a special relationship between the officer and injured subject. Courts have construed a variety of situations as indicative of such a relationship. While variation exists, there are three factors that may create a special relationship and the potential for liability in traffic-related situations.

First, once an officer begins to rescue someone, a special relationship may be established. The officer must then complete the rescue in a non-negligent fashion even though there was no duty to rescue in the first place (*Jackson v. City of Joliet*, 1983). A sufficient showing of negligence is made if an officer fails to take reasonable care not to increase the risk of harm. Similarly, liability may be imposed if harm is suffered because of the injured person's reliance on the officer's undertaking.

Once an officer has begun a rescue attempt, he/she must essentially perform that rescue in a non-negligent fashion.

Second, failure to take simple actions to reduce the risk of harm to an incapacitated individual may lead to liability. Failure of a police officer to summon or render medical aid or to transport an injured person from the scene of an accident has been considered a breach of duty by some courts (*Battista v. Olson*, 1986; *Torres v. The City of Chicago*, 2000). These courts traditionally have recognized a greater duty to persons who are incapable of assisting themselves due to intoxication, injury, or unconsciousness.

Third, liability may be found where an officer impedes medical aid or another's attempt at assistance (*Baldi v. City of Philadelphia*, 1985). This breach of duty may be either explicit or implicit. An officer's presence at the scene of an accident can create a situation where others will not assist because of the officer's presence. Courts reason that the public views police officers as trained experts. Would-be rescuers might, therefore, decline to render assistance if they see that police officers have taken charge at the scene of an accident. Compounding the problem is the fact that police officers often direct other drivers away from the scene of an accident, reducing the possibility that others will render aid. If any of these situations arise, a special relationship and a breach of duty may be found.

These three possibilities are illustrated in the case of *Ramundo v. Town of Guiderland, Albany City* (1984). In this case, a driver was injured in a traffic accident. Police officers were summoned. Upon arrival at the scene they found the plaintiff lying unconscious with a hot exhaust system on his face. The officers failed to act to correct the situation, and the plaintiff sustained serious facial burns.

Civil suit was brought against the officers and municipality. The plaintiff argued that when the police officers arrived at the scene, they had voluntarily assumed a duty of assistance to the plaintiff and that officers breached that duty by failing to act to prevent the plaintiff's facial burns. The New York Supreme Court applied the public duty/ special duty doctrine noting that while police officers have no duty to provide assistance or protection to the general public, when a special relationship arises, liability may be found.

The court reasoned that the presence of the officer at the scene of the accident acted as a deterrent to others who may have come forth to aid the injured party since the public views police officers as trained to deal with these situations. Accordingly, the plaintiff's cause of action against the police and municipality was affirmed. Ironically, the court used the public duty/special duty doctrine (intended to reduce police liability) to create a duty in a situation where it is traditionally recognized that no duty exists.

The ability of the judiciary to use the public duty doctrine to arrive at almost any outcome it chooses and the conflicting applications of the doctrine are illustrated in the case of *Allison Gas Turbine v. District of Columbia* (1994). In this case, a helicopter crashed into the Potomac River. The pilot freed himself and was rescued by civilian divers. The three passengers, however, were trapped inside the helicopter. Harbor Patrol Police arrived at the scene but because they did not have diving equipment, they did not undertake a rescue. Civilian divers at the scene offered to assist while the police waited for equipment, but the would-be rescuers were ordered by the police to stay out of the water. By the time the diving equipment was obtained and a police rescue attempt was made, the passengers drowned.

The pilot and the passengers' survivors brought a claim against the District of Columbia. The District moved for summary judgment, arguing that the public duty doctrine precluded liability. Evidence at trial established that more than twenty minutes elapsed between the time of the crash and the time the Harbor Patrol began to dive and that the passengers died from being submerged in the river rather than as a result of the accident. Expert testimony also established that the passengers would have had a better than fifty percent chance of survival if the rescue had been attempted sooner.

In a summary judgment, the district court ruled that the public duty doctrine protects municipalities from liability for the discretionary acts committed by their police officers during a rescue operation. The decision was appealed and the United States Court of Appeals affirmed but certified the following question to the district court of appeals:

> Does the public duty doctrine render the District of Columbia immune from tort liability in a case in which the District police officers interfered with the private rescue efforts of civilians at the scene of an accident, thereby worsening the condition of the victims? (p. 844)

The court ruled that the actions of the Harbor Patrol officers were directly related to their on-scene responsibility for conducting a rescue operation. This responsibility, reasoned the court, is an integral part of the officers' general duty to the public and, therefore, did not create a special relationship. The court continued reasoning that this responsibility necessarily requires discretion on how to proceed, including making the judgment of who should take part in the rescue. The court therefore concluded that the public duty doctrine barred plaintiff's recovery.

The Duty to Investigate Accidents

Police officers have no duty and are not liable for failure to collect or maintain information for traffic accident reports (*Poland v. Glenn*, 1993). This includes information that would assist in attempts to recover damages from accidents in a civil proceeding. Neither are police officers under any duty to investigate the circumstances surrounding a traffic accident (e.g., *Caldwell v. City of Philadelphia*, 1986). Decisions of several courts have reinforced this position, despite existing statutes and departmental policies to the contrary (e.g., *Williams v. State of California*, 1983).

The California Supreme Court decided a major case on this issue. This case warrants consideration for a number of reasons. First, the case is illustrative of the above-mentioned principles of nonliability. Second, the case provides numerous insights into the judicial decision-making process on police liability for failure to investigate traffic accidents. Third, the case shows how alternative doctrines and the temporal sequence of judicial decisions can affect the outcome of a police liability case.

In *Williams v. California* (1983), a passenger in a motor vehicle was struck with a hot piece of brake drum expelled from a passing truck. Within minutes of the incident, California Highway Patrol officers arrived at the scene of the accident and took control of the injured individual. The injured passenger brought a negligence action against the state, the California Highway Patrol, and the individual officers. The complaint alleged that police officers negligently failed to investigate the traffic accident. Specifically, the plaintiff charged that defendant-officers failed: (1) to measure the temperature of the brake drum; (2) to obtain the identity of witnesses present at the accident scene; and (3) to attempt to apprehend or at least identify the truck's operator (p. 139). The plaintiff maintained that any possibility of civil recovery against the truck driver was destroyed by the negligence of the investigating officers.

The defendants made a motion for summary judgment based on statutory immunity and the discretionary function doctrine. The trial court granted the motion, and the plaintiff appealed the decision to the California Supreme Court. The court determined that the trial court's consideration of statutory and discretionary immunity was premature and that these considerations were secondary to a determination of the existence of a police duty to the plaintiff. The court stated, "conceptually, the question of the applicability of a statutory immunity does not even arise until it is determined that a defendant otherwise owes a duty of care to the plaintiff and thus would be liable in the absence of such immunity" (p. 139). The court then analyzed the nature of the police duty to render aid and assistance, noting that there exists no duty by citizens or police officers to take affirmative actions to come to the aid of another, unless the officer created the initial peril.

This analysis confused the issue. Plaintiff did not say that the officers failed to assist but rather that the officers were negligent in their investigation. The court had adopted a traditional approach to negligence. If it had been consistent, the logical conclusion would have been to deny a cause of action because of the absence of a duty to the plaintiff.

If the issue were addressed as presented by the plaintiff (under a theory of duty to investigate), the court would have had to examine statutes that could be interpreted as creating a duty to investigate traffic accidents. From this approach, the court would have had little alternative but to rule that the police have a duty to investigate traffic accidents (pp. 145–48). Probably for this reason, the court adopted the public duty/special duty doctrine and departed from the traditional principles of negligence, failing to examine either the issue as presented or the existing statutes. The majority also failed to note that the public duty doctrine was developed to limit liability for existing duties and that the doctrine is used almost exclusively in protection cases. The court further held that liability will not attach unless there is a special relationship and a subsequent breach of that relationship (p. 139).

By switching between doctrines and altering the normal sequence of considerations, the court provided the potential for a liability ruling without finding an initial duty to the plaintiff. The court outlined two factors that would lead to a special relationship and duty by the police. First, a duty may be breached when affirmative acts by police officers increase the risk of harm to the plaintiff. Second, a duty may be established when an officer undertakes a duty of protection that causes reliance and then damage results. When applying these factors to this case, the majority failed to find a special relationship between the officer and the traffic accident victim. Accordingly, the court reversed summary judgment and allowed the plaintiff to amend the complaint. The decision, however, gave little possibility of the plaintiff obtaining a favorable judgment in the absence of the necessary special relationship.

The *Williams* decision mixes negligence theories and resequences the customary judicial decision-making process. First, the court created the possibility of police liability for failure to investigate traffic accidents through the special duty doctrine. Second, the court fell short of establishing a duty based on statute, using the public duty doctrine to avoid a consideration of statutes that would have created an absolute duty by the police. Third, the court narrowed those situations of liability by applying the special relationship exception to the public duty doctrine. The decision severely limited the number of situations from which a plaintiff could recover damages from negligent police investigations. In essence, by providing a very limited potential for police liability, the court avoided having to establish a general duty to investigate.

The court left open the door to a finding of police liability based on a theory of reliance, but this possibility is not very likely. Later decisions of the California courts have rejected the notion that a breach of a special relationship can be based on a police inducement of reliance. In the case of *Van Truag v. James* (1985) a California court of appeals flatly rejected the plaintiff's contention that state police officers breached a special and protective relationship based on the inducement of a sense of false security. The California courts have effectively barred findings of police liability for negligent traffic accident investigations by manipulating the doctrines of negligence.

Other courts have not been as calculating. Besides the *Williams* conception of special relationship, one further liability possibility exists. When both a statute and a policy prescribe an officer's behavior and when there are unique circumstances where the plaintiff is in no condition to retrieve the needed information or assistance. Some courts use the public duty doctrine and its special relationship exception coupled with a standard of reasonable care to create a duty and impose police liability. This was the situation in *Duncan v. Town of Jackson* (1995). An off-duty police officer, Foster, responded to a call about an injury accident in his unmarked police car. Upon arrival, he found a pickup in a field off the highway and down an embankment. Foster proceeded down the embankment to investigate, but part way down he began to worry about leaving his young son alone in the car. Foster decided to go back up the embankment and get his son. After retrieving his son he once again began down the embankment but stopped when another officer arrived at the scene. The two officers looked for tire tracks going off the roadway, got binoculars to look at a broken fence in the field, and viewed damage to the truck rather than going down the embankment. A few minutes later an ambulance arrived and was instructed to leave because the officers had determined the report to be false. The next morning David Duncan was found dead in the truck.

Duncan's family filed a wrongful death claim alleging that Foster was negligent in investigating the accident. The district court granted the defendant-officer's motion for summary judgment, ruling that off-duty police officers, not acting in the scope of employment, are not liable absent a special relationship.

The decision was appealed and the appeals court found that the appellant had put forth sufficient evidence that Foster owed Duncan a legal duty and held that the district court erred in concluding that no duty was owed. The court also found genuine issues of material fact as to whether Foster discharged his duty of ordinary prudence as a reasonable police officer under the circumstances. The case was therefore reversed and remanded.

Courts generally have been reluctant to impose liability for police failure to investigate traffic accidents. In some circumstances liability may attach where police officers owe a duty to exercise reasonable care or where the investigation evidences misconduct. This duty depends on whether the officer is exercising a duty to the public at large or to an individual. Thus, a special relationship must be found in order for a suit to succeed in failure to investigate traffic accident cases.

The Duty to Secure Accident Scenes

Following their arrival at the scene of an accident, police officers owe a duty of protection to the general motoring public. This duty extends to persons directly involved in an accident and to third parties not involved in the initial accident. This duty, however, cannot result in police liability unless there is a special relationship between the police and a specific individual. Under this theory of negligence, the single act of a police officer of failing to remain at the scene of an accident to ensure the safety of innocent third parties is not sufficient to cause liability. However, leaving the scene of an accident, coupled with additional factors indicative of negligence, can constitute the basis for a finding of liability. In this area of duty, courts have opted again to apply the public duty/ special duty doctrine.

While case law in this area of liability is relatively scant, the analysis of several existing cases illustrates behaviors that may constitute a special relationship. In the case of *Johnson v. Larson*, (1983), a Louisiana court of appeals addressed such an issue. Johnson was driving his vehicle down an interstate when he overtook a disabled vehicle, which was in the right lane. The driver of the disabled vehicle flagged Johnson down. Both vehicles pulled off the travel portion of the roadway, and Johnson attempted to repair the disabled vehicle. A few minutes later, two deputy sheriffs arrived at the scene and inquired as to the motorist's trouble. The deputies remained at the scene a few minutes and determined that no assistance was required. They left the area. Shortly thereafter, a soldier traveling down the same roadway rear-ended one of the parked vehicles. Johnson was standing between the vehicles. As a result of the collision, he received serious injuries.

Johnson brought action against the two deputies arguing that the officers could have taken precautionary measures to ensure his safety. The trial court ruled that the officers had no duty to protect the plaintiff from the type of injury he sustained. On appeal, the trial court's decision was affirmed. The appellate court reasoned that the special relationship exception to the public duty doctrine was controlling. A special relationship would have been found if the following circumstances were present: if the officer had had knowledge of the impending danger (*Curry v. Iberville Parish Sheriff's Office*, 1981); if the danger had been obvious; if a traffic hazard had existed at the time (*Duvernay v. State*, 1983); and if the officers had had ample opportunity to correct the situation but failed to do so. If these factors were present, liability might have arisen.

Similar results were achieved in the case of *Long v. Soderquist* (1984). In this case, a motorist struck a guardrail. The road conditions at the time of the accident were icy, and the driver's vehicle slid off the road. Another motorist saw the accident and stopped to assist the injured party. Shortly thereafter, a deputy sheriff arrived at the accident scene. After inquiring as to the subject's physical condition, the officer observed another traffic accident. Instructing the traffic accident victim and the would-be rescuer to remain in their respective vehicles, the officer went to investigate the second accident. Then, the officer left the scene without taking adequate measures to protect the parked vehicles. A few moments later, a third vehicle approached the first accident scene and struck the parked vehicles.

The driver of the third vehicle brought civil suit against the officer and argued that he was negligent in failing to: light flares, direct other vehicles away from the accident scene, remove the parked vehicles, warn other motorists of the hazard, and call for assistance. Applying the public duty doctrine, the appellate court held that, "although a municipality is generally not liable for failure to provide adequate police protection or service, this rule does not apply where the police have assumed a special duty to a person that elevates his status to something more than a member of the general public" (p. 1157). The court went on to determine that a special relationship requires the following:

1. the municipality must be uniquely aware of the particular danger or risk to which the plaintiff is exposed;
2. there must be allegations of specific acts or omissions on the part of the municipality;
3. the specific acts or omissions must be either affirmative or willful in nature; and
4. the injury must occur while the plaintiff is under the direct and immediate control of employees or agents of the municipality. (p. 1157)

Concluding that the plaintiff failed to establish a special relationship in that he was not under the immediate control of the police, the appellate court affirmed the lower court's summary judgment in favor of the defendant-officer.

Under this theory of negligence, the municipality or police officer must be aware of the particular danger or risk to establish a special relationship. Knowing such risk, the officer must subsequently make an act or omission and have direct or immediate control over the situation. If these factors are present, the courts may find a special relationship and duty to persons injured following an accident. However, reliance of the plaintiff or inducement by the state in providing a false sense of security is not sufficient to create a special relationship or cause liability (*Van Truag v. James*, 1985).

Summary

States and municipalities have a duty to use reasonable care in maintaining roadways for the safety of the public. This duty of care is extended to police officers and law enforcement agencies where a police officer or agency has actual or constructive knowledge of a potentially dangerous condition. A variety of conditions are sufficient to be considered hazardous. Liability may attach if an officer fails to take reasonable action to correct existing road hazards. There are two primary facets of police liability for failure to warn. A duty to warn can arise when a municipality or a police agency creates a danger to the public, or it may arise when the municipality or police agency has knowledge of a dangerous situation but does not take precautionary measures to prevent injury or damages.

Police officers are not liable for their failure to provide aid or assistance to endangered individuals absent a statutory or special duty. Existing statutes can create a duty by police officers to render aid and save lives at accident scenes. Similarly, unique circumstances can create a special duty to rescue persons in distress; in such cases, a breach may constitute negligence. While variations exist, there are three common factors that may create a special duty and the potential for police liability. First, once an officer begins to rescue someone, a special relationship may be established even though there may have been no duty to rescue in the first place. Second, failure to take simple actions to reduce the risk of harm to an incapacitated individual may lead to liability. Third, liability may be found where an officer explicitly or implicitly impedes medical aid or another's attempt at assistance.

Police officers owe a duty of protection to the general public following the officers' arrival at the scene of an accident (cf. *Susko v. Pennsylvania*, 1990). This duty, however, cannot result in police liability unless there is a special relationship between the police and a specific individual. A special duty may be found if the officer has knowledge of the impending danger, if the danger is obvious, if a traffic hazard had existed at the time, if the officer is in direct and immediate control, and if the officer had ample opportunity to correct the situation but failed to do so.

Law in this area of police liability is in a state of transition. There is much confusion as to which theory of negligence should be applied to a given police service. Several trends can be noted. First, while the public duty doctrine has declined in other areas of police liability, it seems to be enjoying new vitality in accident-related police liability cases. Second, courts seem to be split on whether to apply the traditional concepts of negligence or the public duty doctrine. Whether these trends will continue in the future and whether there will be consistency in this area of case law remains to be seen.

Police Liability for Failure to Prevent Detainee Suicide 10

Police officers have greater prisoner responsibilities than are often recognized by the general public. Many law enforcement officials have authority and responsibility for the operation of short-term detention facilities. According to the Bureau of Justice Statistics, local and county law enforcement agencies operate approximately 4,095 local jails, and 94 percent of local police agencies servicing cities with a population of 1 million or more operate lockup facilities (BJS, 2000a). That same study showed that 30 percent of all the local law enforcement agencies surveyed operated some form of detention facility. Even though many law enforcement agencies do not operate formal jails, most have holding cells where detainees are held for limited periods of time until they can be transported to jail facilities. The custodial role of sheriffs' agencies adds to these totals. According to the Bureau of Justice Statistics, 80 percent of all sheriffs' agencies operate jails (BJS, 1999). Law enforcement officers make more than 14 million arrests each year (BJS, 2000b). Each of those arrests required some type of custody, even if involving only a brief detention or transportation. These figures indicate that many law enforcement agencies serve supplemental roles that include custodial responsibilities; in fact, the data suggest that for police officers, the line between corrections and law enforcement is often blurred.

Police custody of detainees entails certain legal responsibilities. This includes a duty of care to persons in custody who pose danger to themselves. Because the suicide rate for persons detained in local jails is 9 times greater than that experienced by the general public (Hayes, 1989; see also Kennedy and Homant, 1988), police officers must be particularly aware of their duty of care to detainees. Since suicide is one of the leading causes of death among persons detained in local jails and holding facilities (Hayes, 1989; Kennedy, 1984; Kennedy and Homant, 1988), the custodial duties entrusted to law enforcement officers raise important questions regarding police legal responsibility.

This chapter analyzes state case law on police liability for negligent failure to protect detainees from self-inflicted injury and suicide. It focuses on jurisdictions that impose civil liability against the police for failure to prevent suicide. First we will look at the standard of care, then we will explore the circumstances necessary for that special duty of care to arise. We will discuss measures taken by the police to prevent self-inflicted injury and suicide in the context of negligence cases under state law. The chapter outlines four areas of potential liability for the police: supervision of suicidal detainees; construction of the custodial facility; the effect of agency rules, regulations, and procedures; and failure to render assistance. The chapter concludes with principles of law on police liability for failure to prevent suicide.

The Framework of Negligence Litigation

Actions against police officers involving detainee suicide are usually wrongful death or negligence claims based on state tort law. As discussed in chapter 2, negligence is inadvertent behavior that results in damage or injury. Negligence tort is distinguished from other tort actions in that it requires a lesser degree of foreseeability of danger. In negligence tort, the mental state of the police officer is not an issue; even inadvertent behavior resulting in a suicide can lead to liability. The standard applied in negligence tort is whether the officer's act or failure to act created an unreasonable risk to a detainee. Proving negligence, however, is more complicated than showing inadvertent behavior and injury. The four elements presented in previous chapters must be established in a negligence claim: legal duty, breach of duty, proximate cause of injury or damage, and actual damage or injury.

To review, legal duties are obligations recognized by the courts, which require police officers either to act or to refrain from acting in particular situations. Police legal duties arise from several sources, including laws, customs, judicial decisions, and various agency rules and regulations. Once a plaintiff has shown a legal duty and has demonstrated that the police breached that duty to a specific detainee, the petitioner must prove further that the officer's conduct was the proximate cause of the suicide. As we have mentioned previously, the proximate cause of an injury or damage can be determined by asking the question, "but for the officer's conduct, would the detainee have sustained the injury?" If the answer is yes, then proximate cause may be established.

The determination of proximate cause is the source of considerable difference among courts. In many cases it may only be necessary to establish that the officer's behavior or failure to act was a material element or a substantial factor in the injury. Similarly, state courts differ as to the requisite level of negligence needed to establish liability. The level of culpability for establishing liability can range from mere to gross negligence and, in some rare cases, may require the establishment of reckless or wanton conduct. If proximate cause is established, a police officer, agency, or government may be found liable for the injury, provided that the other elements of negligence are present.

The Special Duty of Care

State courts generally recognize that law enforcement officials have a duty of care to persons in their custody (e.g., *Sauders v. County of Steuben*, 1998; *Thomas v. Williams*, 1962). This means that police officers have a legal responsibility to take reasonable precautions to ensure the health and safety of persons in their custody. This general duty of care requires that custodial officers keep detainees free from harm, render medical assistance when necessary, and treat detainees humanely (*Thomas v. Williams*, 1962). While the legal definition of custody is not all-encompassing, it generally includes those incarcerated in a detention or holding facility. Custody is not restricted, however, only to those who are incarcerated. Police officers, for example, also owe the same duty of care to persons in their physical custody outside a jail setting. This standard applies to officers arresting or transporting prisoners and mental patients as well as to law enforcement agents detaining persons in booking or interrogation areas, regardless of whether they have been formally charged with a crime (*Hake v. Manchester Township*, 1985; *Morris v. Blake*, 1988).

The general duty of care owed to persons in police custody seldom results in liability for self-inflicted injury or suicide because these acts are normally considered intentional, resulting from a detainee's own conduct instead of from police negligence (*Guice v. Enfinger*, 1980; *Pretty on Top v. City of Hardin*, 1979). Some courts view custody as a form of law enforcement. In states where officers are shielded by immunity for the performance of law enforcement functions, there can be no liability for negligence in failing to prevent a detainee's suicide (see, *Sauders v. County of Steuben*, 1991). There are, however, exceptions to this general rule. In certain circumstances, behavior of a police officer or a detainee can create a "special duty" for the police (*Manuel v. City of Jeanerette*, 1997). "If the suicidal tendencies of the inmate are known, the standard of care required of the custodian is elevated" (*Sauders v. County of Steuben*, 1998, p. 19; see also, *Breese v. State*, 1983; *Fowler v. Norways Sanitorium*, 1942).

The term *special duty* lacks a precise legal definition. In the context of suicide liability cases, it implies the presence of factors that transcend the usual police-detainee relationship. The courts often view such factors as intervening causes that transcend the intentional nature of a detainee's suicide (*Pretty on Top v. City of Hardin*, 1979). Other courts view police behavior in detainee suicide cases not as intervening causes but rather as part of the circumstances surrounding the suicide. As the Indiana Supreme Court has remarked "the focus is on the defendant's conduct under the circumstances. The plaintiff's actions are relevant only insofar as they are a part of the circumstances of which the custodian is or should be aware, or they bear on whether any breach of defendant's duty is causally related to the injury" (*Sauders v. County of Steuben*, 1998, p. 19). In detainee-suicide police liability cases, these include specific circumstances surrounding the suicide and the behavior of the officers involved. The presence of either may give rise to a cause of action and create the potential for police liability.

A special duty may arise when police officers have reason to believe that a detainee presents a danger to him- or herself. When circumstances suggest that a particular detainee may create foreseeable danger, the duty of care required of law enforcement officers is transformed and becomes a special duty. This special duty of care carries greater responsibilities and extends to cases of detainee suicide. The custodial environment, coupled with other circumstances indicating that a suicide may occur, create a special duty of care and can lead to liability if that duty is breached. Under this analysis, police officers take on a superior caretaker's role over the detainee and are seen as imbued with specialized training or experience that allows them to recognize potential dangers to individuals entrusted to their custody.

This special duty of care may arise when it is recognizable that a particular detainee has a diminished ability to prevent self-injury or cannot exercise judgment with the same level of caution as an ordinary detainee. In these cases, officers must ensure that measures are taken to prevent self-inflicted harm. Two types of persons fall under this category: detainees who suffer from a disturbed state of mind and have a diminished ability for self-protection and those who are impaired by drugs or alcohol (*Manuel v. City of Jeanerette*, 1997).

Detainee Condition and Foreseeability of Suicide

Foreseeability is reasonable anticipation that injury or damage may occur as a result of an act or omission. Foreseeability depends on a combination of several factors. As the number and severity of factors multiply, courts become more likely to find that the police owe a special duty, as long as the police are aware that these factors exist. While the following list of foreseeability indicators is not inclusive of every possible factor, the courts have included:

1. previous suicide attempts while in custody;
2. detainee's statements of intent to commit suicide;
3. detainee's history of mental illness;
4. health care professionals' determinations of suicidal tendencies;
5. the emotional state and behavior of the detainee;
6. the circumstances surrounding the detainee's arrest;
7. the detainee's level of intoxication or drug dependence; and
8. the precautionary removal of shoes, belts, and other articles from the detainee.

When it is evident that a particular detainee has a diminished ability to prevent self-injury or cannot exercise the same level of care as an ordinary person because of mental illness or intoxication, police officers must take reasonable measures to prevent self-inflicted injury. This includes removing shoes, belts, and other articles from the detainee (e.g., *Manuel v. City of Jeanerette*, 1997; *Shuff v. Zurich*, 1965). The determination of a special duty in these cases hinges on two factors: first, the courts consider the extent to which a condition renders a detainee unable to exercise ordinary care and control; second, courts consider the officer's knowledge of the detainee's mental incapacitation and propensity for suicide.

A special duty arises if an officer has sufficient knowledge that a particular detainee is intoxicated or is under the influence of drugs to the extent that he or she cannot exercise reasonable caution. In *Thomas v. Williams* (1962), the Georgia Court of Appeals found that a police chief owed a greater duty of care to an arrestee who was semiconscious as a result of intoxication. The intoxicated detainee was incarcerated with matches and a cigarette, which he later used to start a fire that resulted in his death. The court, rejecting the defendant-officer's argument that the decedent was voluntarily drunk and that he placed himself in peril, stated "the prisoner may have been voluntarily drunk, but he was not in the cell voluntarily . . . [he] was helpless and partially unconscious and that the officer knew this and knew there was a means of harm on his person and in his surroundings" (p. 414). The court stated that with this information the police officer "was bound to deal with him with his condition in mind" (p. 414).

Similar results were achieved in *Barlow v. New Orleans* (1970), where two city of New Orleans police officers entered a bar on private business and found a man slumped across a table in a state of intoxication. The officers arrested Barlow and, since he could not walk, assisted him to the patrol car. After the officers locked the plaintiff in the back seat of the police vehicle for transportation to jail, they returned to the bar leaving the arrestee locked in the unattended squad car. The arrestee started a fire that consumed the locked police vehicle and resulted in severe burns to various parts of his body. The Louisiana Supreme Court stated that "it seems manifest that where a person is arrested for drunkenness and confined in an automobile from which he cannot escape, it would be unrealistic to conclude that the arresting officers owe no duty to see that he may not be harmed . . . from his own unconscious acts while he is in custody" (pp. 503–4). The Louisiana Appeals Court's finding of police negligence was affirmed.

Emotionally disturbed arrestees can create a greater duty for police officers to prevent injury or suicide. In *Kanayurak v. North Slope Borough* (1984), the Alaska Supreme Court refused to affirm summary judgment for city-defendants in a jail suicide case. The decedent was arrested for public intoxication in a hotel. At the time of her arrest she was visibly intoxicated and had trouble standing, walking, and speaking. Arresting officers placed the decedent in a holding cell. Evidence showed that the decedent had a blood-alcohol level of 0.264 percent and that during her incarceration she had been screaming about her children. Because of the noise, officers closed the cell door. Approximately two and a half hours later, when officers checked the cell, they found her hanging by her sweater from mesh wiring in the cell.

Defendants argued that they should be granted summary judgment because a special duty did not attach, nor was the suicide foreseeable. The Alaska Supreme Court stated:

> The Borough Police had reason to believe that Kanayurak was severely depressed. They knew that in the past few months one of her sons had been burned to death, another son had been stabbed to death, and her mother had died. Furthermore, shortly before her suicide, Kanayurak had pled for assistance in locating her children. (p. 897)

Given the evidence, the Alaska Supreme Court concluded that a "genuine issue of material facts existed as to whether the borough had reason to anticipate that Kanayurak would attempt suicide . . ." and "whether Kanayurak was incapable of exercising due care by virtue of her intoxication" (pp. 898–99). The court therefore denied summary judgment for the defendant-officers.

In *City of Belen v. Harrell* (1979), the Supreme Court of New Mexico heard the case of a seventeen-year-old boy who was arrested for armed robbery. While in the detention center, the youth's mother paid him a visit, at which time he told her "that he'd die before he would go [to the penitentiary], he would kill himself . . ." (p. 712). As the mother was leaving the facility, the young man tried to cut his wrists with an aluminum can top. After being restrained by officers, he repeated his threats to kill himself. The detainee's mother notified the assistant chief about the events, and he ordered a dispatcher to keep watch over the detainee. Sometime during the early morning hours, the detainee hanged himself using his shirt as a noose. The Supreme Court of New Mexico stated that "knowledge on the part of the custodian that the charge may injure himself unless precautionary measures are taken is an important factor to be considered" in determining an officer's negligence and liability (p. 713).

In *Harrell*, the officers were aware of the suicidal intentions of a detainee and of an actual previous suicide attempt. Despite this information, the officers failed to remove articles from the detainee that were later used to commit suicide. In other cases, an officer's knowledge of a detainee's intent to commit suicide is less obvious. These situations often call for law enforcement officers to make difficult judgments concerning the possibility of suicide. A few cases will illustrate.

In *Hake v. Manchester Township* (1985), a police officer arrested a young man following the pursuit of a suspicious vehicle. The young man was under the influence of alcohol when he was stopped and arrested. Although the youth was depressed at the time of the arrest, he began to "cheer up as the afternoon wore on" (p. 840). Officers placed the youth in a holding cell, but did not remove his leather belt, which he later used to take his own life. This, coupled with the officer's failure to call medical personnel to attempt to resuscitate the unconscious detainee, led the New Jersey Supreme Court to find that the officer's conduct could have been a "substantial" factor in the detainee's death.

Similarly, in *Overby v. Wille* (1982), a Florida court of appeals considered the emotional state and behavior of an arrestee as a basis for negligence. Overby was arrested and later committed suicide in a cell at the Palm Beach County Jail. Overby had a history of mental illness, although this information was not directly known to the officer-defendants. Police officers came into contact with the arrestee when he requested to be transported to a mental health facility, stating that he had injured someone and needed medical attention. Upon arrival at the police station, the arrestee struck a police officer. The officer contacted a mental health agency, but he was erroneously informed that they had no record of the arrestee ever being treated. After the arrestee was transported to the county jail, he again became violent and requested mental health care. After the second altercation, the arrestee was transported to a hospital where wounds sustained in the fight could be treated. When he was later returned to detention, an entry was made in jail records that the arrestee was mentally incompetent. Clad in street clothes, the arrestee was placed in a cell and later hanged himself with his belt.

The district court entered summary judgment for the defendants, noting that the decedent's act was an independent, intervening cause that the officials could not have reasonably foreseen. On appeal, a Florida appeals court stated that the police had "heard from Overby's own lips that he had emotional problems requiring that he be immediately transported to the Mental Health Center or similar facility" (p. 1333). The court noted that the sheriff's department had recorded that Overby was a mental incompetent and that he had engaged in several outbursts of antisocial behavior. "Notwithstanding, they [police officers] caused his arrest and subsequent transfer to and detention in the county jail as a common criminal" (p. 1333). From these facts, the court found sufficient evidence of the foreseeability of suicide as to preclude summary judgment.

The above cases identify several factors courts use to determine whether the police have a special duty to prevent a detainee's suicide. Courts weigh the detainee's mental incapacitation and the officer's knowledge of the possibility of a suicide attempt (*Sauders v. County of Steuben*, 1998). Although the facts in each of the above cases vary, they indicate that detention and the determination of foreseeability of suicide elevates the police duty of care to a special duty.

Since courts determine foreseeability on a case-by-case basis, there is no litmus test to ascertain its existence. Most courts say, however, that there is foreseeability if circumstances foretell a detainee's impending suicide. Circumstances creating a special duty to prevent detainee suicide include an officer's knowledge of detainee's previous suicide attempts, detainee's statements threatening suicide, and police knowledge of detainee's mental illness. In addition, a detainee's despondent emotional condition, incapacitation due to drugs or alcohol, as well as the unique events surrounding a detainee's detention, may lead to circumstances in which police officers owe a special duty to prevent suicide.

Police Conduct and Breach of Duty

In addition to establishing the requirement of special duty, a plaintiff in a negligence lawsuit must prove a breach of that special duty on a case-by-case basis. While plaintiffs can rely on existing legal precedent, each suicide situation is unique, and courts must consider the suicide in its situational context. To establish a breach, an operative element of duty must be found that allows the reviewing court to assess surrounding circumstances. Hence, the formulation of a breach of special duty is related to both situational factors and existing law. In other words, a breach of a duty is, in part, the result of some act or omission of the officer-defendant that violates a recognized special duty. In cases where a duty has not been established, an officer cannot be held liable even if misconduct occurs. Conversely, even if a duty is established, an officer cannot be held liable absent behavior that breaches the duty.

To succeed, plaintiffs must establish foreseeability by showing that not only did the officers have a duty to prevent the suicide attempt but that the officers breached the duty in such a manner that the act or omission substantially contributed to the suicide (*Helmly v. Bebber*, 1985). The courts have considered various behaviors by law enforcement officers as evidence of a causal link between an officer's conduct and a suicide. These factors include failure to: follow agency rules, regulations and procedures; properly supervise the suicidal or incapacitated detainee; provide a safe custodial facility; and render medical aid or assistance.

Violation of Rules and Regulations

Legislative bodies and professional organizations have developed standards applicable to detainee suicides for corrections and law enforcement personnel. These organizations include the American Medical Association (AMA), the National Commission of Correctional Health Standards (NCCHS), the American Correctional Association (ACA), and the Commission on Accreditation for Law Enforcement Agencies (CALEA). The standards promoted by these bodies do not carry the force of law because they are not legally binding on municipalities, agencies, or employees. "Agency protocols and procedures, like agency manuals, do not have the force or effect of a statute or an administrative regulation," rather "they provide officials with guidance on how they should perform those duties which are mandated by statute or regulation" (*Phillips v. District of Columbia*, 1998, p. 774, citing *Wanzer v. District of Columbia*, 1990). Standards, however, have been recognized by some courts as objective criteria that can offer guidance in determining what constitutes "reasonable" conduct (*Falkenstein v. City of Bismarck*, 1978; see also, *Richards v. Southeast Alabama Youth Ser. Diversion*, 2000) and "duty" of care (see, *Bell v. Wolfish*, 1979; *Rhodes v. Chapman*, 1981).

The violation of national standards as well as agency rules, regulations, and procedures can provide evidence of negligence by an officer or agency (*Keeton v. Fayette County*, 1989; *Phillips v. District of Columbia*, 1998). One court has instructed that "failure of an employee to operate in compliance with practices adopted by a governmental entity for the welfare of persons similarly situated to the plaintiff [detainees] constitutes evidence of negligence in a tort action" (*Silva v. State*, 1987, p. 386). In several other cases, courts have held that agency rules and regulations, even if they are promoted by authorities other than governmental entities or by an agency not involved in the lawsuit, can show negligence. In one suicide case, the Michigan Appeals Court noted that the Department of Corrections' rules and regulations for jail facilities apply to police holding cells (*People v. Bland*, 1974).

In another Michigan case, the court stated that the Department of Corrections' rules and regulations apply and that

> even if we were to hold that those rules and regulations did not apply in this case, the rules of the MSU Department of Public Safety

required that if a prisoner has objects that he could use as weapons against himself or others, such objects must be removed from his person before lockup. (*Hickey v. Zezulka*, 1989, p. 187)

The court therefore found that the officer's failure to follow both sets of rules and regulations was evidence of negligence in failure to prevent the detainee's suicide.

In *Young v. City of Ann Arbor* (1982), a case involving a detainee suicide, the Michigan Court of Appeals instructed "The Ann Arbor facility was required to follow the [Michigan Corrections] Department's rules... which required belts to be removed from inmates and [a] visual inspection of inmates at least once every sixty minutes" (p. 550). The court added that as chief of police, the defendant was responsible for observing and enforcing all policies and practices in that jail. "Therefore [defendant's] potential negligence in failing to require his subordinates to follow the department's rules and regulations is an issue that properly should have been determined by the jury" (p. 551). The lower court's directed verdict for the defendant was reversed and the case was remanded for a new trial.

Police Supervision

Statutes in some states require law enforcement agents to provide constant supervision for detainees exhibiting emotional or physical conditions that could result in harm to self or others. In *Kozlowski v. City of Amsterdam* (1985), for example, a man was arrested for drunken driving and had a blood-alcohol level of 0.23 percent. During the booking process, he told officers he would take his life. Because of the arrestee's suicidal nature, officers handcuffed him to the processing desk, pursuant to "state regulations requiring 30-minute interval checks on prisoners in city jail cells . . . that . . . warrant . . . constant observation and supervision" (p. 864). After the arrestee "calmed down," however, he was placed in a holding cell without shoes or belt. He later hung himself with his socks (p. 863). Plaintiff-administratrix filed a wrongful death action contending that the negligent supervision resulted in decedent's death. Denying plaintiff's motion to set aside a verdict in favor of the defendant, the Appellate Division of a New York Supreme Court held that although "the jury could have determined that the police acted reasonably in keeping decedent under constant supervision at the booking area until he appeared calmer" (p. 864), it was prejudicial error for the trial court not to allow in evidence a medical report required by state law, which stated "that defendant failed to maintain constant supervision of decedent after placing him in a cell in view of his intoxication and expressions of suicidal ideation" (p. 864).

In *Wilson v. Sponable* (1981), the plaintiff, who had a history of mental disorders, was arrested for murder and placed in jail. The prosecutor informed the sheriff that Wilson should be kept under surveillance because of attempts to hurt himself. Before his arrest, Wilson had attempted to commit suicide and had a gauze bandage on his wrists when placed in jail (p. 550). Aware of the potential harm arrestee could cause, the sheriff ordered that he be guarded. Pursuant to the sheriff's directive, arrestee was placed in a cell under officer supervision. The next day, however, he was placed in a cell with other inmates, out of the range of officer supervision. Arrestee, thereafter, attempted to asphyxiate himself by forming a noose from the gauze bandage on his arm. Because of these injuries, plaintiff stayed comatose for 13 weeks. The court held that the relevant statute did not require the county to provide "special facilities for suicidal patients, or psychiatric care from outside agencies" (p. 552). The court stated that even though these services are desirable, failure to provide them did not give rise to liability. In addition, although the county did have a duty of care to prevent suicide, "reasonable care does not require supervision 24 hours per day" (p. 553). For these latter two claims, the court granted county-defendant summary judgment.

In *Lucas v. City of Long Beach* (1976), a seventeen-year-old juvenile was arrested pursuant to a penal code provision for public drunkenness. After the arrestee was transported to the police station, the breathalyzer results showed no significant amount of alcohol in his system, so the officers concluded that the arrestee was under the influence of a drug. The arrestee showed no signs of impending suicide to police officers. Forty-five minutes after arrest, the suspect was placed in a holding cell for juveniles. Approximately three hours later, officers found him hanging in the cell.

Wrongful death action was brought against the officer and city for failure to follow state regulations requiring hourly inspections of juveniles in police detention. The California Court of Appeals concluded that since the decedent acted voluntarily and since no amount of supervision—barring constant supervision that was not required—could have prevented the suicide, the arrestee's act was a superseding cause and relieved the officer of liability. The court rejected plaintiff's constant supervision argument, saying that under the statute, liability only attaches "for [an] injury resulting from the failure to treat the physical condition requiring treatment and not for some other incidental injury that might have been permitted by the mere presence of medical personnel" (p. 475). In addition, even if the police officer had made the hourly inspections as required by state regulations, the decedent would still have committed suicide because he concealed all evidence of suicidal intentions and tore off a piece of the mattress to fashion the noose with which he took his life (see also, *Keeton v. Fayette County*, 1989).

Some courts require that a failure to supervise be coupled with prior notice of suicide before liability will be imposed on an officer. For example in *McDay v. City of Atlanta* (1992) police arrested Robert Wadley on a murder charge. The murder weapon, a loaded pistol, was confiscated, Wadley was handcuffed and brought to a police station for questioning. At the station, Officer Price placed two unsealed evidence envelopes on his desk. One envelope contained Wadley's gun and the other contained bullets. When police left Wadley unattended and unrestrained in the room, he took the pistol from the envelope, loaded it, and shot himself.

Negligence action was brought against the police, but the trial court granted the defendant-officer summary judgment. The decision was appealed. On appeal the defendant-officer argued the decision to uncuff a suspect during an interview is a discretionary act that affords an officer immunity when exercising discretion in the performance of official duties. The appeals court held that although the officer failed to anticipate and prevent the suicide, he had no prior notice of the event. In the absence of prior notice or malice the officer was to be afforded immunity. Accordingly, the appeals court affirmed the trial court's grant of summary judgment.

The idea of constant supervision by police or correctional officers is problematic. First, the courts have yet to define "constant supervision." Second there is confusion as to whether supervision by means of video monitoring is a ministerial or discretionary function. A Texas Court of Appeals in *City of Coppell v. Waltman* (1998) explained,

> although the City's policies require a prisoner be "constantly" monitored, the manner in which the monitoring is to be carried out is left to the discretion of the dispatcher . . . [T]he manner in which the dispatcher does the monitoring is discretionary, but . . . the requirement the prisoner be "constantly" monitored imposes a ministerial duty.

> The term "constantly" is not defined in the City's policy and could be subject to interpretation under these facts. The video monitor was placed on the desk in front of the dispatcher, who was to perform other duties besides monitoring the prisoners, including answering the telephone. Further, the video camera was situated in a manner to provide the prisoner some limited privacy; the toilet in the jail cell was placed behind a wall so the prisoner would be out of the view of the camera while using the toilet facilities. The manner in which the dispatcher monitored the prisoner while performing her other duties was subject to personal deliberation, decision, and judgment. We therefore conclude . . . monitoring. . . [was] . . . a discretionary duty. (p. 637)

The courts have, however, alluded to the use of electronic monitoring devices as well as human visual contact. The Indiana Supreme Court has held that local government has

> no duty to purchase the monitoring equipment, and immunity for the decision not to purchase the equipment—are distinct from the

question of what constitutes reasonable care under the circumstances, one of which was the known absence of the equipment. The jury should have been able to consider whether, without the equipment, the County should have been more vigilant in making personal checks on Sowles. As the court correctly concluded, there is no duty to provide the equipment and its absence is not evidence of negligence. However, its absence is one of the circumstances together with all others that are relevant to the issue of the defendant's conduct. The instruction that the absence of the equipment "shall not be considered" in determining the County's liability, went too far in precluding the jury from considering all relevant circumstances (*Sauders v. County of Steuben*, 1998, p. 21).

Some criminal justice scholars have suggested that certain measures—including constant supervision—may have dehumanizing effects that could create an environment more conducive to detainee suicide (Kennedy and Homant, 1988).

Providing a Safe Facility

Courts have also considered the design of detention facilities as a source of negligence. In *Davis v. City of Detroit* (1986), the Michigan Appeals Court noted that the construction of the holding cell did not allow officers to observe a detainee's movements unless the detainee was standing directly in front of the cell door. The construction of the precinct's cell doors hampered detainee supervision, and there were no electronic monitoring devices by which a detainee's actions could be observed (see also, *Keeton v. Fayette County*, 1989). Additionally, there was an absence of detoxification cells required under Department of Corrections rules. Following a suicide in this facility, the court concluded that the absence of a detoxification cell was a proximate cause of decedent's death and constituted a building defect.

In *Hickey v. Zezulka* (1989), the Michigan Court of Appeals addressed the issue of providing detainees with a safe and secure environment for their detention. Hickey, a student at Michigan State University (MSU), was stopped by a university police officer for driving erratically. Unable to produce a valid driver's license and deemed intoxicated by the officer, he was arrested and transported to the East Lansing Police Department for a breath test. The test results indicated that he had blood-alcohol levels between 0.15 and 0.16 percent. A supervisor directed that Hickey be taken to the university's public safety building for processing. Thereafter, Hickey was placed in a holding cell at that facility. "Cell 171 had a nine- to ten-foot-high ceiling and a concrete bench along one side. Above the bench was a heater with a metal mesh that was supported by four metal brackets which extended one to two inches from the wall" (p. 183). When Officer Zezulka checked Hickey approximately forty minutes later, he was hanging from the heating device by the noose he had fashioned from his socks and belt.

The Michigan Court of Claims found that MSU was liable for the operation of a defective building and awarded plaintiff $650,000. On appeal, the Michigan Appeals Court noted that the Claims Court found that the heating device was the proximate cause of the suspect's death and that the university had been aware of the defective condition of the cell. Additionally, the court stated that the absence of a detoxification cell may have contributed to the suspect's suicide. Reviewing the record, the court stated "we are convinced that the lower court did not err in finding a defect in MSU's Department of Public Safety which was the proximate cause of the decedent's death" (p. 184).

The case, however, was appealed to the state supreme court in 1992. On appeal the court considered whether the public building exception to governmental immunity was applicable to the claims against Michigan State University and whether Zezulka's actions were discretionary-decisional so as to afford her the protection of state governmental immunity. The state supreme court concluded that the plaintiff's claim against MSU was barred by state governmental immunity because the public building exception was inapplicable to the case but found that Zezulka's actions were ministerial-operational so as not to afford her the protection of governmental immunity. Therefore the decision was reversed as to MSU but remanded in regard to the negligence claim for reconsideration of damages only. Since the *Hickey* decision, the Michigan Supreme Court has consistently held that claims by detainees that they were injured because of unsafe construction in detention facilities is not an exception to legislative immunity. The court has, however, allowed claims of negligence and deliberate indifference to go forward against individual officers and cities (see, *Jackson v. City of Detroit*, 1995).

The need to provide a secure environment for detainees extends beyond the confines of the detention center. In *Morris v. Blake* (1988), a constable used his private vehicle to transport mental patients. Although the constable was aware that there were specially equipped police vehicles with safety features for transporting patients, he had not been told to use those vehicles. Upon arrival at the medical complex, the constable was told that the patient/plaintiff had tried to take away a police officer's service revolver. After the constable placed the patient securely in his vehicle, the patient requested that the handcuffs and leg shackles be removed. The officer removed them. While the vehicle was in motion, the patient told the officer that he intended to kill himself; some time later, he "unfastened his seatbelt, unlocked the door, and jumped out of the vehicle while it was in motion" (p. 845). The plaintiff died of the injuries sustained.

The Delaware Superior Court found that the constable's misconduct constituted wantonness and that he "forewent his normal practice of cuffing the patient with his hands behind his back . . ." (p. 846). The constable knew the vehicle was not adequate for transporting patients, heard the decedent state his intention to commit suicide, and failed to take precautions. The court therefore denied summary judgment for the constable and the county.

Failure to Rescue

Behavior of law enforcement officers following a suicide or attempted suicide may also indicate a breach of duty. Failure to rescue or to give aid to an injured detainee or to one who has attempted suicide can establish negligence. An officer's inaction can also be seen as the proximate cause of an injury if that action substantially contributed to the injury or death. The line between detainee supervision and a rescue attempt is often fine and interrelated to other circumstances surrounding a suicide. In *Manuel v. City of Jeanerette* (1997) a Louisiana court of appeals found failure to supervise and attempt a rescue of a suicidal detainee were significant factors in determining liability. The court found,

> The Jeanerette Police Department breached the duty owed to the prisoner by not having a specific policy or rule regarding regular checks on the prisoners. Chief Kahn testified that the dispatcher was supposed to use her common sense in determining whether or when to check on the prisoners. However, the dispatcher had virtually no training prior to starting her job and had only three months experience as a dispatcher at the time this incident occurred. Also, both prisoners in cell one testified that Mr. Manuel called for help a few times and the dispatcher did not respond. When the dispatcher heard a bunk turning over in the cell area she did not investigate the source of the noise or check the prisoners. Jesus Arriaga testified that, approximately five to ten minutes after the bunk turned over, he heard Mr. Manuel choking and gurgling. Mr. Arriaga testified that he could not be sure of the time but he believed it to be around midnight. The trial judge's observation that "Jimette Hebert's failure to provide adequate, and indeed any, observation of the deceased Wilbert Manuel while he was in custody of the Jeanerette Police Department, was a breach of the duty owed to the prisoner" has ample support in the record and is reasonably based. (p. 713)

In the *Hake v. Manchester Township* case discussed earlier, the New Jersey Supreme Court held that, in detainee suicide cases, plaintiffs need only establish that defendants had a duty to try to save a life and that there was a chance the decedent would have recovered from self-inflicted injuries had the officer rendered assistance. When the officers checked on the detained youth, they found him slumped in a chair with his belt around his neck. Instead of trying to aid him or call for medical assistance, the officers left him in that position while they notified other authorities. This behavior, according to the New Jersey

Supreme Court, established a causal link between the officers' inaction and the boy's death.

Defenses to Detainee Suicide

The traditional defenses associated with negligence actions are available to a police officer facing liability for failure to prevent a detainee's suicide. As discussed in chapters 2 and 7, officers can employ the defense of either contributory or comparative negligence. These defenses, however, have conceptual problems when applied to cases of detainee suicide; they are highly speculative and very dependant on the jurisdiction in which the case is heard, the specific court reviewing the case, and facts of the case before the court.

Recall that contributory negligence basically holds that if an officer can show the plaintiff was also negligent in causing the damage or injury, the officer will not be held liable. This defense is based on the idea that all persons owe a duty to carry out their day-to-day activities in a reasonable manner. It is thought that if the plaintiff was engaged in unreasonable behavior that increased the likelihood of damage or injury, the officer should not be held liable. Comparative negligence does not totally bar an officer's liability but mitigates the size of the damage award. When the defense comes to court in a jurisdiction using comparative negligence, the court would attempt to determine the degree of negligence of both the officer and the injured party and assess fault to both parties to the extent each party contributed to the injury.

Several courts have rejected the contributory negligence defense in cases of detainee suicide when the act of suicide is alleged to have been the contributing factor in the death. In *Sauders v. County of Steuben* (1998), the Indiana Supreme Court reasoned that:

> If the act of suicide (or attempted suicide) is a defense to a claim for failure to take reasonable steps to protect an inmate from harm, the cause of action evaporates in any instance of suicide or attempted suicide. This would completely obviate the custodian's legal duty to protect its detainees from that form of harm. (p. 19)

The court did not totally close the door on contributory negligence but clearly removed the act of suicide from the defense stating, "Although we have no example to offer, we do not exclude the possibility that contributory negligence or incurred risk might constitute a defense if based on some act other than the suicide or attempted suicide" (p. 19).

Concern about the application of contributory negligence in these cases has also been expressed by at least one federal court that stated "a duty to prevent someone from acting in a particular way logically cannot be defeated by the very action sought to be avoided" (*Myers v. County of Lake, Ind.*, 1994, p. 853). Other courts have reached similar positions, concluding "the acts which plaintiff's mental illness alleg-edly caused him to commit were the very acts which defendants had a duty to prevent, and these same acts cannot, as a matter of law, consti-tute contributory negligence" (*Cole v. Multnomah County*, 1979, p. 223).

Under unique circumstances other courts have reached a differ-ent conclusion on the issue of contributory negligence in detainee sui-cide cases. In *City of Belen v. Harrell* (1979), the court held, without analysis, that contributory negligence in a jail suicide case was a deci-sion for the jury. Similarly, in *Dezort v. Village of Hinsdale* (1976) the court concluded that contributory negligence was a defense under the Illinois Wrongful Death Act and that it applied to jail suicide cases.

There is even less precedent and more conceptual confusion about the applicability of the comparative negligence defense for police officers facing liability for failure to prevent detainee suicide. In at least two common-law jurisdictions, the courts have considered the issue and held that a jury instruction on comparative fault in jail sui-cide cases is sometimes appropriate and that the apportion of fault should be left to the jury (*Heflin v. Stewart County, Tennessee*, 1995; *Hickey v. Zezulka*, 1992). But as the *Sauders* court has reasoned

> custodial suicide is not an area that lends itself to comparative fault analysis. . . . The conduct of importance in this tort is the custodi-an's and not the decedent's. Further, it is hard to conceive of assign-ing a percentage of fault to an act of suicide. The suicide can be viewed as entirely responsible for the harm, or not relevant at all to an assessment of a custodian's breach of duty. A comparative bal-ance of "fault" in a suicide case would seem to risk random "all or nothing" results based on a given jury's predilections. (p. 20)

Summary

Local and county law enforcement agents have a broad range of custo-dial responsibilities over detainees. Because suicide is a major cause of detention deaths, the legal responsibilities associated with detainee custody is a concern for the law enforcement community. When a detainee commits suicide in police custody, law enforcement agencies are frequently sued in state court under negligence and wrongful death claims. Many of these claims have succeeded.

In negligence tort, the general duty of care owed to persons in police custody normally does not result in police negligence or liability because the suicide is construed as voluntary and a direct result of the detainee's behavior. In unique circumstances, however, conduct by the officer or the detainee can create a "special duty" for the police. The special duty arises only if events give the officer reason to believe the detainee may be a hazard to self or others. When officers are aware that a detainee is unable to prevent self-injury or cannot exercise the care that an ordinary reasonable person demonstrates, officers are under a special duty to prevent the potential harm. If foreseeability is present, law enforcement officers are required to take extra precautions to prevent suicide. If special precautions are not taken, law enforcement agents could be held liable for breaching their duty to prevent a detainee from committing suicide or other self-inflicted injuries.

An analysis of state tort case law shows that to succeed in negligence or wrongful death claims, plaintiffs, in addition to foreseeability, must establish a duty to prevent suicide and a breach of that duty. Special duty is imposed in a number of ways that are often beyond an officer's control; a breach of that duty is determined through a convergence of facts and applicable law. A host of factors indicates a possible breach of duty, among them: failure to provide safe facilities for detainees, negligent supervision, failure to remove facilitating suicide materials, failure to provide medical care after a suicide attempt, and failure to follow agency rules.

The success plaintiffs have had in death in detention cases reflects the continuing trend for care and accountability in law enforcement and corrections. Accountability preference is likely to continue and perhaps accelerate in the future as judicial precedents are established that make it easier for plaintiffs to succeed. Law enforcement and corrections officials must be properly informed about judicial trends in hopes that egregious cases that lead to liability can be avoided.

Shifting Conceptions of Police Civil Liability and Law Enforcement

11

Prior to the 1960s, the study of potential governmental civil liabilities, specifically those associated with providing critical police service, were not viable academic pursuits. There simply was no adequate body of knowledge or legal doctrine to make police liability a topic of scholarly concern. During the last four decades, however, the law of police civil liability has evolved rapidly. For the first time in the nation's history, citizens can successfully sue governmental entities for police conduct resulting in damage or injury (Kappeler, 1989). Municipal governments, police organizations, and police personnel still feel the effects of this legal revolution.

It is often thought the future of police liability depends solely on the judicial branch of government. Police executives often feel that they can only sit back and wait for the next pronouncement of the judiciary to shape department policy and operation. Street-level officers are often more concerned with the personal financial devastation a lawsuit brings than they are with the social purpose it serves (Alpert and Smith, 1990). The police often feel they are being placed in a no-win situation. The public expects the police to ferret out crime aggressively, yet the courts expect them to do so within legal boundaries of acceptable conduct. Unfortunately, this concern exists because of a lack of awareness of the interrelationships among shifting judicial philosophies of law enforcement, innovative police practice, and the way civil liability law develops. More important for liability law and police executives than the pronouncements of the judiciary are the changing underpinnings of policing and the evolving perception of police responsibility to society. While it is certainly important for the police to understand the law of civil liability and its judicial interpretation, it is equally important for police executives to realize that they shape the contours of liability law as it affects critical police operations.

This chapter examines directions in policing and civil liability law that may affect the future police executive. First, the chapter explores the premises of actors involved in litigating police civil liability cases. It explores conceptualizations regarding the filing and pleading of cases including assumptions about police and their role in society. Second, practices of the police are examined to understand the relationship between innovation and police civil liability. The chapter concludes with a discussion of the implications these shifting conceptions and evolving police practices may have on the future police executive.

Legal Assumptions and Police Civil Liability

It is incorrect to assume that the values and assumptions held by those litigating police liability cases are shaped solely by legal standards. The presumptions that litigators and judges have concerning law enforcement—including the proper way to file, plead, and adjudicate civil liability cases—shape litigation. These assumptions are currently changing and promise to influence the course of police civil liability.

Assumptions of Litigators

Several legal developments and assumptions made by litigators shape the law of police liability. To varying extents, these attitudes determine the volume of cases filed against the police and how these cases are litigated. From the 1960s through the middle part of the 1980s, litigation of police liability cases was influenced by the following factors: (1) passage of the Civil Rights Attorney's Fees Award Act of 1976; (2) lack of a substantial body of law on governmental liability, particularly relating to police service; and (3) the absence of legal doctrine that precluded filing of police civil liability claims in both state and federal courts.

The Civil Rights Attorney's Fees Act of 1976 reads in part: "In any action or proceeding to enforce a provision of sections 1981, 1982, 1983, 1985 and 1986 of this title . . . the court, in its discretion may allow the *prevailing* party . . . a reasonable attorney's fee as part of the costs" (emphasis added; 42 U.S.C. Sec. 1988). This legislation was used to allow attorneys to bring new and novel claims and to strengthen the enforcement aspect of the Civil Rights Acts. Since the passage of the Act in 1976, counsel for plaintiffs has been encouraged to file civil liability claims against the police even where these cases were previously considered less than fruitful. The effect of this legislation has been that

claimants with a grievance against the police are assured to find counsel willing to represent them. Under some interpretations of the legislation, attorneys do not necessarily have to "win" the civil rights case
to collect a fee (*Venegas v. Mitchell*, 1990). This motivates attorneys to
file claims with slim chances of success. An attorney who fails can only
lose the time and trouble of preparing the case. This, of course, can be
a costly investment, but it can also result in substantial rewards. In
essence, some attorneys are willing to gamble with the court system. If
they win, they are compensated; if they lose, but put on a "good show"
(prevail on a substantive issue) or are granted some relief on their
claim, they may be compensated (*Ramos Padro v. Commonwealth of
Puerto Rico*, 2000).

A second factor prompting the filing of cases against the police is
that much of the law on police civil liability is newly created. Until
recently, there existed no body of law governing the litigation of police
liability cases. The legal community as well as the police needed established legal doctrine to guide decision making. This need, coupled with
the change in compensation discussed above, prompted attorneys to
advance new claims and novel lines of argument. The possibility always
exists that a court will recognize a new claim or overturn an existing
principle of law that had earlier barred recovery. Attorneys are rewarded
for their successful attempts by the federal legislation guaranteeing fees.

The lack of uniformity and the absence of established doctrine
have resulted in no mutually exclusive division between federal and
state courts. Historically, under any given set of case facts, counsel
could file a claim in both federal and state courts alleging violation of
constitutional rights and negligent police conduct. This approach was
seen as a way of increasing the odds of successfully litigating a claim
against the police. If federal courts failed to find a constitutional violation, the state courts could still recognize the conduct as tortious.

These legal duplications and the corresponding strategies that
were encouraged in the legal community are coming under attack.
Attorneys are now required to examine the merit of their cases before
going forward with their claims. The courts are in effect reducing the
motivation to file flimsy cases by imposing sanctions. This could eventually reduce frivolous claims filed in federal court and raise the quality and merit of litigated cases.

Since the United States Supreme Court's determination that a
claim brought under Section 1983 must exceed negligence and be a
product of deliberate indifference (*Board of County Commissioners of
Bryan County, Oklahoma v. Brown*, 1997; *Harris v. City of Canton*,
1989), lawyers have become less likely to file a claim in federal court
if that case amounts to mere negligence and does not meet the deliberate indifference threshold. The Supreme Court is beginning to make
a clearer demarcation between negligence and constitutional viola-

tions. This has created a division between federal and state courts that
may evolve into mutually exclusive forums for adjudicating police liability cases. This trend is evidenced in the reduction of federal claims
filed against the police for negligent operation of emergency vehicles
and hiring practices. This change may reduce the overall number of
cases filed in the federal courts against the police, but it will also have
the chilling effect of retarding the legal community's desire to use
innovative lines of argument to plead new cases and to seek exceptions to existing legal doctrine—presumably what the legislature
intended when it enacted the Attorney's Fees Act. This could conceiv-
ably retard the development of legal doctrine on police civil liability
and leave the police without established legal precedent for many of
their functions. Questions currently left unanswered by the courts
may never be fully considered if the courts overuse their power of
sanction against attorneys.

Assumptions of Pleading and Litigating Cases

Before the 1980s, plaintiffs filing Section 1983 actions approached
police liability cases from a situational, incident-specific, and fact-based
strategy. There was an overemphasis on the facts surrounding a particular incident to prove a constitutional violation by the police. Cases
were largely won and lost based on facts of the individual incident
under review. Attorneys would know the facts of a case, conform to the
requirements of pleading, and present their case in the most favorable
light. Policy of the municipality or police agency was introduced as part
of the factual scenario surrounding the incident, but scant attention
was given to the role custom played in the nexus between police conduct and the injury inflicted.

The fact-based approach to pleading police liability cases is rapidly changing. Attorneys now construct detailed histories of the police
departments they sue. The more detailed the historical account of similar abuses of authority, the more likely the plaintiff is to win a case
against the police. This historical picture need not be limited to a single
incident or necessarily be overtly related to the conduct that caused
injury. The more a department's recorded history indicates administrative apathy, the likelier it is for a plaintiff to succeed in a police liability
case. Police policy, custom, and practice are now significant factors in
the determination of police liability at both the state and federal levels.
Externally derived standards of professionalism and practice, such as
those promoted by CALEA, ACA, and AMA (see chapter 10), are emerging as sources of determining the appropriateness of law enforcement
conduct. From this approach, issues of personnel selection, evaluation,
retention, and training become as important as the constitutionality of
the incident under review.

Judicial Assumptions and Law Enforcement

Several assumptions held by the judiciary about the police and their law enforcement role traditionally determined liability outcomes. These judicial assumptions included: (1) the imposition of liability hampers effective law enforcement; (2) it would place an unnecessary burden on government to demand educating and training; and (3) police officers and agencies owed no duty of protection to specific members of the general public.

Today, fewer courts are willing to accept the proposition that imposing civil liability hampers effective law enforcement. This position is reflected frequently in cases related to police use of force and pursuit driving. Courts had once maintained that the imposition of civil liability would force officers to choose between allowing criminal suspects to escape or facing the possibility of legal liability. With increasing regularity, courts are making the value judgment that law enforcement and criminal apprehension should be subordinate to general public safety. This represents a dramatic shift in judicial value and assumption about the importance of law enforcement, public safety, and civil liability. Public safety—not law enforcement—is becoming the issue on which liability hinges. Likewise, courts are becoming less willing to accept blindly political and media constructions of crime and policing. Many courts will, for example, no longer accept the construction of drug traffickers as inherently dangerous individuals or police use of force as the result of split second decisions in dangerous situations.

During the early development of police liability law, courts generally assumed law enforcement personnel were largely uneducated and lacked sufficient legal knowledge to be held accountable for a variety of behaviors. Threads of this assumption are still present in the rulings that police officers should not be held liable for conduct that is not clearly established as either tortious or unconstitutional as a matter of law. Officers were not expected to scan the legal horizons to determine which behaviors might become constitutional violations. Similarly, courts viewed policing as a blue-collar occupation not requiring a college education or extensive training. This fact is reflected frequently in early cases arising from the Civil Rights Act of 1964, Title VII litigation for discrimination in employment (Gaines and Kappeler, 1992; Kappeler and del Carmen, 1989).

This judicial view of policing is also changing (Carter and Sapp, 1990; Carter, Sapp and Stephens, 1988; *Davis v. City of Dallas*, 1985). Courts are now recognizing the need for training and college education. One court has stated "law enforcement officials are responsible for keeping abreast of constitutional developments in criminal law" (*Ward v. County of San Diego*, 1986). More recently courts have begun to establish specific areas of the law where police officers are expected to have legal knowledge. Police officers, for example, are now expected to know the subtleties of probable cause and warrant requirement (*Franz v. Lytle*, 1993) and their applicability to criminal, civil, and private actions (*Anaya v. Crossroads Managed Care Systems*, Inc., 1997). It remains to be seen whether this will become a formal legal principle in criminal or civil law, but the trend is becoming more evident. We can say, however, that as more principles of law become clearly established, fewer officers will be granted qualified immunity for misconduct.

The Supreme Court has all but mandated police training in several critical areas of law enforcement, namely: use of force, basic medical care, and to a lesser extent, pursuit driving (*Hockenberry v. Village of Carrollton*, 2000). The future may bring a further articulation and clarification of the areas in which police departments must provide adequate training. Failure to train has been one elusive link in establishing liability in many different claims of police abuse of authority. As courts move away from an excessively fact-based approach toward a historical and custom-based approach, training will become an important part of determining liability. With judicial thinking no longer bound to the immediate facts of a case, courts will be free to search for causes of police misconduct that manifest themselves outside the facts of a particular act of misconduct.

It has also been a judicial assumption that police do not owe a duty of protection to specific members of the general public they serve. Courts generally reasoned that to place the burden of protection on government would be to hamper the development of municipal government and to encumber needed resources from other public services. Courts are now less likely to assume that police owe no duty to persons who are either the victims of crimes or injured by behaviors the police could have prevented. The overused argument that police owe no duty to specific members of the general public is losing its legal effectiveness as courts carve out exceptions to the once blanket protection of the public duty doctrine. This trend is evident from even a cursory examination of current cases involving inadequate police response to incidents of domestic violence, failure to protect citizens, failure to arrest drunk drivers, and detainee suicide.

Police Innovation and Liability

Evolving police practice will bring about more liability litigation. Consider the use of deadly force and high-speed police pursuits as techniques for criminal apprehension. These practices were once accepted by most police organizations as traditional means for apprehending suspected criminals. Civil liability litigation did not cause the dramatic changes in these two areas that have occurred in the last twenty years. Before the Supreme Court's decision in *Tennessee v. Garner* (1985), many innovative police departments had begun to develop policy curtailing the use of deadly force by the police (Fyfe and Walker, 1990). Similarly, police organizations began developing policy restricting the use of high-speed police pursuit before the onset of litigation. In both areas, police executives were the forerunners of change.

Courts are not the leaders of change in either police practice or civil liability; instead they are the followers of change. Courts conceptually cling to the common-law notion of "the reasonable and prudent man." Generally speaking, an officer's behavior is "reasonable and prudent" if it is commonly accepted practice. Once a behavior becomes questionable regarding its "reasonableness," the potential for police liability exists. This situation is illustrated by the Supreme Court's consideration of police use of roadblocks (*Brower v. County of Inyo*, 1989). Almost since the inception of the automobile, the police have used roadblocks as a technique for apprehending suspected criminals. Only after leading innovators in the law enforcement community began to question the viability of such a practice did the Court express its opinion. The courts have followed the trend set by leading police executives instead of carving out new liability territory on their own. What was once reasonable is no longer accepted. What is now reasonable may become unreasonable in the future.

Proactive Training Prescriptions

The idea that police executives should take proactive approaches to reducing liability is a frequently prescribed remedy for civil liability litigation. Consider two scholars' comments about police training and liability, "Of course, a positive, proactive training model is most beneficial to officers and citizens alike" (Alpert and Smith, 1990). Another commentator states, "The best advice one could give to criminal justice practitioners and agencies is to take the 'proactive' position and attempt to prevent the lawsuits" (Barrineau, 1994). These proactive prescriptions are fine advice for the individual department that has the immediate concern of reducing litigation. They are, however, potential sources of liability in the broad and long-term sense. If police executives in leading departments begin to refine and develop elaborate training courses designed to prevent litigation, departments that fail to adopt such programs will be deemed "unreasonable and imprudent." Such departments will be open to liability. The innovation of leading police executives today can become the liability of less progressive administrators of the future. Similarly, the creation of new approaches to training, criminal apprehension, and record keeping can become the fuel for an expert witness claim that a department was negligent or indifferent when it failed to adopt the new and more prudent police practice.

The Supreme Court's decision in *City of Canton v. Harris* (1989) addressed specific areas of training critical to law enforcement operations. Leading police executives already recognized these areas of training. However, a pronouncement from the Supreme Court on the need for police training makes it mandatory that the entire law enforcement community accelerate the development of such programs. Once this evolution is complete, the Court will again await further innovation (brought to its attention through litigation), which eventually will be routinely mandated throughout the system. If a maxim can be stated it might read as follows: innovation equals litigation, but stagnation ensures liability.

Community Policing

Yet another example of innovation and the potential for civil liability is community policing. Will community policing become a source of civil liability? The answer depends on the definition of community policing as well as on the short- and long-term effects of community policing. If by community policing we mean, as Trojanowicz and Bucqueroux have stated, a "continuous, sustained contact with the law-abiding people in the community . . ." where the goal of the program involves officers "so deeply in the life of the community that the officers feel responsible for what happens in their beat areas, and the people who live there learn to trust them and work with them and hold them accountable for their success and failures" (Trojanowicz, Kappeler, Gaines, and Bucqueroux, 1998, p. 13), then there is the short-term likelihood of increased litigation and a longer term likelihood of decreased liability. As Trojanowicz and his associates note, "Allowing officers the freedom to attempt creative solutions to problems carries with it the risk of mistakes that can range from the embarrassing to the disastrous" (Trojanowicz, et al., 1998, p. 22).

Increased claims of police negligent failure to protect are some of these potentially disastrous results. This would be predicated on the increased contact between citizens and police and a greater reliance from citizens on the police. A substantial portion of liability case law is generated from special relationships between police and the public. These relationships require close contact and special knowledge by the police. Such reliance and contact can be promoted by community policing and can render police liable if they do not take measures to ensure the safety of particular citizens.

John L. Worrall and Otwin Marenin (1998) built on this concern about community policing and its potential sources of liability. They noted that community policing can generate liability in a number of ways. They suggest that community policing:

1. thrives in neighborhoods that are most receptive; that is, in more affluent and socially homogeneous neighborhoods (citations omitted). If so, new and innovative practices would seem to place officers in a risky predicament, especially those who serve in neighborhoods that are not responsive to the change in policing philosophy. If citizens in neglected communities learn that partnership and informality is practiced mainly in wealthier neighborhoods while they continue to receive formal crime control policing, the knowledge of such discrimination could increase their distrust of the police and result in suits against officers and agencies because of the absence of COP innovations.

2. expands officers' duties, hence increasing their capacity to act under color of state law. COP places officers in contact with citizens through such means as storefront stations, special task units, victim contact programs, or educational programs (citations omitted). As officers perform heretofore private and community roles and do so under the "color of law," they are risking an expansion (and perhaps clouding) of the courts' interpretations of this "threshold requirement." By virtue of assimilating duties previously delegated to citizens and interest groups into official police functions, departments could become more vulnerable to lawsuits.

3. justifies and enlarges the definition of the job of the police and multiplies approved encounters (it is legitimate to have a cup of coffee with a citizen who wants to chat about the neighborhood), but also changes the formally approved or demanded style of dealing with people in encounters (from formal to informal interactions) and the criteria for measuring success (crime and order but also quality of life and community well-being). . . . The standard of "legal duty" is hazy to begin with and will be made more so by adoption of COP (p. 126–28).

These researchers then cite cases where liability issues were raised in functions closely associated with community policing. These functions ranged from foot and bike patrols to the overly aggressive enforcement of so called "broken windows" violations like panhandling. In short, drastic changes in police practice are almost certain to bring about legal issues and the potential for new forms of civil liability. These observations are not included to dispel the merits of community policing but rather to illustrate that change in crime control practice can have civil liability consequences.

Technology

As policing begins to embrace the computer age, new liability issues will confront the courts. Although policing has been slow to adopt technology and the use of computers, there are signs that liability problems are beginning to surface in the courts. In recent years several courts have addressed the issue of police failure to use technology to prevent civil rights violations as well as abuses of technology that amounted to civil rights violations. Although not a civil liability case, a Supreme Court decision may give insight into how the courts will view law enforcement's use of computers and the information they store. The case of *Arizona v. Evans* (1995) arose because a Phoenix police officer, Bryan Sargent, observed Isaac Evans driving the wrong way on a one-way street. Sargent stopped Evans and asked him to produce a driver's license. After Evans told the officer that his driver's license was suspended, Sargent entered Evans's name into a computer data terminal in his patrol car. The inquiry confirmed the license suspension and an outstanding warrant. While arresting Evans, Sargent located a marijuana cigarette, and a subsequent search of Evans's car uncovered a bag of marijuana. Evans was charged with possession of marijuana. When police notified the justice court of the arrest, they discovered the warrant had been "quashed."

A clerk of the justice court testified at the suppression hearing that Evans had appeared in court on the traffic violations, and the justice of the peace quashed the warrant. The clerk testified that the standard court procedure for quashing a warrant was to inform the sheriff's office. The sheriff's office then removes the warrant from its computer records. Both parties are then to make notations of the recall and the transaction. The clerk testified that there was no indication in Evans's file that the sheriff's office was notified of the quashed warrant. A sheriff's records clerk testified that the office had no record of a telephone call informing it that Evans's warrant had been quashed.

Evans argued that the evidence obtained by arrest should be suppressed because application of the exclusionary rule would make the responsible parties "more careful about making sure that warrants are removed from the records." The trial court granted the motion to suppress. The Arizona Court of Appeals reversed, finding that the exclusionary rule was not intended to deter misconduct by justice court employees or sheriff's office employees not directly associated with the arresting officer or the arresting officer's agency. The Arizona Supreme Court reversed, rejecting the distinction "between clerical errors committed by law enforcement personnel and similar mistakes by court employees." The court predicted that application of the exclusionary rule would "serve to improve the efficiency of those who keep records in our criminal justice system."

The U.S. Supreme Court granted certiorari to decide whether the exclusionary rule requires "suppression of evidence seized incident to an arrest resulting from an inaccurate computer record, regardless of whether police personnel or court personnel were responsible for the record's continued presence in the police computer." The Court reversed the state supreme court's decision, reasoning that just because responsibility for the error rested with the court, it does not follow that the exclusionary rule should be applicable. The Court reasoned the exclusionary rule was developed to deter police misconduct, not mistakes by court employees. Evans "offered no evidence that court employees are inclined to ignore or subvert the Fourth Amendment or that lawlessness among these employees requires application of the extreme sanction of exclusion." The Court stated "there is no basis for believing that application of the exclusionary rule in these circumstances will have a significant effect on court employees responsible for informing the police that a warrant has been quashed."

The Court was careful to limit its decision and placed emphasis on the fact that court employees were responsible for failing to notify the sheriff's office of information necessary for them to maintain accurate computer records. The Court may have reached an alternative conclusion had the record indicated that the sheriff's office failed to update their computer files.

The decision provides a warning of potential problems associated with the automation of police records. It also provides some insight into the Court's thoughts on the automation of law enforcement records. In a concurring opinion Justice O'Connor made the following remark:

> We have witnessed the advent of powerful, computer-based record keeping systems that facilitate arrests in ways that have never before been possible. The police, of course, are entitled to enjoy the substantial advantages this technology confers. They may not, however, rely on it blindly. With the benefits of more efficient law enforcement mechanisms comes the burden of corresponding constitutional responsibilities.

Justice Ginsburg's dissenting opinion was more pointed. She wrote:

> Widespread reliance on computers to store and convey information generates, along with manifold benefits, new possibilities of error, due to both computer malfunctions and operator mistakes . . . computerization greatly amplifies an error's effect, and correspondingly intensifies the need for prompt correction; for inaccurate data can infect not only one agency, but the many agencies that share access to the database.

One can only interpret this decision and the justices' concerns as putting law enforcement on notice that failure to use technology and information properly will be an area closely watched by the courts.

Implications for the Future Police Executive

There are several important implications of these shifting judicial concepts of police liability and responsibility. The future police executive's function will be altered by changing police practice as well as by the course of judicial thoughts. Police executives will have to become aware of the histories of the departments with which they are entrusted. Future police executives will no longer be able to take over police organizations with a legal clean slate, hence limiting transitional administrative periods to mop-up operations of pending liability lawsuits created by past administrations. Police executives of the future will inherit not only these pending liability cases but also the problems associated with past innovations and stagnation, including the department's historical record of custom and policy. This will place executives in a position of defending past behavior or of trying to distance their administration from past administrations.

Police executives of the future will have to sift innovations through a civil liability filter. This will require executive analysis of the short-term possibility of increased litigation and the longer term potential for reduced liability. The double-edged sword of innovation and liability has other consequences as well. In this setting, innovative police executives will have a substantial advantage over those who are less inclined toward change. As the courts recognize the necessity for change, those agencies that do not conform will find themselves in a liability quandary of someone else's making. Policy and procedures that were acceptable in the past will become legally obsolete. In this environment it will not suffice for police executives to be aware of their own agency's histories and practices; they will also be required to stay abreast of the ever-changing field of police management. Stagnating will no longer simply result in a backward agency, it will render an agency susceptible to legal challenge. In other words, innovative chiefs may be sued in the short run over their innovations, but uninnovative chiefs will be sued and found liable over their failure to follow the lead of the innovators.

The new responsibility of managing change will require the future police executive to become the disseminator of workable adaptations. Police executives will have to become the creators and transmitters of new customs and traditions, not just policy and directives. As police executives begin to take responsibility for the effects of their innovations on other police organizations, they will have to teach new methods to their counterparts. The importance of membership in organizations dedicated to providing this conduit for knowledge will become paramount. These organizations will not only disseminate information on existing innovations but will become forums for discussions on the ramifications of innovations and the necessity for change before it occurs.

The role of police supervisors should be expanded to include responsibility for the development and preservation of departmental history. The supervisory function of lower-level managers will have to allow for these new responsibilities. Lower-level supervisors will become the personnel managers of police organizations, thus assuming many of the duties and responsibilities normally associated with city personnel directors. Municipal personnel departments are ill-equipped and often poorly versed in the demands of this liability revolution. With this responsibility will come the need to create systems capable of merging selection, evaluation, retention, and training records of individual personnel with actual departmental activities. These systems will document departmental actions, on both a micro and macro level, as well as individual officer behavior—allowing police executives to present information on departmental history, policy, and custom. It will no longer be sufficient for agencies to pull individual personnel jackets without the ability to relate these records to actual performance and departmental policy and custom.

This means an even greater emphasis on education and training. With each passing year it will become more important to increase the educational standards of newly hired officers. The selection criteria, "high school or equivalent," is evolving to "college-educated." Departments will see an increasing need for training in communication and human relation skills as opposed to skills involved in the use of weapons. The police duty to protect life will come into greater conflict with police actions that threaten life. Failure to recognize the changing court attitude toward the police responsibility to avoid the use of force will increase police liability.

Finally, future police executives will be trapped between two evolving forces that will tax severely their administrative skills. On the one side we will see increased pressures for decentralized decision making. Both the community-oriented policing and problem-oriented policing models require decision making at the lowest level of the organization. As innovative executives decentralize their agencies to make them more responsive to the citizen, the administrator will run headlong into the opposing trend. Courts, through the liability process, are demanding ever-increasing administrative control over the organization. With each successful civil suit, the administrator is being held more accountable for the actions of each member of the organization. The executive is being pressured to establish a tight rein over the organization. While other innovations transform the quality of service delivered by the police, the most important innovations—those involving transforming the structure of the police—may run into a solid barrier. Decentralization will be in direct conflict with court-mandated centralization and control. This conflict will have to be resolved.

While concerns over police civil liability should not paralyze innovation in policing, it should be taken seriously as one of many important factors to consider when police executives plan for the future. Innovation has its costs, among them the possibility of litigation and police civil liability. Police executives must begin to monitor shifting judicial philosophies of law enforcement and police responsibility to society while being mindful that today's actions directly affect both the future of liability law and their colleagues in law enforcement.

References

Alpert, G. P., and Dunham, R. G. (1996). *Policing urban America* (3rd ed.). Prospect Heights, IL: Waveland Press.

Alpert, G., and Smith, W. (1990). Defensibility of law enforcement training. *Criminal Law Bulletin, 26*(5), 452-58.

Americans for Effective Law Enforcement (AELE). (1974). *Survey of police misconduct litigation: 1967-1971.* San Francisco: AELE.

Americans for Effective Law Enforcement (AELE). (1980). *Lawsuits Against Police Skyrocket.* San Francisco: AELE.

Americans for Effective Law Enforcement (AELE). (1982). *Impact.* San Francisco: AELE.

Barrineau, H. E. (1994). *Civil liability in criminal justice* (2nd ed.). Cincinnati, OH: Anderson.

Bates, R. D., Culter, R. F., and Clink, M. J. (1981). *Prepared statement on behalf of the national institute of municipal law officers*, presented before the Subcommittee on the Constitution, Senate Committee on the Judiciary, May 6, 1981 (as cited in Barrineau, 1994).

Bittner, E. (1970). *The functions of police in modern society.* Washington, DC: National Institute of Mental Health.

Black, H. C. (1990). *Black's law dictionary* (6th ed.). St. Paul, MN: West Publishing Co.

Bureau of Justice Statistics (1999). *Executive summary: Sheriffs' departments, 1997.* Washington, DC: U.S. Department of Justice.

Bureau of Justice Statistics (2000a). *Local police departments, 1997.* Washington, DC: U.S. Department of Justice.

Bureau of Justice Statistics (2000b). *Sourcebook.* Washington, DC: U.S. Department of Justice.

Carter, D. (1994). Contemporary issues facing police administrators: Guideposts for the academic community. *Police Forum, 4*(1), 9-10.

Carter, D., and Sapp, A. (1990). Higher education as a policy alternative to reduce police liability. *Police Liability Review, 2*(4), 1-3.

Carter, D., Sapp, A., and Stephens, D. (1988). Higher education as a bona fide occupational qualification (BFOQ) for police: A blueprint. *American Journal of Police, 7*(2), 1-28.

Christopher, W. (1991). *Report of the independent commission on the Los Angeles Police Department.* Los Angeles: City of Los Angeles.

203

Comment (1990). *City of Canton v. Harris*: Municipal liability under 42 U.S.C. Section 1983 for inadequate police training. *George Mason University Law Review, 12*(4), 757–74.

Cunningham, C. (1986). Tactical driving: A multifaceted approach. *FBI Law Enforcement Bulletin, 55*, 18–19.

del Carmen, R. V. (1981). An overview of civil and criminal liabilities of police officers and departments. *American Journal of Criminal Law, 9*, 33.

del Carmen, R. V. (1994). Civil and criminal liabilities of police officers. In T. Barker and D. L. Carter (Eds.), *Police Deviance.* Cincinnati, OH: Pilgrimage.

del Carmen, R. V. (1995). *Criminal procedure for law enforcement personnel* (3rd ed.). Monterey, CA: Brooks/Cole.

del Carmen, R. V. (2001). *Criminal procedure for law enforcement personnel* (5th ed.). Monterey, CA: Brooks/Cole.

del Carmen, R. V., and Kappeler, V. E. (1991). Municipal and police agencies as defendants: Liability for official policy and custom. *American Journal of Police, 10*(1), 1–17.

del Carmen, R. V., and Saucier, R. (1985, September). Of sniffs and bites: Legal issues in police dog use. *Police Chief,* 50–53.

Fyfe, J. J. (1983). Fleeing felons and the Fourth Amendment. *Criminal Law Bulletin, 19*(6), 525–28.

Fyfe, J., and Walker, J. (1990). Garner plus five years: An examination of Supreme Court intervention into police discretion and legislative prerogatives. *American Journal of Criminal Justice, 14*(2), 167–88.

Gaines, L. K., and Kappeler, V. E. (1992). Selection and testing. In G. Cordner and D. Hale (Eds.), *What works in policing.* Alexandria, VA: Academy of Criminal Justice Sciences/Cincinnati, OH: Anderson.

Gaines, L. K., Kappeler, V. E., and Vaughn, J. B. (1999). *Policing in America* (3rd ed). Cincinnati, OH: Anderson.

Gallagher, G. P. (1989, August 7). The crisis in police pursuit driver training: An action plan. *Crime Control Digest,* 9.

Garner, G. (1991). Off-duty: Off the hook? *Police, 15*(9), 32–34, 71–73.

Garrison, A. H. (1995). Law enforcement civil liability under federal law and attitudes on civil liability: A survey of university, municipal and state police officers. *Police Studies, 18*(3), 19–37.

Gotham, D. (1992). The duty to serve and protect: 42 U.S.C. Section 1983 and police officers' liability following roadside abandonment. *Washington Law Review, 67*(3), 647–68.

Green, L. (1995). Cleaning up drug hot spots in Oakland, California: The displacement and diffusion effects. *Justice Quarterly, 12*(4), 737–54.

Hayes, L. (1989). National study of jail suicides: Seven years later. *Psychiatric Quarterly, 60*(1), 7–29.

Human Rights Watch (1998). *Shielded from justice: Police brutality and accountability in the United States.* New York: Human Rights Watch.

International Association of Chiefs of Police (1976). *Survey of police misconduct litigation 1967–1976.* Fairfax, VA: IACP.

Kappeler, S. F., and Kappeler, V. E. (1992). A research note on Section 1983 claims against the police: Cases before the federal district courts in 1990. *American Journal of Police, 11*(1), 65–73.

Kappeler, V. E. (1989). Preface to special issue: Police civil liability. *American Journal of Police, 8*(1), i–iii.

Kappeler, V. E. (1996). The fear of civil liability among Kentucky police cadets. Richmond, KY: Eastern Kentucky University (unpublished paper).

Kappeler, V. E., and del Carmen, R. V. (1989). The personal staff exemption to Title VII of the Civil Rights Act of 1964: May some criminal justice personnel be dismissed at will? *Criminal Law Bulletin, 25*(4), 340-61.

Kappeler, V. E., Kappeler, S. F., and del Carmen, R V. (1993). A content analysis of police civil liability cases: Decisions of the federal district courts, 1978-1990. *Journal of Criminal Justice, 21*(4), 325-37; updated 1996.

Kappeler, V. E., and Vaughn, J. B. (1989). The historical development of negligence theory. *American Journal of Police, 8*(1), 1-36.

Katz, D. M. (1998). L. A. cops lop $10M off tort costs. *National Underwriter/ Property & Casualty Risk & Benefits, 102*(26), 11-12.

Kennedy, D. B. (1984). A theory of suicide while in police custody. *Journal of Police Science and Administration, 12*(2), 191-200.

Kennedy, D. B., and Homant, R. J. (1988). Predicting custodial suicides: Problems with the use of profiles. *Justice Quarterly, 5*(3), 441-56.

Kingston, K. (1989). Hounding drug traffickers: The use of drug detection dogs. *FBI Law Enforcement Bulletin, 58*(8), 26-32.

Koper, C. S. (1995). Just enough police presence: Reducing crime and disorderly behavior by optimizing patrol time in crime hot spots. *Justice Quarterly, 12*(4), 649-72.

Kraska, P. B., and Kappeler, V. E. (1997). Militarizing American police: The rise and normalization of paramilitary units. *Social Problems, 44*(1), 1-18.

Kritzer, H., Marshall, L., and Zemans, F. (1992). Rule 11: Moving beyond the cosmic anecdote. *Judicature, 75*(5), 269-72.

Littlejohn, E. J. (1976). Civil liability and the police officer: The need for new deterrents to police misconduct. *University of Detroit Urban Law, 58,* 365-70.

MacManus, S. A. (1997). Litigation costs, budget impacts, and cost containment strategies: Evidence from California cities. *Public Budgeting and Finance, 17*(4), 28-47.

McCoy, C. (1987). Police legal liability is "Not a Crisis" 99 chiefs say. *Crime Control Digest, 21,* 1.

National League of Cities (1985, November 25). Seeking solutions on liability insurance. *Nations Cities Weekly.* Washington, DC: N.C.W.

Prosser, W., and Keeton, P. (1984). *The law of torts.* St. Paul, MN: West Publishing.

Reynolds, C. D. (1988, December). Unjust civil litigation—A constant threat. *Police Chief, 7.*

Ross, D. L. (2000). Emerging trends in police failure to train liability. *Policing: An International Journal of Police Strategies and Management, 23*(2), 169-93.

Ryals, S. M. (1995). *Discovery and proof in police misconduct cases.* New York: John Wiley and Sons.

Schmidt, W. W. (1974). Recent developments in police civil liability. *Journal of Police Science and Administration, 4*(2): 197-202.

Schofield, D. L. (1990). Personal liability: The qualified immunity defense. *FBI Law Enforcement Bulletin, 59*(3), 26-32.

Scogin, F., and Brodsky, S. L. (1991). Fear of litigation among law enforcement officers. *American Journal of Police, 10*(1), 41-45.

Sherman, L., Gartin, P., and Buerger, M. (1989). Hot spots or predatory crime: Routine activities and the criminology of place. *Criminology, 27*(1), 27-55.

Sherman, L., and Weisburd, D. (1995). General deterrent effects of police patrol in crime "hot spots": A randomized, controlled trial. *Justice Quarterly, 12*(4), 625–48.

Silver, I. (2000). *Police civil liability.* New York: Matthew Bender.

Skogan, W. (1990). *Disorder and decline: Crime and the spiral of decay in American neighborhoods.* New York: Free Press.

St. Louis Globe (1904, July 10).

St. Louis Globe (1905, September 3).

Staff (1992, March 6). NYPD fails to monitor police misconduct suits. *Chief Leader.*

Stevens, D. J. (2000). Civil liabilities and arrest decisions. *The Police Journal, 73,* 119–42.

Terry, D. (1996, June 25). Philadelphia held liable in calamitous MOVE fire. *New York Times,* p. A7.

Trautman, N. (1997). *The cutting edge of police integrity.* Longwood, FL: National Institute of Ethics.

Trickett, A., Osborn, D., Seymour, J., and Pease, K. (1992). What is different about high crime areas? *British Journal of Criminology, 32*(1), 81–9.

Trojanowicz, R., Kappeler, V.E., Gaines, L.K., and Bucqueroux, B. (1998). *Community policing: A contemporary perspective.* (2nd ed.). Cincinnati, OH: Anderson.

Vaughn, M. S. (1994). Police civil liability for abandonment in high crime areas and other high risk situations. *Journal of Criminal Justice, 22*(5), 407–24.

Vaughn, M. S., and Coomers, L. F. (1995). Police civil liability under Section 1983: When do police officers act under Color of Law? *Journal of Criminal Justice, 23*(5), 395–415.

Vaughn, M. S., Cooper, T. W., and del Carmen, R. V. (2001). Assessing legal liabilities in law enforcement: Police chiefs' views. *Crime & Delinquency, 47*(1), 3–27.

Warner, B. D., and Pierce, G. L. (1993). Reexamining social disorganization theory using calls to the police as a measure of crime. *Criminology, 31*(4), 493–517.

Worrall, J. L., and Marenin, O. (1998). Emerging liability issues in the implementation and adoption of community oriented policing. *Policing: An International Journal of Police Strategies & Management, 21*(1), 121–36.

Zevitz, R. (1987). Police civil liability and the law of high speed. *Marquette Law Review,* 237–38.

Cases

Abraham v. Raso, No. 98-5305, 98-5406 (3rd. Cir. 1999).

Abrahante v. City of New York, 606 N.Y.S.2d 689 (A.D. 1 Dept. 1994).

Adams v. State, 555 P.2d 235, 24–42 (Alaska 1976).

Albright v. Oliver, 510 U.S. 266 (1994).

Allen v. Muskogee, 119 F.3d 837 (10th Cir.1997).

Allison Gas Turbine v. District of Columbia, 642 A.2d 841 (D.C. App. 1994).

Anaya v. Crossroads Managed Care Systems, Inc., No. 97-1358 (10th Cir. 1997).

Anderson v. Creighton, 483 U.S. 635 (1987).

Anderson v. Jones, 902 S.W.2d 889 (Mo. App. E.D. 1995).

Anderson v. Liberty Lobby, Inc., 477 U.S. 242 (1986).

Angle v. Miller, 629 A.2d 238 (Pa. Cmwlth. 1993).

Arizona v. Evans, 115 S. Ct. 1185 (1995).

Ashburn v. Anne Arundel County, 510 A.2d 1078 (Md. App. 1986).

Atchinson v. District of Columbia, 73 F.3d 418 (D.C. Cir. 1996).

Atkins v. New York, 143 F.3d 100 (2nd Cir. 1998).

Babcock v. Mason County Fire Dist., 101 Wn. App. 677 (Wa. 2000).

Bailey v. Town of Forks, 688 P.2d 526 (Wash. App. 1985).

Baldi v. City of Philadelphia, 607 F. Supp. 162 (E.D. Pa. 1985).

Barlow v. New Orleans, 241 So.2d 501 (La. 1970).

Barratt v. Burlingham, 492 A.2d 1219 (R.I. 1985).

Battista v. Olson, 516 A.2d 117 (N.J. Super. A.D. 1986).

Baum v. Ohio State Hwy. Patrol, 650 N.E.2d 1347 (Ohio 1995).

Bell v. Wolfish, 441 U.S. 520 (1979).

Bennett v. City of Slidell, 735 F.2d 861 (5th Cir. 1984).

Bennett v. Pippin, 74 F.3d 578 (5th Cir. 1996).

Bickel v. City of Downey, 238 Cal. Rptr. 351 (Ct. App. 1987).

Black v. Shrewsbury Borough, 675 A.2d 381 (Pa. Cmwlth. 1996).

Blea v. City of Espanola, 870 P.2d 755 (N.M. App. 1994).

Board of County Commissioners of Bryan County, Oklahoma v. Brown, 520 U.S. 397 (1997).

Bonner v. Anderson, 81 F.3d 472 (4th Cir. 1996).

Bordanaro v. McLeod, 871 F.2d 1151 (1st Cir. 1989); cert. denied, 493 U.S. 820 (1989).

Bordeau v. Village of Deposit, 113 F. Supp.2d 292 (N.D. N.Y. 2000).

Bouye v. Marshall, 102 F. Supp.2d 1357 (N.D. Ga. 2000).

Boyd v. Baeppler, 2000 FED APP 0188p (6th Cir. 2000).
Brady v. Dill, No. 98-2293 (1st Cir. 1999).
Brady v. Ft. Bend Cty., 145 F.3d 691 (5th Cir. 1998).
Breese v. State, 449 N.E.2d 1098 (Ind. Ct. App. 1983).
Brisco v. LaHue, 103 S. Ct. 1108 (1983).
Brower v. County of Inyo, 489 U.S. 593 (1989).
Brown v. Bryan County, Okla., 1410 F.3d 1410 (5th Cir. 1995).
Brown v. City of New Orleans, 464 So.2d 976 (La. App. 1985).
Brown v. City of Pinellas Park, 557 So.2d 161 (Fla. Dist. Ct. App. 1990).
Brown v. Glossip, 878 F.2d 871 (5th Cir 1989).
Brown v. Gray, Denver Manager of Public Safety, Nos. 99-1134, 99-1164
    & 99-1232 (10th Cir. 2000).
Brown v. Noe, 711 F. Supp. 1114 (N.D. Ga. 1989).
Brown v. Tate, 888 S.W.2d 413 (Mo. App.1994).
Browning v. Snead, 886 F. Supp. 547 (S.D. W.Va. 1995).
Buffkins v. City of Omaha, Douglas County, Neb., 922 F.2d 465 (8th Cir. 1990).
Burchins v. State, 360 N.Y.S.2d 92 (S. Ct. App. Div. 1974).
Burke v. Miller, 580 F.2d 108 (4th Cir.1978), cert. denied, 440 U.S. 930 (1979).
Burns v. Loranger, 907 F.2d 233 (1st Cir. 1990).
Butler v. City of Detroit, 386 N.W.2d 645 (Mich. App. 1985).
Cain v. Leake, 695 P.2d 794 (Co. App. 1984).
Caldwell v. City of Philadelphia, 517 A.2d 1296 (Penn. 1986).
Carlin v. Blanchard, 537 So.2d 303 (La. App. 1 Cir. 1988).
Carroll v. U.S., 267 U.S. 132 (1925).
Cathey v. Guenther, 47 F.3d 162 (5th Cir. 1995).
Cavigliano v. County of Livingston, 678 N.Y.S. 2d 187 (A.D. 4 Dept. 1998).
Chambers-Castaner v. King County, 669 P.2d 452 (Wash. 1983).
Chatman v. Slagle, 1997 FED App. 0064P, No. 95-3885 (6th Cir.1997).
Chimel v. California, 395 U.S. 752 (1969).
Chisholm v. Georgia, 2 U.S. (Dell.) 419 (1793).
City of Belen v. Harrell, 603 P.2d 711 (N.M. 1979).
City of Canton v. Harris, 489 U.S. 378, 109 S. Ct. 1197 (1989).
City of Coppell v. Waltman, 997 S.W. 2d 633 (Tex. All-Dallas 1998).
City of St. Louis v. Praprotnik, 108 S. Ct. 915 (1988).
City of Winter Haven v. Allen, 541 So.2d 125 (Fla. App. 1989).
Coco v. State, 474 N.Y.S.2d 397 (Ct. Cl. 1984).
Cohens v. Virginia, 19 U.S. (6 Wheat.) 264 (1921).
Cole v. Multnomah County, 592 P.2d 221 (Or. Ct. App. 1979).
Collins v. Harker Heights, 503 U.S. 115 (1992).
Comfort v. Town of Pittsfield, 924 F. Supp. 1219 (D. Me. 1996).
Commonwealth of Pa. Dept. of Trans. v. Philips, 488 A.2d 77 (Pa. Comm. Ct.
    1985).
Conrod v. Missouri State Highway Patrol, 614 S.W.2d 614 (Mo. App. 1991).
Cornfiled by Lewis v. Consolidated High School District No. 230, 991 F.2d 1316
    (7th Cir. 1993).
Cortez v. Close, 101 F. Supp.2d 1013 (N.D. Ill. 2000).
Costello v. City of Ellisville, 921 S.W.2d 134 (Mo. App. E.D. 1996).
County of Sacramento v. Lewis, 523 U.S. 833 (1998).
Courson v. McMillian, 939 F.2d 1479 (11th Cir. 1991).
Crosby v. Town of Bethlehem, 457 N.Y.S.2d 618 (A.D. 1982).
Cuffy v. City of New York, 513 N.Y.S.2d 372 (NY 1987).

Curry v. Iberville Parish Sheriff's Office, 405 So.2d 1387 (La. App. 1981).
Dalehite v. United States, 346 U.S. 15 (1953).
Daniels v. Wilson, 5 T.R. 1, 101 Eng. Rep. 1. (1810).
Davis v. City of Dallas, 777 F.2d 205 (5th Cir. 1985).
Davis v. City of Detroit, 386 N.W.2d 169 (Mich. App. 1986).
Day v. Willis, 897 P.2d 78 (Alaska 1995).
de Koning v. Mellema, 534 N.W.2d 391 (Iowa, 1995).
Dennis v. City of Philadelphia, 620 A.2d 625 (Pa. Cmwlth. 1993).
Dennision v. Plumb, 18 Barb. N.Y. 89 (1854).
DeShaney v. Winnebago County Department of Social Services, 489 U.S. 189, 109 S. Ct. 998 (1989).
DeWald v. State, 719 P.2d 643 (Wyo. 1986).
Dezort v. Village of Hinsdale, 342 N.E.2d 468 (Ill. App. Ct. 1976).
Dickerson v. Monroe County Sheriff's Department, 114 F. Supp.2d 187 (W.D. N.Y. 2000).
Dillenback v. City of Los Angeles, 446 P.2d 129 (Cal. 1968).
Donaldson v. City of Seattle, 831 P.2d 1098 (Wash. App. Div. 1 1992).
Drawbridge v. Douglas City, 311 N.W.2d 898 (Neb. 1981).
Duncan v. Town of Jackson, 903 P.2d 548 (Wyo. 1995).
Dunn v. Denk, 54 F.3d 248 (5th Cir. 1995).
Dunn v. Denk, 79 F.3d 401 (5th Cir. 1996).
Duvernay v. State, 433 So.2d 254 (La. App. 1983).
Dwares v. City of New York, 985 F.2d 94 (2nd Cir. 1993).
Ealy v. City of Detroit, 375 N.W.2d 435 (Mich. App. 1985).
Eberle v. City of Anaheim, 901 F.2d 814 (9th Cir. 1990).
Erwin v. County of Manitowoc, 872 F.2d 1292 (7th Cir. 1989).
Estate of Aten v. City of Tucson, 817 P.2d 951 (Ariz. App 1991).
Estate of Macias v. Lopez, 42 F. Supp.2d 957 (N.D. Cal. 1999).
Estate v. Willis, 897 P.2d 78 (Alaska 1995).
Evans v. Hawley, 559 So.2d 500 (La. App. 2 Cir. 1990).
Eversole v. Steele, 59 F.3d 710 (7th Cir. 1995).
Everton v. Willard, 468 So.2d 936 (Fla. 1985).
Ewing v. City of Detroit, 543 N.W.2d 1 (Mich. App. 1995).
Ezell v. Cockrell, 902 S.W.2d 394 (Tenn. 1995).
Falkenstein v. City of Bismarck, 268 N.W.2d 787 (N.D. 1978).
Fielder v. Jenkins, 633 A.2d 906 (N.J. Super. A.D. 1993).
Fiser v. City of Ann Arbor, 339 N.W.2d 413 (Mich. 1983).
Fitzpatrick v. City of Chicago, 507 N.E.2d 310 (Ill. App. 1987).
Floyd v. Laws, 929 F.2d 1390 (9th Cir. 1991).
Ford v. Childress, 650 F. Supp. 110 (D.C. Ill. 1986).
Foremost Dairies v. State, 232 Cal.Rptr. 71 (Cal. Ct. App. 1986).
Fowler v. North Carolina Dept. of Crime Control, 376 So.2d 11 (N.C. App. 1989).
Fowler v. Norways Sanitorium, 112 Ind. App. 347, 42 N.E.2d 415 (1942).
Franz v. Lytle, 997 F.2d 784 (10th Cir. 1993).
Fudge v. City of Kansas City, 720 P.2d 1093 (Kan. 1986).
Fusilier v. Russell, 345 So.2d 543 (La. App. 1977).
Gabriel v. City of Plano, Texas, No. 98-41022 (5th Cir. 2000).
Gary Police Department v. Loera, 604 N.E.2d 6 (Ind. App. 3 Dist. 1992).
George v. City of Long Beach, 973 F.2d 706 (9th Cir. 1992).
Gibson v. Pasadena, 148 Cal. Rptr. 68 (Cal. App. 2nd Dist. 1987).
Gillette v. Delmore, 979 F.2d 1342 (9th Cir. 1992), cert. denied 114 S. Ct. 345 (1993).

Graham v. Connor, 490 U.S. 386, 109 S. Ct. 1865 (1989).
Gregory v. Cardenaz, 402 S.E.2d 757 (Ga. App. 1991).
Guice v. Enfinger, 389 So.2d 270 (Fla. App. 1980).
Gumz v. Morrissette, 772 F.2d 1395 (7th Cir. 1985).
Gutierrez v. City of San Antonio, 139 F.3d 441 (5th Cir. 1998).
Hafer v. Melo, 502 U.S. 21 (1991).
Hainze v. Allison, No. 99-56222 (5th Cir. 2000).
Hake v. Manchester Township, 486 A.2d 836 (N.J. 1985).
Hamilton v. Town of Palo, 244 N.W.2d 329 (Iowa, 1976).
Harlow v. Fitzgerald, 457 U.S. 800 (1982).
Harper v. Harris County, Texas, 21 F.3d 597 (5th Cir. 1994).
Harsen v. Black, 885 F.2d 642 (9th Cir. 1989).
Heflin v. Stewart County, Tennessee, 1995 WL 614201 (Tenn. Ct. App. 1995).
Hegarty v. Somerset County, 53 F.3d 1367 (1st Cir. 1995).
Hegarty v. Somerset County, 848 F. Supp. 257 (D. Me. 1994).
Helmly v. Bebber, 335 S.E.2d 182 (N.C. App. 1985).
Helseth v. Burch, 109 F. Supp.2d 1066 (D. Minn. 2000).
Hemphill v. Schott, 141 F.3d 412 (2nd Cir. 1998).
Henderson v. Bowden, 737 So. 2d 532 (Fla, 1999).
Hernandez v. Maxell, 905 F.2d 94 (5th Cir. 1990).
Hervey v. Estes, 65 F.3d 784 (9th Cir. 1995).
Hickey v. Zezulka, 443 N.W.2d 180 (Mich. App. 1989).
Hickey v. Zezulka, 487 N.W.2d 106 (Mich. 1992).
Hicks v. Woodruff, No. 99-6303 (10th Cir. 1999).
Hill v. Clifton, 74 F.3d 1150 (11th Cir. 1996).
Hilliard v. City and County of Denver, 930 F.2d 1516 (10th Cir. 1991).
Hinton v. City of Elwood, Kansas, 997 F.2d 774 (10th Cir. 1993).
Hockenberry v. Village of Carrollton, 110 F. Supp.2d 597 (N.D. Ill. 2000).
Hoffman v. Warden, 457 N.W.2d 367 (Mich. App. 1990).
Holsten v. Massey, 490 S.E. 2d 864 (W.Va. 1997).
Horton v. Californnia, 496 U.S. 128 (1990).
Horton v. Flenory, 889 F.2d 454 (3rd Cir. 1989).
Hudson v. Carton, 141 S.E. 222 (Ga. 1929).
Hunter v. Bryant, 502 U.S. 224, 112 S. Ct. 634 (1991).
Illinois v. Rodriguz, 495 U.S. 177 (1990).
Imbler v. Pachtman, 424 U.S. 409 (1976).
Irwin v. Ware, 467 N.E.2d 1292 (Mass. 1984).
J. B. v. Washington Cty., 127 F.3d 919 (10th Cir. 1997).
Jackson v. City of Detroit, 537 N.W.2d 151 (Mich. 1995).
Jackson v. City of Joliet, 715 F.2d 1200 (7th Cir. 1983).
Jackson v. Marion County, 66 F.3d 151 (7th Cir. 1995).
Jeffers v. Heavrin, 932 F.2d 1160 (6th Cir. 1991).
Jennings v. Joshua Independent School District, 869 F.2d 870 (5th Cir. 1989).
Jensen v. City of Oxnard, No. 97-55936 (9th Cir. 1998).
Jett v. Dallas independent School Dist., 491 U.S. 701 (1989).
Jocks v. Tavernier, 97 F. Supp.2d 303 (E.D. N.Y. 2000).
Johnson v. Glick, 481 F.2d 1028 (2nd Cir. 1973).
Johnson v. Jones, 115 S. Ct. 2151 (1995).
Johnson v. Larson, 441 So.2d 5 (La. App. 1983).
Johnson v. Morel, 876 F.2d 477 (5th Cir. 1989).
Johnson v. State, 447 P.2d 352 (Cal. 1968).

Jones v. Chieffo, 664 A.2d 1091 (Pa. Cmwlth. 1995).

Jones v. Maryland-National Capital, 571 A.2d 859 (Md. App. 1990).

Jordan v. Jackson, 15 F.3d 333 (4th Cir. 1994).

Kaisner v. Kolb, 543 So. 2d 732 (Fla. 1989).

Kanayurak v. North Slope Borough, 677 P.2d 892 (Alaska 1984).

Karnes v. Skrutski, 62 F.3d 485 (3rd Cir. 1995).

Keating v. Holston's Ambulance Serv., Inc., 546 So.2d 911 (La. Ct. App. 1989).

Keeton v. Fayette County, 558 So.2d 844 (Ala. 1989), rehearing denied Feb. 9, 1990.

Kelleher v. New York State Trooper Fearon, 90 F. Supp.2d 354 (S.D. N.Y. 2000).

Kendrick v. City of Lake Charles, 500 So.2d 866 (La. App. 1986).

Ketcham v. Alameda County, 811 F.2d 1243 (9th Cir. 1987).

Kibbe v. City of Springfield, 777 F.2d 801 (1st Cir. 1985).

Kisbey v. California, 682 P.2d 1093 (Cal. 1984).

Kozlowski v. City of Amsterdam, 488 N.Y.S.2d 862 (A.D. 3 Dept. 1985).

Lakoduk v. Cruger, 296 P.2d 690 (Wash. 1956).

Landis v. Rockdale County, 427 S.E.2d 286 (Ga. App. 1992).

Leake v. Cain, 720 P.2d 152 (Co. 1986).

Lehto v. City of Oxnard, 217 Cal. Rptr. 450 (Cal. App. 1985).

Lewis v. McDorman, 820 F. Supp. 1001 (W.D. Va. 1992).

Liggins v. Morris, 749 F. Supp. 967 (D. Minn. 1990).

Lindsey v. Storey, 936 F.2d 554 (11th Cir. 1991).

Little v. Smith, 114 F. Supp.2d 437 (W.D. N.C. 2000).

Long v. Soderquist, 467 N.E.2d 1153 (Ill. App. 2nd Dist. 1984).

Louie v. United States, 776 F.2d 819 (9th Cir. 1985).

Lucas v. City of Long Beach, 131 Cal.Rptr. 470 (App. 1976).

Lugar v. Edmondson Oil Co., 457 U.S. 922 (1993).

Macias v. Ihde, No. 9915662 (9th Cir. 1999).

Makris v. City of Gross Pointe Park, 448 N.W.2d 352 (Mich. App. 1989).

Malley v. Briggs, 475 U.S. 335 (1986).

Manuel v. City of Jeanerette, 702 So. 2d 709 (La. App. 3 Cir. 1997).

Maple v. City of Omaha, 384 N.W.2d 254 (Neb. 1986).

Marchese v. Lucas, 758 F.2d 181 (6th Cir. 1985).

Marriott v. Smith, 931 F.2d 517 (8th Cir. 1991).

Martin v. Board of County Commissioners, 909 F.2d 402 (10th Cir. 1990).

Martinez v. California, 444 U.S. 277 (1980).

Martinez v. Colon, 54 F.2d 980 (1st Cir. 1995).

Maryland v. Buie, 494 U.S. 752 (1990).

Mason v. Britton, 534 P.2d 1360 (Wash. 1975).

Massengill v. Yuma County, 456 P.2d 376 (Ariz. 1969).

McDay v. City of Atlanta, 420 S.E.2d 75 (Ga. App. 1992).

McMillian v. Johnson, 88 F.3d 1573 (11th Cir. 1996).

McMillian v. Monroe County, Alabama, 520 U.S. 781, 117 S. Ct. 1734 (1997).

McNabola v. Chicago Transit Authority, 10 F.3d 1316 (7th Cir. 1993).

Medina v. City of Chicago, 606 N.E.2d 490 (Ill. App. 1 Dist. 1992).

Merzon v. County of Suffolk, 767 F. Supp 432 (E.D. W.Y. 1991).

Messico v. City of Amsterdam, 215 N.E.2d 163 (N.Y. 1983).

Miami v. Horne, 198 So.2d 10 (Fla. 1967).

Mills v. Graves, 930 F.2d 729 (9th Cir. 1991).

Monell v. Department of Social Services, 436 U.S. 658 (1978).

Monroe v. Pape, 365 U.S. 167 (1961).

Moore v. Marketplace Restaurant, Inc., 754 F.2d 1336 (7th Cir. 1985).
Morris v. Blake, 552 A.2d 844 (Del. Super. 1988).
Morro v. City of Birmingham, 117 F.3d 508 (11th Cir. 1997).
Murray v. Leyshock, 915 F.2d 1196 (8th Cir. 1990).
Myers v. County of Lake, Ind., 30 F.3d 847 (7th Cir. 1994).
Napolitano v. County of Suffolk, 460 N.Y.S.2d 353 (App. 1983).
Narney v. Daniels, 846 P.2d 347 (N.M. App. 1992).
Navarro v. Block, 72 F.3d 712 (9th Cir. 1996).
Naylor v. Louisiana Dept. of Public Highways, 423 So.2d 674 (La. App. 1982).
Nelson v. City of Cambridge, 101 F. Supp.2d 44 (D. Mass. 2000).
Nelson v. County of Wright, No. 98-2026 (5th Cir. 1998).
Nelson v. Strawn, 897 F. Supp. 252 (D. S.C. 1995).
Nereida-Gonzalez v. Tirado-Delgado, 990 F.2d 701 (1st Cir. 1993).
Norton v. City of Chicago, 676 N.E.2d 985 (Ill. App. 1 Dist. 1997).
Oklahoma City v. Tuttle, 471 U.S. 808 (1985).
Orozco v. County of Yolo, 814 F. Supp. 885 (E.D. Cal. 1993).
Overby v. Wille, 411 So.2d 1331 (Fla. App. 1982).
Owen v. City of Independence, 445 U.S. 622 (1980).
Owens v. Haas, 601 F.2d 1242 (2nd Cir. 1983).
Palmer v. Williamson, 717 F. Supp. 1218 (W.D. Texas 1989).
Palmquist v. Selvik, 111 F. 3d 1332 (7th Cir. 1997).
Parrilla-Burgos v. Hernandez-Rivera, 108 F.3d 445 (1st Cir. 1997).
Payton v. New York, 445 U.S. 573, 100 S. Ct. 1371 (1980).
Peak v. Ratliff, 408 S.E.2d 300 (W.Va. 1991).
Pembaur v. City of Cincinnati, 475 U.S. 469 (1986).
Pennsylvania v. Lubron, 378 U.S. 938 (1996).
People v. Bland, 218 N.W.2d 56 (Mich. App. 1974).
People v. Schuyler, 4 N.Y. 173 (1850).
Phillips v. District of Columbia, 714 A. 2d 768 (D.C. 1998).
Pierson v. Ray, 386 U.S. 547 (1967).
Pinder v. Johnson, 33 F.3d 368 (4th Cir. 1995).
Pino v. Higgs, 75 F.3d 1461 (10th Cir. 1996).
Pittman v. Nelms III, 87 F. 3d 116 (4th Cir. 1996).
Plaza v. City of Reno, 898 P.2d 114 (Nev. 1995).
Poland v. Glenn, 623 So.2d 227 (La. App. 2 Cir. 1993).
Pretty On Top v. City of Hardin, 597 P.2d 58 (Mt. 1979).
Ramos Padro v. Commonwealth of Puerto Rico, 100 F. Supp.2d 99 (D. Puerto
    Rico, 2000).
Ramos v. City of Chicago, 707 F. Supp. 345 (N.D. Ill. 1989).
Ramundo v. Town of Guiderland, Albany City, 475 N.Y.S.2d 752 (N.Y. Albany
    County 1984).
Reed v. Gardner, 986 F.2d 1122 (7th Cir.), cert. denied, 114 S. Ct. 389 (1993).
Reiff v. City of Philadelphia, 471 F. Supp. 1262 (E.D. Pa. 1979).
Reynolds v. County of San Diego, 84 F.3d 1162 (9th Cir. 1996).
Rhiner v. City of Clive, 373 N.W.2d 466 (Iowa 1985).
Rhode v. Denson, 776 F.2d 107 (5th Cir. 1985).
Rhoder v. McDannel, 945 F.2d 117 (6th Cir. 1991).
Rhodes v. Chapman, 452 U.S. 337 (1981).
Richards v. Southeast Alabama Youth Ser. Diversion, 105 F. Supp.2d 1268 (M.D.
    Ala. 2000).
Richards v. Wisconsin, 520 U.S. 385 (1997).

Riggs v. State, 488 So.2d 443 (La. App. 1986).

Riley v. Dorton, 93 F.3d 113 (4th Cir. 1996).

Ringuette v. City of Fall River, 146 F.3d 1 (1st Cir. 1998).

Rivera v. Vargas, 168 F.3d 42 (1st. Cir. 1999).

Rodriguez v. Jones, 473 F.2d 599 (5th Cir. 1973).

Ross v. United States, 910 F.2d 1422, 1425 (7th Cir. 1990).

Ryan v. State, 656 P.2d 597 (Ariz. 1982).

Ryder v. City of Topeka, 814 F.2d 1412 (10th Cir. 1987).

Sansonetti v. City of St. Joseph, 976 S.W. 2d 572 (Mo. App. W. D. 1998).

Santiago v. Fenton, 891 F.2d 373 (1st. Cir. 1989).

Sarno v. Whalen, 659 A.2d 181 (Conn. 1995).

Sauders v. County of Steuben, 564 N.E.2d 948 (Ind. App. 3 Dist. 1991).

Sauders v. County of Steuben, 693 N.E.2d 16 (Ind. 1998).

Schear v. Board of County Commissioners of Bernalillo, 687 P.2d 728 (N.M. 1984).

Schillingford v. Holmes, 634 F.2d 263 (5th Cir. 1981).

Scott v. City of Opa Locka, 311 So.2d 825 (Fla. Dist. Ct. App. 1975).

Sheth v. Webster, 137 F.3d 1447 (11th Cir. 1998).

Shore v. Stonington, 444 A.2d 1380 (Conn. 1982).

Shuff v. Zurich, 173 So.2d 393 (La. App. 1965).

Silva v. State, 745 P.2d 380 (N.M. 1987).

Simpson v. City of Pickens, Mississippi, 887 F. Supp. 126 (S.D. Miss. 1995).

Sims v. Forehand 112 F. Supp.2d 1260 (M.D. Ala. 2000).

Singer v. Fulton County Sheriff, 63 F.3d 110 (2nd Cir. 1995).

Siren, 74 U.S. (7 Wall.) 152 (1869).

Smith v. Bradford, 475 So.2d 526 (Ala. 1985).

Snyder v. Trepagnier, 142 F.3d 791 (5th Cir. 1998).

Soldal v. Cook County, Illinois, 506 U.S. 56, 113 S. Ct. 538 (1992).

Somavia v. Las Vegas Metropolitan Police Dept., 816 F. Supp. 638 (D. Nev. 1993).

South v. Maryland, 59 U.S. (18 How.) 396 (1856).

Sova v. City of Mt. Pleasant, 142 F.3d 898 (6th Cir. 1998).

Spotts v. City of Kansas City, 728 S.W.2d 242 (Mo. App. W. D. 1987).

Sterling v. Bloom, 723 P.2d 755 (Idaho, 1986).

Stewart v. City of Omaha, 494 N.W.2d 130 (Neb. 1995).

Strickler v. Waters, 989 F.2d 1375 (CA4 1993).

Susko v. Pennsylvania State Police, 572 A.2d 831 (Pa. Cmwlth. 1990).

Swint v. Chambers County Comm'n, 115 S. Ct. 1203 (1995).

Tennessee v. Garner, 471 U.S. 1 (1985).

Terry v. Ohio, 392 U.S. 1 (1968).

Tetro v. Town of Stratford, 485 A.2d 5 (Conn. 1983).

Thomas v. Williams, 124 S.E.2d 409 (Ga. App. 1962).

Thompson v. City of Los Angeles, 885 F.2d 1439 (9th Cir. 1989).

Thompson v. Duke, 882 F.2d 1180 (CA7 1989).

Thorton v. City of Macon, 132 F.3d 1395 (11th Cir. 1998).

Tittle v. Mahan, 566 N.E.2d 1064 (Ind. App. 3 Dist. 1991).

Torres v. City of Anacortes, 97 Wn. App. 64 (Wa. 1999).

Torres v. The City of Chicago, 123 F. Supp.2d 1130 (W.D. Ill. 2000).

Torres v. State, 894 P.2d 386 (N.M. 1995).

Townley v. City Of Iowa, 702 So. 2d 323 (La. App. 2 Cir. 1997).

Trejo v. Wattles, 654 F. Supp. 1143 (D. Colo. 1987).

Trout v. Frega, 926 F. Supp. 117 (N.D. Ill. 1996).

Trull v. Town of Conway, 669 A.2d 807 (N.H. 1995).

United States of America v. Kip R. Jones, No. 99-2527 (7th Cir. 2000).

United States v. Beale, 674 F.2d 137 (9th Cir. 1982).

United States v. Lanier, 520 U.S. 259 (1997).

United States v. Place, 462 U.S. 696 (1983).

U.S. v. Clark, 33 U.S. (8 Pct.) 436 (1834).

Urban v. Village of Lincolnshire, 651 N.E.2d 683 (Ill. App. 1 Dist. 1995).

Van Truag v. James, 215 Cal.Rptr. 33 (Cal. App. 2 Dist. 1985).

Venegas v. Mitchell 495 U.S. 82 (1990).

Venter v. City of Delphi, 123 F.3d 956 (7th Cir. 1997).

Vera v. Tue, 73 F.3d 604 (5th Cir. 1996).

Walsweer v. Harris County, 796 S.W.2d 269 (Texas App. 1990).

Walton v. City of Southfield, 995 F.2d 1331 (6th Cir. 1993).

Wanzer v. District of Columbia, 580 A.2d 127 (D.C. 1990).

Ward v. County of San Diego, 791 F.2d 1329 (1986).

Warden v. Hayden, 387 U.S. 294 (1967).

Wells v. Bonner, 45 F.3d 90 (5th Cir. 1995).

Wells v. Stephenson, 651 So.2d 1215 (Fla. App. 2 Dist. 1990).

West v. Atkins, 487 U.S. 42 (1988).

West v. United States, 617 F. Supp. 1015 (C.D. Cal. 1985).

Westbrooks v. State, 219 Cal.Rptr. 674 (Cal. App. 1985).

White v. Humbert, WL 482445, 2 (Mich. App. 1994).

White v. Rockford, 592 F.2d 381 (7th Cir. 1979).

Whitney v. Worcester, 373 Mass. 208, 218–29 (1977).

Will v. Michigan Department of State Police, 492 U.S. 58 (1989).

Williams v. City of Detroit, 843 F. Supp. 1183 (E.D. Mich. 1994).

Williams v. State of California, 664 P.2d 137 (Cal. 1983).

Wilson v. Layne, 119 S. Ct. 1692 (1999).

Wilson v. Sponable, 439 N.Y.S.2d 549 (App. Div. 1981).

Wingerter v. State of New York, 438 N.E.2d 885 (N.Y. 1984).

Wisniewski v. Kennard, 901 F.2d 1276 (5th Cir. 1990).

Wood v. Ostrander, 879 F.2d 583 (9th Cir. 1989), cert. denied, 498 U.S. 938 (1990).

Wright v. Whiddon, 747 F. Supp. 694 (N.D. Ga. 1990).

Ying Jing Gan v. City of New York, 996 F.2d 522 (2nd Cir. 1993).

York v. City of San Pablo, 626 F. Supp. 34 (N.D. Cal. 1985).

Young v. City of Ann Arbor, 326 N.W.2d 547 (Mich. App. 1982).

Young v. Woodall, 458 S.E.2d 225 (N.C. App. 1995).

Zambranan-Marrero v. Suarez-Cruz, No. 98-1601 (1st. Cir. 1998).

Zuchel v. Spinarney, 890 F.2d 273 (10th Cir. 1989).

Index

Abandonment
　of assault victims, 115–117
　case analysis, 117–119
　of children, and severity of injury,
　　113–115
　third-party criminal victimization
　　and, 108–110
　of vehicle occupants, and quali-
　　fied immunity, 110–113
Absolute immunity, 61
Accidents
　duty to investigate, 163–166
　duty to secure accident scenes,
　　166–168
Administrative negligence, 27, 52–54
Africa, Ramona, 2
*Allison Gas Turbine v. District of
　Columbia,* 162
Appeals, automatic, 13
Arizona v. Evans, 198
Arrest, false, 21–22
Assault
　intentional torts and, 21
　prior knowledge of, 115–117
Assignment, negligent, 27
Assumption of risk doctrine, 32–33
Attorney's Fees Act of 1976, 36

Bailey v. Town of Forks, 149
Barlow v. New Orleans, 175
Barratt v. Burlingham, 150
Battery, assault and, 21
Bittner, Egon, 65
*Board of the County Commissioners
　of Bryan County, Oklahoma v.
　Brown,* 53
Bordanaro v. McLeod, 55–56

Branch Davidians, 2
Breach of duty
　failure to prevent detainee sui-
　　cide, 178–186
　intentional tort and, 24–25
　liability of traffic officers and,
　　161
　negligence tort and, 24
　negligent failure to discipline and
　　investigate, 27
　negligent failure to warn, 157, 159
　police pursuit and, 133
　standard of care and, 127–128
Brisco v. LaHue, 61
Brodsky, S. L., 5
Brower v. Inyo County, 66, 79
Buffkins v. City of Omaha, 99
Burchins v. State, 150
Burns v. Loranger, 92

Cain v. Leake, 140–141
Canine Drug Enforcement Unit. *See*
　Dogs, drug-sniffing
Care, duty of, 125, 173–174
Carter, David, 4
Causation, judicial constructions of,
　in pursuit negligence, 130–134
Cavigliano v. County of Livingston,
　130
Chatman v. Slagle, 95–96
Child abandonment, 113–115
Chisholm v. Georgia, 29
City of Belen v. Harrell, 176–177, 187
City of Canton v. Harris, 55, 57, 196
City of Coppell v. Waltman, 182
City of St. Louis v. Praprotnik, 46, 48
City of Winter Haven v. Allen, 90

Civil liability. *See also* Litigation, civil
abandonment issues, 107-120
benefit of, 11
cost of, 8-11
failure to arrest intoxicated drivers, 137-153
for indirect excessive force, 78-80
frequency of, 3-5
implications for the future, 199-
201
in drug enforcement operations,
81-104
judicial assumptions and law
enforcement, 193
legal assumptions about, 190-194
negligent operation of vehicles in
emergencies, 121-136
police fear of, 5-8
scope and impact of, 1-15
Civil litigation. See Litigation, civil
Civil Rights Act of 1871, 35-36. *See
also* Section 1983
Civil Rights Attorney's Fees Act of
1976, 190
Cohens v. Virginia, 29
*Collins v. City of Harker Heights,
Texas*, 57-58
Color of law, acting under, 37-39
Community policing, 196-197
Comparative negligence, 32
Complaints, 12-13
Constitutional amendments. *See* indi-
vidual amendments.
Constitutional rights, violation of,
39-44
Contributory negligence, 32, 186-187
Cooper, T. W., 6
Courson v. McMillian, 111
Crosby v. Town of Bethlehem, 146
Custom, knowledge of, 50-52

Danger, immediate and serious, 72-74
Dangerousness, past, 74-75
Daniels v. Wilson, 30
Davis v. City of Detroit, 183
Deadly force
defined, 67
immediate and serious danger,
72-74
past dangerousness, 74-75
del Carmen, R. V., 6

Deliberate indifference, 45, 52-59,
109, 113, 119, 184, 191
*DeShaney v. Winnebago County
Department of Social Services*, 109
Detainee suicide
defenses to, 186-187
foreseeability of, 174-178
Detainees
failure to rescue, 185
providing a safe facility for, 183-
185
Detention, of drug suspects, 91-92
DeWald v. State, 147
Dezort v. Village of Hinsdale, 187
Diallo, Amadou, 2
Discipline, negative failure to, 27
Discretionary vs. ministerial function, 124-125, 138-144
Dismissal, motion for, explanation
of, 13
Doctrinal barrier, proximate cause as,
131
Dogs, drug-sniffing, 99-103
Drug enforcement
confiscation of property, 96-98
detection and probable cause, 98-
103
detention and search of suspects,
91-95
emergency response teams, 84-88
search and seizure law in, 82, 98
securing drug houses, 88-91
substance identification and
analysis, 103-104
Drunk drivers, failure to arrest, 137-
153
Duncan v. Town of Jackson, 165
Duty
breach of, 24-25, 27, 127-128,
133, 157, 159, 161, 178-186
of care, 125, 127, 173-174
legal, and intentional tort, 23-24
to investigate accidents, 163-166
to secure accident scenes, 166-168
Dwares v. City of New York, 117

Eighth Amendment
and excessive force, 69
and protection of fleeing felons, 68
search and seizure, 41
verbatim, 40

Eleventh Amendment, and sovereign
    immunity, 29
Emergency response teams, 84–88
Emergency use of vehicles. *See also*
    Pursuit driving
    negligence principles and police
        pursuit, 125–133
    statutory immunity, 122–124
    traditional barriers to liability,
        124–125
Entrustment and assignment, negli-
    gent, 27
Erwin v. County of Manitowoc, 89
Everton v. Willard, 141–142
Excessive force. *See also* Deadly force
    deadly vs. nondeadly, 66–67
    liability for indirect, 78–80
    standards governing, 71–78
    state and federal claims, 67–70

Failure
    to arrest, 26
    to arrest intoxicated drivers, 137–
        153
    to discipline and investigate, 27
    to prevent detainee suicide, 171–
        188
    to protect, 26
    to render assistance, 26
    to rescue suicidal detainees, 185
    to train, 54–60
False arrest/imprisonment, as inten-
    tional tort, 21–23
Federal liability law
    acting under color of law, 37–39
    administrative negligence and
        deliberate indifference, 52–54
    Civil Rights Act of 1871, 35–36
    municipal liability, 45–52
    proof of constitutional violation
        (significance level), 42–44
    violation of constitutional rights,
        39, 42
Fifth Amendment, verbatim, 40
First Amendment, and police policy-
    makers, 47
First Amendment, verbatim, 40
Fiser v. City of Ann Arbor, 123, 131
Force. *See also* Deadly force
    federal standards governing
        deadly, 71–75

indirect excessive, 78–80
    standards governing nondeadly,
        76–78
    types of, 66–67
Foreseeability, 20, 118, 130, 133, 141,
    144, 146, 149, 152, 172
    of detainee suicide, 174–178
Fourteenth Amendment
    abandonment and, 108, 111–117
    excessive force and, 58, 67, 76
    failure to train and, 58
    failure to warn and, 57
    search and seizure and, 41, 97
    third-party criminal victimization
        and, 108–110
    verbatim, 40
Fourth Amendment
    excessive force and, 58, 68–69, 79
    nondeadly force and, 76
    physical abuse of a prisoner, 41
    search and seizure and, 39, 41,
        71, 82–83, 85–86, 92–97, 100,
        102, 104
    verbatim, 40
Fusilier v. Russell, 145
Fyfe, J., 68

Gaines, L. K., 10
Garrison, A. H., 5, 7
Gary Police Department v. Loera,
    157–158
Good faith, and municipal liability,
    63–64
Graham v. Connor, 41, 66, 76, 78

Hake v. Manchester Township, 177, 185
Harlow v. Fitzgerald, 110
Hegarty v. Somerset County, 73–74
Henderson v. Bowden, 143
Hernandez v. Maxell, 96
Hervey v. Estes, 87
Hickey v. Zezulka, 183
Hill v. Clifton, 47
Hilliard v. City and County of Denver,
    110–111
Hinton v. City of Elwood, Kansas, 43, 68
Hiring, negligent, 27
Horton v. Flenory, 116
"Hot spots," urban, 107–108
Hudson v. McMillian, 69–70
Hunter v. Bryant, 62

Immunity
    absolute, 61
    qualified, 61-62, 110-113
    sovereign, 28-30, 138
    statutory, 122-124
Imprisonment, false, 22-23
Injury, and child abandonment, 113-
    115
Insurance, liability, 8
Intentional torts, 19-21
    assault and battery, 21
    false arrest and imprisonment,
        21-23
    wrongful death, 20
Investigate, negligent failure to, 27
Irwin v. Ware, 140-141, 149

Jeffers v. Heavrin, 103
Jennings v. Joshua Independent
    School District, 101
Jensen v. City of Oxnard, 58-59
Johnson v. Glick, 67
Johnson v. Larson, 166
Johnson v. State, 142
Judicial assumptions about law
    enforcement, 193-194
Jury deliberation and selection, 13-14

Kaisner v. Kolb, 143
Kanayurak v. North Slope Borough, 176
Kappeler, V. E., 10
Karnes v. Skrutski, 102-103
Katz, D. M., 10
King, Rodney, 1-2
Kingston, K., 102
Kisbey v. California, 124
Kozlowski v. City of Amsterdam, 180

Landis v. Rockdale County, 139
Law enforcement, and civil liability,
    189-201
Legal duty, as negligence tort, 23-24
Liability defenses
    assumption of risk, 32-33
    contributory and comparative
        negligence, 32
    public duty doctrine, 30-32
    sovereign immunity doctrine, 28-30
    sudden peril, 33
Liggins v. Morris, 85-86
Lindsey v. Storey, 97

Litigation, civil
    assumptions about, 192
    benefit of, 11
    cost of, 8-11
    detainee suicides and, 172-173
    frequency of, 3-5
    police fear of, 5-8
    process of, 12-14
Litigators, assumptions of, 190-192
Long v. Soderquist, 167
Louima, Abner, 2
Lucas v. City of Long Beach, 181

Macias v. Ihde, 44
Manuel v. City of Jeanerette, 185
Maple v. City of Omaha, 135
Marenin, O., 196
Marriott v. Smith, 94
Martin v. Board of County Commis-
    sioners, 69
Martinez v. California, 109
Martinez v. Colon, 38
Massengill v. Yuma County, 145
McDay v. City of Atlanta, 182
McMillian v. Monroe County, Ala-
    bama, 48
Ministerial vs. discretionary function,
    123-144
Monell v. Department of Social Ser-
    vices, 45
Moore v. Marketplace Restaurant,
    Inc., 115
Morris v. Blake, 184
Municipal liability
    cost of, 8-9
    failure to train, 54-60
    good faith and, 63
    knowledge of policy and custom,
        50-52
    policy and policymakers, 45-49
    under Section 1983, 45-52
Murray v. Leyshock, 89

Narcotics. See Drug enforcement
Naylor v. Louisiana Department of
    Public Highways, 156-158
Negligence
    administrative, 52-54
    at accident scenes, 155-169
    common claims of, 25-27
    contributory and comparative, 32

emergency use of vehicles, 124
failure to arrest drunk drivers,
    137-153
vehicle operation during emer-
    gencies, 121-136
Negligence tort, 23
    breach of duty, 24
    damage or injury, 25
    detainee suicides and, 172
    legal duty, 23-24
    proximate cause, 25
Norton v. City of Chicago, 133

Oklahoma City v. Tuttle, 51
Orozco v. County of Yolo, 91
Overby v. Wille, 177
Owen v. City of Independence, 63

Pembaur v. City of Cincinnati, 46
People v. Schuyler, 30
Personnel administration, negligence
    in, 27
Pierson v. Ray, 146
Pinder v. Johnson, 112
Police
    community policing, 196-197
    conduct of, and breach of duty,
        178-186
    conduct of, and detainee suicide,
        178-179
    developing pursuit policies of, 126
    effect of technology on, 197-199
    fear of civil litigation, 5-8
    implications for future police
        executives, 199-201
    innovations of, and liability, 194-
        195
    judicial assumptions about, 193-
        194
    lack of concern re liability suits, 4
    misconduct, 1-3
    policy on pursuit driving, 126-127
    proactive training prescriptions
        for, 195-196
    supervision of detainees, 180-183
Policy and policymakers, of munici-
    pal law, 45-52
Probable cause
    and drug detection, 98-99
    municipal liability and, 62-63
Property, confiscation of, 96-98

Prosser, W., 152
Proximate cause
    as negligence tort, 25
    negligence litigation and, 172-
        173
    police pursuit liability, 130-133
    situational factors and, 132-133
Proximity, temporal, 75
Public duty doctrine, 30-32, 108-
    109, 144-148
    demise of, 147-148
    exceptions to, 148-152, 164
Pursuit driving. *See also* Emergency
    use of vehicles
    breach of reasonableness, 127-
        130
    defenses to negligent operation,
        134-135
    developing police policy on, 126-
        127
    duty of care, 125-127
    police policy on, 127
    judicial construction of causation,
        130-133

Qualified immunity, 61-62, 110-113

Racial profiling, 2
*Ramundo v. Town of Guiderland,
    Albany City*, 161
Reasonableness, breaches of, in
    emergency vehicular operation,
    127-130
Reed v. Gardner, 112
Risk, assumption of, 32-33
Ruby Ridge, 2
Ryan v. State, 147

Sanctions, judicial, 7
Sarno v. Whalen, 151
Sauders v. County of Steuben, 186
*Schear v. Board of County Commis-
    sioners of Bernalillo County*, 148
Schillingford v. Holmes, 68
Scogin, F., 5
Search and seizure
    in drug enforcement operations,
        82-98, 91-100
    unreasonable, 71, 77
Search warrants, 82-83, 87-90, 96,
    101

Section 1983
    acting under color of law, 37–39
    administrative negligence and
        deliberate indifference, 52–54
    constitutional level, 42–44
    court decisions, claims against
        police, 42
    defenses to lawsuits, 60–64
    defined (verbatim), 36
    municipal liability, 45–52
    violation of constitutional right,
        39–42
Seizure, defined, 82, *See also* Search
    and seizure
Selection, hiring and retention, negli-
    gent, 27
Shore v. Stonington, 151–152
Single act exception, in municipal lia-
    bility, 51–52
Sixth Amendment, 40
Smith v. Bradford, 135
South v. Maryland, 30–31, 108
Sova v. City of Mt. Pleasant, 51
Sovereign immunity doctrine, 28–30,
    138
Special duty, and suicide liability
    cases, 174
Special relationship, 148
    circumstances and, 150, 153
    statutorily established, 149–150
State tort law. *See also* Torts
    barriers and defenses to claims,
        28–33
    police civil liability and, 17–25
    strict liability torts, 19
Statutory immunity, 122–123
    traditional barriers to liability,
        124–125
Sterling v. Bloom, 143, 152
Stevens, D. J., 7
Strict liability torts, 19
Strip searches, guidelines for, 93
Substance identification and analy-
    sis, 103–104
Sudden peril, 33
Suicide, detainee
    defenses to, 186
    design of detention facilities and,
        183–185
    failure to rescue, 185–186
    foreseeability of, 174–178

police legal duties and, 172
    violation of rules and regulations,
        179–180
Summary judgment, explanation of, 13
Supervision
    negligent (and direction), 27
    of detainees by police, 180–183
SWAT teams, 84–85, 89

Technology, 197–199
Temporal proximity, 75
Tennessee v. Garner, 20, 66, 68, 71–72,
    78–79
Third-party criminal victimization,
    108–110
    pursuit victimization and proxi-
        mate cause, 130–133
Thomas v. Williams, 175
Torts
    defined, 17–18
    intentional, 19–21
    strict liability, 19
    types of, 19–25
Torts, intentional
    assault and battery, 21
    false arrest and imprisonment,
        21–23
Torts, negligence
    breach of duty, 24
    damage or injury, 25
    legal duty, 23–24
    proximate cause, 25
Traffic regulation violations, 123, 134
Training
    municipal liability and, 54–60
    proactive prescriptions for, 195–
        196
Trautman, N., 1
Trial, process of, 12–14
Trojanowicz, R., 196

*United States of America v. Kip R.
    Jones*, 86

Van Truag v. James, 165
Vaughn, J. B., 10
Vaughn, M. S., 6–7
Vehicles, negligent operation of
    emergency, 26, 121–136
Vehicular pursuit. *See* Emergency use
    of vehicles; Pursuit driving

Victimization
    knowledge of impending, 115–117
    third-party criminal, 108–110,
        130–133
Violations of traffic regulations, 134

Walton v. City of Southfield, 114
West v. Atkins, 37
Westbrooks v. State, 158
White v. Humbert, 114–116
White v. Rockford, 113–114

Williams v. California, 163
Williams v. City of Detroit, 83
Wilson v. Sponable, 180
Women in policing, and fear of civil
    litigation, 6
Wood v. Ostrander, 113
Worrall, J. L., 196
Wright v. Whiddon, 75, 78
Wrongful death lawsuits, 20, 91

Young v. City of Ann Arbor, 180